PUERTO RICO

PUERTO RICO

RICO

A NATIONAL
HISTORY

JORELL MELÉNDEZ-BADILLO

PRINCETON UNIVERSITY PRESS
PRINCETON & OXFORD

Princeton University Press is proud to have partnered with Planeta for the
co-publication of this edition in the Spanish language

Published by Princeton University Press
41 William Street, Princeton, New Jersey 08540
99 Banbury Road, Oxford OX2 6JX

press.princeton.edu

Library of Congress Cataloging-in-Publication Data

Names: Meléndez Badillo, Jorell A., author.
Title: Puerto Rico : a national history / Jorell Meléndez-Badillo.
Description: Princeton ; Oxford : Princeton University Press, [2024] |
    Includes bibliographical references and index.
Identifiers: LCCN 2023020859 (print) | LCCN 2023020860 (ebook) |
    ISBN 9780691231273 (hardback) | ISBN 9780691231280 (ebook)
Subjects: LCSH: Puerto Rico—History. | Puerto Rico—Colonial influence. |
    Puerto Rico—History—Autonomy and independence movements. |
    Puerto Rico—Ethnic relations.
Classification: LCC F1971 .M45 2024 (print) | LCC F1971 (ebook) |
    DDC 972.95—dc23/eng/20230522
LC record available at https://lccn.loc.gov/2023020859
LC ebook record available at https://lccn.loc.gov/2023020860

British Library Cataloging-in-Publication Data is available

Editorial: Priya Nelson, Emma Wagh, and Morgan Spehar
Production Editorial: Nathan Carr
Jacket/Cover Design: Chris Ferrante
Production: Danielle Amatucci
Publicity: Julia Haav and Carmen Jimenez

Jacket image credit: Volina / Shutterstock

This book has been composed in Arno

Printed in the United States of America

10 9 8 7 6 5 4 3 2 1

To Blanca G. Silvestrini
in gratitude, admiration, and friendship

CONTENTS

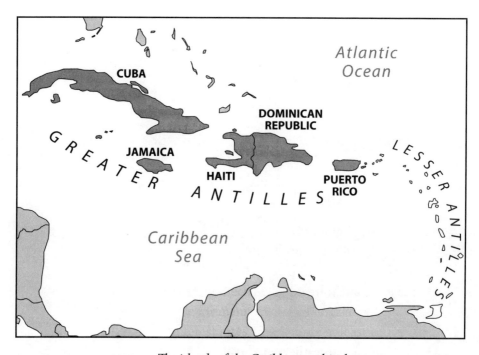

MAP 0.1. The islands of the Caribbean archipelago.

PROLOGUE:

"I AM NEVER COMING BACK HERE"

La realidad puertorriqueña es una realidad caótica en muchos aspectos, sí, pero la tarea del escritor consciente es la de arrojar luz sobre el caos, no la de retratarlo simplemente.

The Puerto Rican reality is chaotic in many aspects, yes, but the conscious writer's task is to cast light on the chaos, not to merely portray it.

—JOSÉ LUIS GONZÁLEZ

Aguadilla, Puerto Rico, 1954: Carlos Alberto Nieves Rivera was unemployed, out of luck, and out of money. Eighteen years old, his only sources of income were odd landscaping and construction jobs for his neighbors. In a tightening economy, his sixth-grade education didn't help. He saved some money for a plane ticket to try his luck *allá 'fuera* (abroad). Three years earlier, in 1951, Pan Am had inaugurated their non-stop flight from San Juan to New York City. Eastern Airlines followed shortly after. Perhaps without realizing it himself, Carlos Alberto would become part of the first large-scale airborne migration in history.[1]

Everyone was dreaming of a better future in 1950s Puerto Rico. The Popular Democratic Party led a titanic effort to industrialize the country and with it came the transformation of national symbols, massive grassroots educational projects, and new historical memories. As literary scholar Arcadio Díaz Quiñones has noted, Puerto Rico broke away from its own memories to create new ones.[2] Anything seemed possible. In San Juan, Doña Fela—the first woman elected mayor of any capital city in the Americas—imported snow from New England on four different occasions to celebrate a white Christmas in the Caribbean archipelago. Nationalists led a revolution in the inland town of Jayuya that was felt all the way to the capital of the United States. And Puerto Rico became an Estado Libre Asociado, simply translated to "Commonwealth."

But not everyone was hopeful. While in Puerto Rico many were dreaming of a glowing future, the reality was that for industrialization to succeed in an archipelago whose main island is only about one hundred miles long and thirty-five miles wide, many people needed to migrate. Carlos Alberto Nieves Rivera was one of hundreds of thousands of Puerto Ricans who packed their bags and headed to the United States, eager to live the American Dream. Before leaving for the airport, he stood on a street corner in his old neighborhood and screamed at the house where he had been raised: "I am never coming back here! Thanks for nothing!" His words were an echo of a generation of working-class families who had been uprooted to make way for modernization.[3]

After two decades of work in low-paying jobs between Boston and New Haven, Carlos Alberto returned to his neighborhood in Aguadilla. He had married, divorced, and left his family behind in Connecticut. After arriving in Puerto Rico, he met and eventually married Ada Nilda Roldán Soto. Like Carlos Alberto, she came from a working-class background and had tried her luck in New York City, only to return to her neighborhood. The majority of her fourteen siblings had done the same, traveling to the United States in search of a better life, only to find themselves living in crowded apartments and facing racism, difficult work conditions, and harsh winters that made them return to Puerto Rico. Ada Nilda had lived with an abusive husband and their three children, moving between the projects in El Barrio and the Bronx. Tired of her husband's abuse, she left him and went back home in search of her community. It was after her divorce that she met Carlos Alberto.

In a brushstroke of irony, on June 12, 2005, Carlos Alberto Nieves Rivera died a few feet away from the place he swore he would never return to. Carlos and Ada were my grandparents. He was not my bio-

FIGURE 0.1. Carlos Alberto Nieves Rivera in Boston, c. 1954.
Author's personal collection.

logical grandfather but raised me like his own. Their stories were hardly
unique. More than 835,000 people migrated north from 1940 to 1970.[4]
Both of my grandparents were part of broader historical and structural
processes that not only forced them to migrate but allowed them to
construct different understandings of Puerto Rico, a nation that remains
legally ambiguous, diasporic, and always "on the move," to borrow a
phrase from anthropologist Jorge Duany.[5]

While the following pages seek to provide a comprehensive narrative
of Puerto Rico—from the indigenous communities that first inhabited
Borikén to the present day—I begin with my grandparents' story to
highlight the personal and intimate dimensions of this history.

My parents and uncles also migrated. They joined the U.S. military to
escape their small towns, and I was born in Fort Benning, Georgia, which
has also served as a military base for the School of the Americas, an institution infamously known for its role in perpetuating violence and coop-
erating with authoritarian regimes across the Americas.[6] Two weeks after
my birth, I was brought to the archipelago and raised by my grandparents

FIGURE 0.2. Ada Nilda Roldán Soto and Carlos Alberto Nieves Rivera at their home in the Muñecas Housing Project, Aguadilla, Puerto Rico, c. 1980s. Author's personal collection.

in a working-class neighborhood. From playing on the corner where *abuelo* swore he would never return to the writing of this book, my life has been shaped by empire and colonialism. But my story, just like my family's, is not unique.

In recent years, Puerto Rico has acquired new visibility in U.S. media outlets, particularly after the destruction caused by Hurricane María in 2017. The storm killed more than four thousand people while millions of others lacked access to potable water, electricity, and the most basic necessities for months on end. Media outlets contended that the U.S. federal government needed to offer assistance because Puerto Ricans were U.S. citizens. While that is an accurate statement, Puerto Rico's relationship to the United States is not that simple. Such arguments overlook the second-class nature of Puerto Ricans' citizenship while portraying them in need of saving. In those conversations, the agency of Puerto Ricans often disappears.[7]

What is also often missing from such conversations is the fact that Puerto Rico is a Caribbean and Latin American country that was colonized by the United States in 1898. But Puerto Rico's colonial history didn't begin there or then. While indigenous communities have lived in Borikén for thousands of years, the archipelago's military conquest by the Spanish Crown started in 1508, fifteen years after a Genovese sailor briefly stopped on its shores on his way to the neighboring island of Hispaniola, known today as the Dominican Republic and Haiti.

Puerto Rico has been called the oldest colony in the world.[8] While some people contest that statement, Puerto Rico's history is marked by five centuries of colonialism, stretching from 1493 to the present day. Colonialism has shaped the ways that Puerto Ricans conceptualize themselves, their politics, and their idea of the nation. This book argues that we cannot understand Puerto Rico's current fiscal, political, and social crises without recognizing its colonial reality. To cast light on Puerto Rico's current moment, we must acknowledge colonialism without overlooking vibrant histories of indigenous resistance and maroon communities to nationalist insurrections and massive mobilizations that demanded the resignation of corrupt elected officials.

Writing a national history is always a complicated and difficult endeavor. I have not attempted to write a history from beginning to end. In fact, the ambiguous nature of the Puerto Rican nation negates the idea of a start or a conclusion. In the absence of a sovereign nation-state, when did Puerto Rico become a "nation"? Was it in the eighteenth century when people began calling themselves Puerto Ricans and not Spaniards?[9] Or was it in the nineteenth century with the consolidation of liberalism and the first works of written national history?[10] Does the cultural nationalism that was produced in the mid-twentieth century count as a legitimate form of nation-building?[11] These questions guide the book's narrative to highlight how for centuries Puerto Ricans have dared to imagine their realities otherwise.

In recent years, scholars have moved away from what some termed "methodological nationalism." Influenced by trends in the humanities and social sciences, these scholars have noted that focusing on nation-states obscures the complex ways that peoples, institutions, and societies function in a highly globalized world. Other scholars further caution that focusing on the nation can reproduce nationalist logics that are inherently exclusionary.[12]

If nationalism justifies the creation of borders, sanctions xenophobia, and excludes peoples, then we should indeed be careful. As American Studies scholar Lisa Lowe has noted, imperialism and other systems of oppression are intimately connected across continents.[13] But in colonized places like Puerto Rico, the idea of the nation and how it has been imagined throughout history offer other possibilities. In spaces without a sovereign nation-state, the idea of the nation becomes a terrain of struggle where different social groups and institutions negotiate understandings of belonging, the past, and, most importantly for this book, other potential futures.

By writing a national history, I do not mean to geographically limit the story to the Puerto Rican archipelago. From the times when indigenous peoples arrived in Borikén to the present day, those who have inhabited Puerto Rico have been in constant flux, engaging frequently with traveling peoples and ideas. While attentive to global events and transnational methodologies, I have chosen to center the nation as an affirmation. In the face of hundreds of years of colonialism, Puerto Ricans have refused to be solely defined by their imperial metropoles.

Centering the nation does not mean that there is consensus about its meaning. As the following pages demonstrate, there have been and continue to be multiple Puerto Ricos that coexist in the archipelago. And although Puerto Rico is not a sovereign nation-state, its inhabitants have created spaces where they enact self-determination and experiment with freedom practices, or what social justice scholar Aurora Santiago Ortiz has termed "circuits of self-determination." In the face of colonial neglect and neoliberal austerity, Puerto Ricans occupy spaces to enact other futures in the present.[14]

By paying attention to the multiple ways that people have negotiated the idea of the nation, I do not seek to romanticize the commonwealth status of Puerto Rico. Affirming the existence of the nation does not negate the fact that Puerto Rico is a colonial possession of the United States in the twenty-first century. But it is also important to highlight that colonialism has not been tacitly accepted by everyone. What follows is a history of struggle. It is a history of resistance. It is the history of a non-sovereign nation along with its contradictions, hopes, and potential futures. It is an attempt to document the agency that has been rendered invisible in U.S. media representations and disaster narratives through willful ignorance. It is intimate and it is painful. But it is also a beautiful and ongoing future-oriented history that is being written, rewritten, and imagined every single day.

PUERTO RICO

CHAPTER 1

BORIKÉN'S FIRST PEOPLES: FROM MIGRATION TO INSURRECTION

Before the arrival of Europeans, the island of Borikén was politically and administratively organized into dozens of *cacicazgos* (chiefdoms). These created a social structure for villages, peoples, and regions, as well as providing a hierarchical chain of command that organized and stratified the island's indigenous societies. While there may have been tensions between some *caciques* (chiefs), others were united by friendships, familial bonds, and networks that transcended the insular borders of Borikén. In fact, these communities likely imagined oceans, rivers, and other bodies of water not as frontiers but as pathways. An indigenous person from the southern coast of Borikén might have felt closer to communities in the neighboring island of Ayití, later renamed Hispaniola, than to the mountainous region of their own.[1]

The caciques of Borikén had known of strange people landing in neighboring islands since the arrival of Europeans in 1492. When the Spaniards disembarked in 1508 to officially begin Borikén's conquest through sword and cross, indigenous communities understood exactly whom they were dealing with. Contrary to myths perpetuated by traditional historiography, the indigenous communities (soon to be named Taínos by the Europeans) did not consider the Spaniards gods. The caciques realized that the colonizers were not to be trusted as they had

1

shown what they were capable of in Ayití. There, they had raped women, beheaded insubordinates, and terrorized indigenous villages.[2]

Agüeybaná I, then one of the most powerful caciques in the Caribbean, had to make a difficult decision. It was up to him whether his people resisted the conquest or negotiated with the conquistadores. His elderly mother advised him to make peace.[3] This was not a sign of weakness or docility but a calculated political move. The Spaniards carried weapons that Agüeybaná I had never seen or imagined. Resisting them could have meant the immediate extermination of his people. The Spaniards also brought with them Bibles, crosses, and germs; their actions were guided by a desire to find and accumulate pieces of a glistening metal found in the island's rivers, often used as décor by indigenous leaders. This object, which the Spaniards called *oro* (gold), seemed to inspire violent greed.[4] This violence, however, did not go unchallenged.

The First Migrations

When the Spaniards first arrived in the Caribbean, they met indigenous people they mistakenly referred to as Indians, thinking that they had arrived at the domain of the Great Khan. These peoples later came to be known as Taínos, though, as historian Ada Ferrer has noted, "how they called themselves in 1492 or 1511, we do not know."[5] There is much that we do not know about pre-conquest indigenous cultures and societies, a testament to the malleability and ever-changing nature of the past.

In the late nineteenth and early twentieth centuries, European thinkers began to create categories to understand time and space. For these scholars, the planet lived in different temporalities, "with Europe in the present and the rest of the world in the past."[6] Such categories were considered universal but inevitably privileged European experiences and knowledge. Scholars created an asymmetric way of understanding the world, with Europe at the center and the peoples without history, to borrow a phrase from anthropologist Eric R. Wolf, on the outside.[7]

History is the documentation and intentional recording of the past, but documentation cannot be solely limited to writing. The people who inhabited the Caribbean centuries before Europeans arrived on its shores had other forms of knowledge, history-keeping, and mythmaking. Oral tradition was a powerful tool to document the past while maintaining tradition and creating community; however, such traditions posed a serious challenge to those attempting to write down what happened in the past. Perhaps those oral traditions accrued their power by evading the gaze of outsiders such as historians writing thousands of years later.[8]

Crafting a history of the indigenous communities who first arrived in the archipelago we now call Puerto Rico requires a careful dance between archaeology, anthropology, and history. In the nineteenth century, the study of Puerto Rico's indigenous communities was done by amateur archaeologists—lawyers and medical doctors with an interest in setting the foundations for Puerto Rican history.[9] Later, in the twentieth century, indigenous histories were taken up by a transnational Caribbean intellectual community who pieced together ceramics, seashells, and other artifacts that allowed them to begin crafting concrete yet fluid and ever-changing narratives of the region's ancestors.[10]

Out of these warring methodologies and debates about the region's first migrations some consensus emerged. It seems that the first migration of peoples to Borikén took place about six thousand years ago.[11] Named by archaeologists as *arcáicos* (archaics), they probably migrated from the estuary of the Orinoco River in the Amazon region by island hopping through the Caribbean. They were semi-nomad societies of hunter-gatherers. What we know of these archaic cultures has been the product of archaeological research. And scholars must grapple with the impossibility of ever fully understanding how these communities lived or the social imaginaries they created.[12]

The term "archaic" is used to identify indigenous societies that only developed rustic tools, but this does not negate the possibility that different ethnic and cultural groups existed in these earlier societies. It seems clear, however, that peoples identified as archaic were part of multiple waves of migration that took place all over the Caribbean. The region might have been more interconnected than we have previously imagined.

The second broad cultural group identified by archaeologists are the Arawak. Much like the archaic, this broad category created by scholars is used to identify peoples who could have belonged to different cultural and ethnic groups. Scholars believe that they might have shared the Arawak language and that they also arrived in several waves of migration. There is also historiographical and scholarly debate about whether they incorporated previous migrant peoples into their societies and whether they clashed with one another.[13]

Anthropologist Irving Rouse famously referred to the Taínos as the people who greeted Columbus. Instead, I propose to think of them as the people who resisted conquest by Columbus.[14] While the term "Taíno" has been traditionally applied to describe a single ethnic or cultural group, there might have been more than just one such group; the people we refer to as Taínos also might have included several ethnicities with different cultural practices that spread throughout the Caribbean region.[15] What seems clear, however, is that those who inhabited Borikén when Columbus arrived had developed sophisticated social systems and hierarchies.

At the beginning of the conquest, Borikén's *yukayekes* (villages) were usually established next to rivers or in fertile valleys. Unlike previous migrations of nomadic groups, the people known as Taínos were farmers. Their diet was composed of tubers or root vegetables along with fish, poultry, reptiles, and insects. Taínos also dedicated some of their time to the production of artworks tied to their religious worldviews. They carved stones or wood to create necklaces, drawings, and ritual artifacts. The *dúho*, for example, was a small seat created out of wood or stone that might have been used for prayer; sacred objects also might have been placed on it. Perhaps the most important artifact in Taíno culture was the *cemí*. These small sculptures were believed to contain gods that represented the forces of nature.[16]

The cacique was at the top of Taíno society. His role was not solely political as he was also expected to lead the religious, military, and intellectual facets of everyday life. Directly below caciques were the *nitainos*, a group usually composed of the cacique's family members or those close to them. The nitainos administered social life on behalf of the cacique. *Bohiques* were those in charge of religious rituals and medicine. And common people were known as *naborías*.[17]

Women played a significant role in Taíno society, which had a matrilineal system where the inheritance of cacicazgos was based on kinship from the mother's side. When a cacique passed away, his siblings—not his children—inherited the cacicazgo. Women also played important roles in decision making. They took an active role in farming, military actions, and even political life. Historian Jalil Sued Badillo has documented the existence of *cacicas* (women chiefs) across the Caribbean region.[18]

Much of what we know about the Taíno culture of the Greater Antilles comes from firsthand accounts by Europeans. In his diary, Columbus wrote how during the first voyage he fooled his crew into believing they were sailing slower than they actually were to avoid mutiny after traveling for weeks without sign of land. Once they arrived in what they thought to be the domain of the Great Khan cited by Marco Polo, Columbus dedicated several pages to trying to comprehend the peoples who inhabited those lands.[19]

Columbus paid particular attention to the gold that adorned their bodies. Early chronicles of the conquest documented the existence of mute dogs, one-eyed humans, and cannibal people with dog snouts. While mute dogs did exist, the one-eyed, dog-snout peoples were pure fiction. Jalil Sued Badillo has argued that such fantastic portrayals of the Indies were used to justify the Spanish Crown's financing of future expeditions. Borikén's communities often went to war with the peoples living in the Lesser Antilles, known by Spaniards as the Caribs. The Caribs were portrayed by Europeans as warlike cannibals and savages. It seems that they did excel in the art of war and frequently attacked the indigenous communities of Borikén. But it is possible that they were not from a different ethnic group. Reports of cannibalism were also used for the purposes of enslaving rebellious indigenous populations.[20] When the Spanish Conquest unleashed its brutal violence, the perceived differences between Taínos and Caribs collapsed, giving way to collaboration and solidarities.[21]

One of the most detailed accounts we have about the Taínos' world-views, mythmaking, and religiosity was written by a self-defined "poor friar of the Order of Saint Jerome" named Ramón Pané. Inspired by Columbus's first voyage, he joined the second expedition and sailed to the Caribbean in September 1493. To comprehend Taíno culture for the purposes of evangelizing and conquering them, Columbus ordered Pané to move to the lands of Guarionex, a powerful cacique from Hispaniola who had shown interest in the Christian religion. Pressured by other caciques, Guarionex abandoned his Christian inclinations to the point of ordering the desecration of Catholic symbols. Pané alleged that Guarionex's people stole religious relics, threw them on the ground, and urinated on them. After these events, Pané settled in the lands of the cacique Mayobanex, where he lived for several years, learning the Taíno language and culture while also continuing his evangelizing mission.[22]

Pané finished his study and delivered his text to Columbus in 1498 during the admiral's third voyage to the Caribbean. After providing the manuscript, Pané disappears from the archival record. After all, he argued that he "wore himself out in order to learn all of this."[23] Just like Columbus's diary, Pané's original text, *An Account of the Antiquities of the Indians,* was lost. Fortunately, it was reproduced in the biography Fernando, Columbus's son, wrote to defend the honor and legacy of his father. Fernando was a bibliophile who built one of the most impressive libraries of his time. Nonetheless, the text of Fernando's biography also disappeared, only to be reproduced in a poor Italian translation published by Spanish historian Alfonso de Ulloa in 1571.[24]

This surviving palimpsest offers a window—through multiple colonizers' gazes—into the ways that Taíno peoples conceptualized their world. It documents origin myths: for example, how the ocean was created and how a woodpecker was used to design female genitalia, thus creating women. It also describes Taíno fears of the dead—believed to walk among the living at night—and how bohiques were in charge of healing the sick, becoming victims of beatings or even death if they failed in their endeavors. One of the stories Pané retold had prophetic undertones. It was said that two caciques from Hispaniola abstained from eating and drinking for days so their cemís would reveal the future to them. After five days, the cemís spoke: "not many years would go by," they said to the caciques, "before a people covered with clothes would reach that island, and they would end all those rites and ceremonies of the island and would kill all their children and deprive them of freedom."[25]

While the Taínos originally thought this premonition referred to the Caribs, it became clear that it was a prophecy about the arrival of the Europeans. After reading Pané's text, the historian and intellectual Pietro Martire d'Anghiera commented on this story in the mid-sixteenth century that "not even a memory is now left of the zemis [sic]."[26] Martire d'Anghiera never set foot in the Americas, but the proliferation of print media allowed him to make an accurate description of what was unraveling on the other side of the Atlantic. The Spaniards soaked the lands and rivers of Borikén with blood. But the Taínos fought back.

1511: The Road to Insurrection

The first recorded clash between indigenous communities and Europeans occurred during Columbus's second voyage. It was November 14, 1493. The Europeans had stopped at the island of Santa Cruz (today St. Croix). They saw a canoe with "four men, two women, and a boy."[27] Twenty-five Europeans decided to go after them. In self-defense, the fleeing indigenous people "daringly put their hands to the arches, the women as well as the men."[28] They were able to wound one Spaniard and kill another before being intercepted. The men were beheaded. The women were raped and later sent to Spain to be showcased as cannibals. Michele de Cuneo, a Spanish soldier who claimed to be on the boat, took pride in raping one of them and argued, "suffice to say that she really seemed trained as a whore."[29] Ten Taíno women were held captive in their ships. Six were able to escape by jumping ship and swimming away in the darkness of night.[30] This was the beginning of a regime of terror sustained by labor and sexual exploitation.

Europeans arrived at the island the Taínos called Burunquén or Borikén a few days later, on November 19, 1493. For decades historians

debated about exactly where Columbus's expedition landed. Nonetheless, it seems that Columbus never actually set foot on the island. His
crew stopped there for two days to restock their food supplies. They
found empty huts, or *bohios*; all the indigenous people had fled. During
his first voyage, Columbus wrote in his diary that the Taínos had feared
them at first glance but were amiable after gaining their trust.[31] In the
Caribbean, bodies of water served as avenues of communication. Columbus noted, "I have seen these canoes with seventy and eighty men
in them, and each had an oar."[32] News of the Spaniards' arrival might
have quickly spread across different cacicazgos, carried by such canoes.
The empty bohios could have meant that the Taínos of Borikén had
already heard the news about the Europeans' brutality.

A few days later, the Europeans returned to Hispaniola and found the
Nativity Fort—their first settlement, established December 24 of the
previous year from the wreckage of Columbus's first ship, the *Santa
María*—burned to the ground with no sign of the thirty-eight men left
behind to protect it. Historians have suggested that the attack was
organized by the cacique Caonabo from Maguana to avenge the brutality of the Spaniards against their people.[33] While we can never recon-
struct what actually happened, the fort's ashes might be imagined as a
symbol of the first indigenous insurrection in the Americas.

The Spanish Crown made Hispaniola their first colonial hub in the
Caribbean. The exploitation of indigenous communities started immediately after the conquest began. Interested in the limited gold reserves
found in the Caribbean, Europeans established a system of forced indigenous labor known as repartimientos (divisions), which later became encomiendas. In this way, Spaniards exploited the land through
forced labor. Each colonizer, known as a *vecino* (neighbor), received
indigenous peoples as subjects.[34] As historian Ida Altman notes, "Indians [*sic*] could be encomienda workers, permanent servants (*naborías*),
or slaves, but in all cases they were subject to Spanish labor demands,
strictures, and punishments."[35] This system was legally consolidated
after a series of royal edicts from 1503 to 1504 ordered *encomenderos*
(grantees) to remunerate indigenous people for their labor, to provide
them time to rest and work in their own fields, and, ultimately, to evan-

gelize them.[36] As historian Juan Ángel Silén has argued, the Taínos' in-
doctrination was part of a longer war Iberians waged against paganism
and Islam. The conquest of the Americas began immediately after Spain
had expelled Muslim communities from the Iberian Peninsula following almost a millennium of conflict.[37]

The official conquest of Borikén, soon renamed the Island of San
Juan Bautista, began in 1508. The original charter for its colonization was
granted in 1505 to Vicente Yáñez Pinzón, who had traveled with Columbus on his first voyage to the Americas. The charter was sold and resold,
passing through different hands until it was granted to Juan Ponce de
León, later immortalized for his death while supposedly searching for
the fountain of youth in Florida. (His true intentions were otherwise—
he was looking for indigenous people to enslave.)[38]

In 1508, the archipelago was organized around two or three geopolitical units divided among dozens of cacicazgos, the most powerful of
whom was Agüeybaná I. He dominated half of the island through alliances and familial relations with other caciques. Ponce de León had met
Agüeybaná on a previous trip.[39] His arrival on August 12, 1508, had been
delayed by two powerful hurricanes that seem to have predicted the
coming storm brought upon by the colonizers.[40] Fernández de Oviedo,
one of the first chroniclers, noted that it was Agüeybaná I's mother who
convinced him to receive the Spaniards in peace because they knew of
the methods used to "pacify" the indigenous communities in their
neighboring island.[41]

In a document written and signed on June 4, 1516, and sent to the
incoming king, Charles I, fourteen priests shed light on the brutality of
the conquest during its first years. I will not reproduce the violence
gruesomely described in the document, but it included infanticide,
sexual terror, brutal dehumanization, and labor exploitation. The friars
carefully described the conquest's genocidal impulse.[42] Agüeybaná I's
decision to negotiate peace with the colonizers should not be understood as an act of docility but one taken after careful political and military reflection.

Back in Spain, Christopher Columbus's son Diego Colón demanded
to be named viceroy of the Indies as part of his inheritance. This meant

that Nicolás de Ovando, the governor of the Indies who had granted Juan Ponce de León a charter to colonize Borikén, would lose his power. Knowing that it was just a matter of time before Diego Colón arrived and reconfigured the political landscape, Ponce de León rushed to establish the town of Caparra, Borikén's first official European settlement.[43] Shortly after, in 1509, Diego Colón sent Cristobal de Sotomayor, a knight from Galicia, to Borikén. Since Ponce de León had already settled in Caparra, it was decided that Sotomayor would establish another town in the southern part of the island, a territory that belonged to the Agüeybaná I cacicazgo.[44]

Two storms had welcomed Ponce de León to Borikén. Now, the winds of war began blowing. In November 1510, a group of indigenous peoples from the Yagüecas region in modern-day Añasco were tasked with ferrying Diego Salcedo, a young Spanish conquistador, across the Guaorabo River. As they carried Salcedo across, his fate turned. The cacique Urayoán had apparently ordered his assassination. The Taínos drowned him, an incident that still carries power today. Some scholars believe that Salcedo might have played and lost a game of *batú* with the Taínos. This ball game was played not only for fun but also for ceremonial purposes, with the loser oftentimes sacrificed.[45] In Puerto Rican mythology, however, the murder was committed to prove the Spaniards' mortality. Recounted in the 1535 chronicles of Gonzalo Fernández de Oviedo, the story gave power to the myth of Taíno docility.[46] However, it can also be understood as a war cry.

Unhappy with the Taínos he had received as part of his repartimientos, Cristobal de Sotomayor began to organize raids to capture indigenous peoples from inland communities and cacicazgos. In fact, Sotomayor was the first person to receive a charter allowing him to enslave indigenous peoples. This created tension between the colonizers and the southern cacicazgos, forcing Cristobal de Sotomayor to move the town of Guánica to the west, soon to be renamed Aguada.[47] Spanish conquistadores began documenting resistance from indigenous communities that refused to be subdued and rumors circulated about the planned assassination of Sotomayor.

FIGURE 1.1. Assassination of conquistador Diego Salcedo.
Source: John Carter Brown Library.

Unfortunately for Cristobal de Sotomayor, Agüeybaná I, who had
been peaceful with the colonizers, died two years after his arrival. His
brother Agüeybaná II inherited Borikén's most powerful cacicazgo.
Known as Agüeybaná the Brave, he probably grew up hearing stories
about the colonizers' actions in neighboring Ayití and was now seeing
that violence unfold in his own land. Unlike his brother, he decided to
act. As a political, religious, and military leader, he began organizing for
war against the colonizers.[48]

In September 1510, Agüeybaná's sister advised Sotomayor to run
away.[49] After receiving confirmation of the planned assassination, Sotomayor gathered four soldiers and made his way to Caparra to alert authorities there about the rebellion. As they traveled along the Jauca river,
Agüeybaná II intercepted them. All the Spaniards were killed except for
Juan González, a Spanish scout who had infiltrated an indigenous ceremony and knew their language. He swore on his life that he would become

loyal to Agüeybaná. He was wounded and left to live—only to promptly alert the Spanish authorities about what had happened that night. The conquistadores' bodies were buried vertically with their feet above-ground, their bodies pointing toward the hell the Christians talked so much about. War was inevitable.[50]

By 1511, Agüeybaná II had amassed an army of 3,000 soldiers. They destroyed the town Sotomayor had established in the south and simul-taneously attacked other settlements throughout the island. They killed 150 to 200 Spaniards at a time when the population was not more than a few hundred.[51] In the chaos of the moment, those who survived fled to Caparra, where Juan Ponce de León was organizing an army. When Ponce de León's soldiers marched toward indigenous territories, they found that the Taínos had swept the dirt roads, symbolically welcom-ing the Spaniards into battle. The Spanish offensive proved successful, and the repression was brutal. Spaniards burned any Taíno town that was in their way and arrested and enslaved a great number of Taínos, burning an F into their heads to remind them that they were property of the Spanish king, Fernando de Aragón.[52]

It was clear that the Taínos had suffered a great defeat. But the war did not end there. When Juan Ponce de León offered a pardon to those caciques in arms, only two accepted. After the initial stage of the war, indigenous communities changed their strategy. Instead of frontal war-fare, they now opted for sneak attacks on Spanish settlements and for a naval strategy. In fact, it seems that many indigenous communities fled Borikén and took shelter in the Lesser Antilles, home to the so-called Carib Indians who had once been their enemies.

One of the most famous early battles took place in Yahuecas in Bor-ikén's central-eastern region. According to chronicler Fernández de Oviedo, Ponce de León killed a cacique carrying a big *guanín* (gold metal necklace). This triggered the long-standing idea that Ponce de León had slain Agüeybaná II in battle. Nonetheless, Jalil Sued Badillo has persuasively demonstrated that the Spaniards recorded sightings of Agüeybaná during the following decades. In fact, the figure of Agüey-baná became a powerful myth, and people reported seeing him fight in multiple battles. It is more likely that he joined those who settled in the

Leeward Islands and continued leading attacks on Borikén's colonizers for years to come.[53]

The war that began in 1511 and continued in the form of attacks for decades marked a turning point in the initial stages of Spain's colonial project in Puerto Rico. After the first battles, the Spaniards viciously murdered and enslaved many indigenous communities while more were killed by European germs. Exploitation and violence consolidated the conquest's genocidal impulse. By 1530, the Spanish reported 1,553 "indians" enslaved or in encomiendas.[54] That number, of course, is questionable if we take into account methods used to generate the data. Many indigenous peoples took to the mountains to live outside the limits of the state and are thus absent from the historical archive. Such silences pose challenges to historians. But if we take an indigenous perspective, absences could also provide a motive for celebration. Disappearing from the archive and from history may have meant surviving the conquest's genocidal thrust. It was in communities that indigenous peoples created on the fringes of societies where some of them befriended another group of people escaping the unspeakable violence of Spain's settler-colonial project: African-descended peoples escaping enslavement.

CHAPTER 2

CONSOLIDATING THE COLONIAL PROJECT

The Spanish successfully and violently suppressed the 1511 indigenous insurrection. But that was just the beginning of indigenous peoples' campaigns against the settlers. There were dozens of attacks organized from within and outside Borikén throughout the sixteenth century. Rebellious caciques from the mountainous interior joined their long-time enemies from nearby islands to fight the Spanish. These attacks varied in size and effectiveness.

In mid-1513, more than 350 Carib Indians attacked the settlement of Caparra. They were able to burn down multiple buildings, including the library of Bishop Alonso Manso, perhaps the first library in the Americas.[1] The attack also left sixteen settlers dead.[2] There were two other strategic attacks that year. These actions targeted not only settlers but also caciques who had betrayed their own and collaborated with the Spaniards. The cacica Luisa was killed during these attacks.[3] By then, some caciques had started to collaborate with Spanish settlers by providing laborers to work in the mines for a set period. When it was the mining season, a person designated as a *recogedor de indios* (Indian collector) traveled through cacicazgos assembling those who were forced to work.[4]

When the attack on the cacica Luisa took place, Francisco Mexía was there as a recogedor de indios. He also died in the battle. Francisco had joined his parents, Antón Mexía and Violante Gómez, in their travels to

Hispaniola and then Borikén during the conquest's early days. The Mexías were probably the first African-descended family to arrive in the Americas. Antón Mexía was able to invest in the mining economy and had accrued enough wealth and social capital by 1514 to be the only Black person to own enslaved indigenous people.[5]

There was a handful of other freed Black people who arrived in Borikén during the first two decades of the sixteenth century. They had received their freedom in Spain and then traveled to the Indies in search of better opportunities. Some took part in the mining economy while others joined the military or became salaried workers for the Spanish Crown. But their opportunities became limited as time went by. In the second half of the century, all official *vecinos*—a title requiring the Crown's recognition, akin to modern-day citizenship—were white Spaniards.[6] As the indigenous population thinned due to illnesses or exploitation or because they ran away to the mountains or other islands, the settlers began to look elsewhere for labor. This period marked the beginnings of African enslaved labor in Puerto Rico.

Since their arrival in the Caribbean, Spaniards had been awed by the abundance of gold. The glistening metal that the Taínos seemed to take for granted was plentiful in the riverbanks and soil. Social and economic life in the conquest's early days was organized around mining gold. The amount of gold produced during the first decades of the sixteenth century was staggering. From 1509 to 1546, for example, the Spanish Crown received two million gold pesos from the Island of San Juan.[7]

The practice of mining was labor-intensive and understood as antithetical to the Spanish settlers' lifestyle. Instead, Spaniards forced indigenous peoples to endure harsh working conditions while they mostly took care of melting the precious metal. But indigenous workers quickly became scarce. The violence of the conquest, the germs brought by the settlers, and the perils of mining took a toll on Borikén's indigenous communities. Early settlers constantly complained to the Crown that there was an abundance of gold but a shortage of workers to mine it. This became the justification for importing enslaved African peoples.

Not all people of African descent enjoyed the privileges of the Mexía family, who had arrived as freed people and were able to accrue a small fortune during the early stages of the conquest. Most Africans disembarking on the Island of San Juan during the early days of the conquest arrived in shackles and were forced to work from sunset to sundown.[8] The settlers argued that the few hundred enslaved people were not enough and asked the Crown to grant them licenses to import more. Most were employed in the gold mines and, later, in the burgeoning sugar industry. The first sugar mill began operation in 1522.[9] Like mining, sugar harvesting was also labor-intensive. By the 1520s, planters were also calling for more enslaved people because the ones on the islands already were dying in large numbers.[10]

Just like indigenous peoples, Africans suffered the brunt of the conquest's genocidal impulse. And just like indigenous peoples had done, they did not passively comply. While records are unclear and vague, it seems that the first enslaved revolt in the Americas took place in Borikén in 1514. In that year a major storm hit the island. Storms, as the indigenous communities had known for centuries and Europeans would quickly find out, are a recurring event in the region.[11] The 1514 storm not only made food scarce but also impacted the mining economy. It seems that the mining schedule was altered that year, affording laborers a mere month of rest between mining seasons. The storm hit as workers returned to the mines, and it was around this time that enslaved peoples revolted.[12] The following year a letter to the Spanish Crown mentioned that Black peoples were *alzados*, a term used for rebellion. The threat was not just that Black peoples were alzados but that they were joining forces with "indios alzados."[13]

Open rebellion was not the only strategy used by indigenous peoples and those of African descent to resist conquest. Others acted individually. In 1527 Juan Garcés, a Taíno man who worked on the Real Hacienda del Toa, the Crown's official estate in Puerto Rico, crossed the Atlantic Ocean for a private meeting with King Charles I. Garcés arrived in Sevilla and made his way to Burgos, where he met with the king on February 15, 1528. The sources are unclear as to what the purpose of the trip was and how he was able to finance it. It seems, however, that the Crown wanted to investigate Blas de Villasante for fiscal and administrative irregularities; he was one of the most powerful men

in Puerto Rico and ran the Real Hacienda. Although there are no records of the conversation between the monarch and Garcés, Villasante,
who was also notoriously violent toward indigenous people, was dismissed from his position and arrested shortly thereafter.[14]

Administering the Colony

The Spaniards first settled in Caparra, a village located in the northeastern part of the island, in 1508. A few years later people began complaining
about the location: access to potable water was limited, commerce was
difficult because the settlement did not have a port, and the poor conditions were leading to the deaths of young children, many before they
turned three years old. Most vecinos argued that the village should be
moved. Juan Ponce de León, by then the island's highest authority, disagreed. He had invested in land that would be lost with the move. After
a series of legal battles, the Crown sided with Caparra's vecinos. The
move to the islet of San Juan, where the capital has been located ever
since, began in 1519. The transfer was officially completed in 1522.[15]

While the ultimate political power resided in the captaincy general
of Santo Domingo, Puerto Rico was administratively divided in two
units: the city of San Juan, which controlled the eastern side, and San
Germán in the western district. Because the Spanish population was so
small—four to five thousand people between 1510 and 1520—these administrative units relied on fictional borders.[16] Much like Caparra,
which was attacked several times by indigenous peoples, the town of
San Germán had to be moved on multiple occasions. Indigenous communities, corsairs, and pirates repeatedly looted it and burned it down.
It was finally settled in its current location in 1573.[17] Beyond San Juan
and San Germán, there were areas where *cimarrones* (runaways) lived
and thrived outside the colonial state.

To properly administer the colony, the Crown implemented a system
of cabildos. These medieval councils managed the colony's political and
economic organization. In the process, they consolidated Spain's settler-
colonial project in an attempt to populate the island and establish
a political apparatus. San Juan's cabildo began operation in 1511 and

San Germán's in 1514.[18] The cabildos supervised the creation of new settlements and towns, collected taxes, and oversaw land distribution, which became particularly important in the second half of the sixteenth century when cattle ranching emerged as the colony's main economic activity.[19]

While the cabildos created an administrative structure, the island remained mostly uninhabited. When news began arriving about the conquest of Mexico in 1521, and later Peru in 1531, most settlers dreamed of leaving Puerto Rico altogether. The phrase "May God take me to Peru" became quite common. The promises of riches must have been an enormous motivator, more so when many people had accrued large debts. This was in part due to the slave trade. It seems that almost every vecino in Puerto Rico had bought an enslaved person even when they could not afford to.[20]

The potential exodus became a real problem for colonial authorities. Governor Francisco Manuel de Lando asked the Spanish Crown to intervene. Lando wrote:

> This is the entry point and key to all the Indies: we are the first with whom the French and English corsairs run into, as they have done so; the Caribs take our vecinos and friends to their lands, and if a ship were to arrive with only fifty people at night, they could burn and kill all of those of us that live here. I ask for your mercy and exception for this noble island, now so uninhabited that you barely see Spaniards, just Black peoples . . . I know that some people had asked for licenses to take their Black enslaved people to Peru; Your Majesty, do not consent to them or to the Black people.[21]

Lando's request was quite telling. He was concerned about the low number of white settlers in relation to the growing number of enslaved Black people. According to a report he ordered, in 1530 there were 347 Spaniards, 2,077 Black people, and 1,537 indigenous people.[22] By then, both indigenous and African workers had organized revolts against the Spaniards, and the Caribs continued their sneak attacks on different parts of coastal Puerto Rico. Because of this, the potential exodus of settlers would be detrimental to Spain. The governor took matters into his own hands. When authorities caught people trying to leave without proper documentation, some were publicly whipped and the soles of their feet slashed with knives.[23]

By the second half of the sixteenth century, indigenous attacks and depopulation were not the only problems colonial authorities faced. New European powers began arriving in the region. Beginning in the 1530s, every war Spain fought in Europe was felt in the Caribbean. It was an age of naval warfare, and the Caribbean islands became another theater of war.[24]

Governor Lando's administration began to shape the island in other ways. He provided loans for the creation of sugar mills and took the initial steps to fortify the capital city of San Juan, which began in 1531. Two years later, the government erected a turret to protect the port. The Crown also began experimenting with different forms of governance. In 1537, a system of ordinary mayors functioned as the island's first self-government. It was a way of empowering vecinos in the administration of the cabildos. This experiment was short-lived, however. In 1545, Santo Domingo's Royal Audience began naming civilian governors to take over the administration of Puerto Rico. In the following years, a series of attacks by French corsairs startled the Crown: because of the wars in Europe that Spain was waging against the French, French corsairs began to attack Spanish colonies in the Caribbean. In 1565, the Spanish Crown decided to remove Puerto Rico from the purview of Santo Domingo and assigned military governors to rule the island.[25]

To protect its interests, the Spanish Crown also relied on corsairs or privateers. Unlike pirates, who attacked and looted any ship they encountered for personal gain, corsairs had royal licenses to do so. They were put under the service of a particular European country to attack their enemies. French corsairs were well-known and feared in Puerto Rico. After all, they had burned down the town of San Germán on eight different occasions.[26] The English and the Dutch also set their sights on the Caribbean islands. In response to this, Spain created a fleet system in 1561 which included a military convoy that accompanied merchant ships to and from Spain. It was later used to protect the Situado Mexicano, money drawn from profits generated in Mexico. The situado was created in 1582 and was sent to the Caribbean colonies to sustain the military apparatus. At times, the situado was the only source of funds flowing to these islands.[27] The fleet system was highly effective in protecting the situado; while it was attacked on multiple occasions, only twice during its more than two centuries in operation did foreign powers seize the treasure the fleet protected.[28]

By the second half of the sixteenth century, Puerto Rico began to lose its economic importance. Mining had been the conquest's initial engine and by the 1530s it was clear that it was losing steam. Sugar production, which required heavy investments and extensive labor, became an important economic enterprise, only to all but disappear the following century.[29] The economy was diversified between cattle raising, agricultural production, and contraband. The latter became a lifeline for many Puerto Ricans at a moment when food was in abundance, to the point of only killing cattle for its skin, while products like fabric for clothing, oil, and wine were scarce.[30]

A letter from Governor Juan de Céspedes in 1581 echoed Lando's earlier assessment: the island was becoming depopulated and constantly under attack from Carib Indians.[31] An earlier letter by Governor Diego de Caraza had also expressed that the island was lacking people who could work because "the very few Indians available are no good . . . and we are out of Blacks."[32] These, of course, were exaggerations, but they reveal the social conditions in the second half of the sixteenth century. Governor Lando noted that there were only 1,043 indigenous people in 1530. That number was certainly higher but, as historian Francisco Moscoso has noted, it seems that no less than 90 percent of Puerto Rico's indigenous population fled to the mountains and other Caribbean islands or died due to exploitative labor, suicide, and epidemics.[33] Contrary to traditional histories, however, they did not simply become "extinct." Those who fled to the mountains continued their practices and traditions, eventually permeating into Puerto Rico's social fabric with Taíno names, foods, and agricultural practices that survived for centuries (and still survive).[34]

While the Caribbean had been the Spanish Crown's first epicenter in the Americas, it lost its economic importance after the depletion of its

FIGURE 2.1. Topographic map of Puerto Rico, c. 1791.
Source: Library of Congress.

gold reserves and after the conquest of Mexico and Peru. But Puerto Rico retained its strategic relevance and became a military outpost of the Spanish Empire. Its location made it ideal to protect Spanish interests in the region. It was, as settlers and even the king often noted in their correspondence, "the key to the Indies." It was of utmost importance to protect it from foreign powers.

In 1595 the Spanish colonial government faced the threat of a potential occupation. That year, Sir Francis Drake, an English privateer feared by the Spanish, sought to take the capital city of San Juan. The attack was not exactly a surprise to Spanish authorities. In 1585, the Crown had sent two messages to San Juan warning them to prepare for a possible English attack.[35] In August 1595, Drake received information that the flagship of the Spanish fleet had stopped in Puerto Rico for some repairs while carrying multiple treasures.[36] Armed with this news, he convinced the English Crown to authorize his expedition. Weeks before his arrival in Puerto Rico, the Spanish Crown's espionage network also received information about Drake's imminent assault. In November 1595, Drake's impressive convoy, composed of twenty-seven ships and 2,500 soldiers, approached the San Juan Bay. The Spanish's Morro fortifications were put to the test for the first time in their history. Early in the battle, on November 22, Drake's ship was hit by a cannonball, wounding him. The following day the English waited until nighttime to try to take San Juan but a ship on fire illuminated the bay—and the target for the Spanish artillery. On November 24, Drake tried again but the Spanish sank three ships in the harbor, forcing him to retreat.[37]

Drake's attack was part of the Anglo-Spanish War, a conflict between Spain and England that took place from 1585 to 1604. Not only fought in Europe, the war led to skirmishes throughout the Caribbean. In 1598 the English once again attacked Puerto Rico. Sir George Clifford, Earl of Cumberland, succeeded in taking the capital city of San Juan and the flag of England was raised in El Morro until events took an unexpected turn.

On June 16, 1598, Sir George Clifford led an expedition of twenty ships and 1,700 men. Unlike Drake, Clifford did not try to take San Juan through the bay. Instead, his troops landed miles away from the capital. After a series of battles, the English were able to force the Spanish troops into retreat. The Spanish locked themselves in El Morro as the English took over the capital city of San Juan. Almost two weeks later, the Spanish troops surrendered and Puerto Rico became an English possession. However, in September a dysentery epidemic spread through the earl's troops, forcing him to leave the island. The occupation had been a disaster. Clifford lost 600 soldiers and was not able to cover the cost of the expedition even after ransacking the capital.[38]

On September 25, 1625, twenty-seven years after Clifford's occupation, another military attack shook colonial authorities in Puerto Rico. After a failed attempt to retake San Salvador de Bahia in Brazil, the Dutch sought to inflict damage on Spanish possessions in the Americas. Puerto Rico became the target of a squadron led by General Boudewijn Hendricksz. His fleet, composed of seventeen Dutch ships, easily entered San Juan Bay, taking the Spanish by surprise. The battle lasted more than a month.[39] When Hendriksz demanded Spain's surrender a second time, he also threatened to burn down the city. The recently appointed Spanish governor, Juan de Haro, noted, "And if you burn the place, our neighbors have courage to make other houses because they have wood in the mountains and other materials from the land."[40] True to his threats, Hendriksz destroyed San Juan. But he was not able to occupy it. The Spanish troops resisted and were joined by militia companies under the orders of Patricio de la Concepción, a man of color.[41] The Dutch abandoned San Juan on November 1, 1625, leaving behind destruction that took decades to recover from.[42] But war was not the only thing affecting the people of Puerto Rico.

Outside Legality

The history of Puerto Rico cannot be limited to European battles or statecraft. Most of the island's inhabitants lived beyond the city centers and were left on their own. While food was never lacking, other necessities were scarce. The Catholic Church constantly complained that because people lacked fabric for clothing, they could not attend mass. The situation was so dire that some church services were moved to the evening so the darkness of night could cover people's bodies.[43]

The Spanish Crown also participated in the era's mercantilist system, which depended on national accumulation of wealth and riches. Spain did this through a state-based monopoly: merchants were not allowed to trade with foreign countries. To make matters more difficult, San Juan was the only port authorized by the Crown. These monopolistic policies were particularly harsh when Spain was at war and a limited number of ships arrived on Puerto Rican shores. From 1651 to 1699, for example, only twenty-eight ships from Spain, seventy-one from the Americas, and three from the Canary Islands arrived in Puerto Rico. Not a single Spanish vessel arrived in Puerto Rico from 1700 to 1706.[44]

Given the dire economic situation, contraband, or unofficial trade, became a lifeline for many during the seventeenth and eighteenth centuries. Those who lived in Puerto Rico often traded with ships that carried multiple flags. This was well known and acknowledged even by religious and secular authorities. Friar Íñigo Abbad y Lasierra, writing in the first wide-ranging history of Puerto Rico, published in 1788, alleged that there were at least twelve different unauthorized ports around the island used for contraband.[45]

By the end of the seventeenth century, Spain had lost its primacy in the seas as France, England, and Holland expanded their naval reach. These countries also claimed territories in the Caribbean. Meanwhile, Puerto Rico's colonial economy went through its most dire contraction yet.[46] This was heightened by a monarchical crisis in the Iberian Peninsula after the death of Charles II of Spain and the House of Habsburg's unsuccessful fight against the House of Bourbon from 1702 to 1713.[47]

The European conflict had immediate consequences in Puerto Rico. The English unsuccessfully attacked the island in 1702 and, as had happened in the past, years passed with no official ships and no outside supplies. Now, Spain used corsairs to defend its coasts. One individual who successfully merged the legal system of privateering with contraband was Miguel Enríquez.

At a moment when Spain was going through the War of Succession, Enríquez rose to power in Puerto Rico by protecting the Crown's interests and successfully opposing European threats to the Spanish Caribbean. By doing so, he became the wealthiest and most powerful person in Puerto Rico. Unlike the rest of San Juan's elite at the time, Enríquez was a *pardo*, the son of a formerly enslaved Black woman and a white father who never recognized him. These two social traits were markers of social inferiority in Spanish colonial society.[48]

Enríquez's story highlights the many ways that individuals had to devise strategies to navigate social hierarchies. Enríquez's actions challenged colonial regulations but did so without resulting in open confrontation. Literary scholar Arcadio Díaz Quiñones has called these maneuvers Puerto Ricans' art of *bregar*. For Díaz Quiñones, bregar—which does not neatly fit its English translation of "struggle"—is a strategic practice of working around colonial violence without necessarily publicly opposing or conceding to it.[49]

Miguel Enríquez was born on September 29, 1674. His grandmother was an enslaved woman who had been born in Africa and was later forcefully brought to Puerto Rico. His mother, Graciana, was born into slavery in Puerto Rico. Although Graciana's father never recognized her, she was granted her freedom as a baby and was later raised in her father's house, where she was forced to serve as a maid during her teenage years.

Enríquez, born free, was also the son of a white man. It was not unusual for white men to rape or have unrecognized relationships with freed or enslaved women of color.[50]

At a young age, Enríquez was mentored by a clergyman who was also well-connected in San Juan's world of politics. Under his tutelage, Enríquez learned to write and eventually secured an apprenticeship in a shoemaking workshop. When Enríquez first tried his luck with contraband in 1700, he was caught and arrested. He was sentenced to hard labor in El Morro, but the clergyman's contacts helped him get a lighter sentence working in the artillery. The clergyman, Enríquez later learned, was his father.

While serving his sentence, Enríquez's skills caught the eye of Governor Gabriel Gutiérrez de la Riba. The governor eventually made Enríquez his right-hand man in contraband activities. To protect himself, the governor put several properties, including houses and sailboats, under Enríquez's name. When Gutiérrez de la Riba unexpectedly died in 1703, Enríquez inherited all these properties along with contacts he had accrued while secretly collaborating with the governor. This would launch his career as a corsair and contrabandist.[51]

During the first three decades of the eighteenth century, Enríquez amassed one of the largest fortunes in the Americas; he held more wealth than all other Puerto Ricans combined. His fleet of ships numbered more than 150; he also owned around 300 enslaved people. Enríquez could also buy political positions for allies, including governorships. At a moment when most lived in precarity, Enríquez enjoyed the finest wines, meats, and cheeses. His role in defending the island did not go unnoticed by the Crown. The king made him a captain and later granted him the Royal Effigy, effectively making him a knight with the title of "don." These were the highest honors any Puerto Rican ever received during Spanish colonial rule, all while being an illegitimate pardo, something that his enemies constantly repeated.[52]

When the Crown consolidated its control over the Caribbean in the 1730s he lost royal protection once he had ceased to be an asset to Spain.[53] In Puerto Rico, the elite also conspired against him. Once the most powerful man on the island, in 1735 he was forced to seek shelter in a Catholic convent. He spent the last seven years of his life there and died penniless. Although he had paid for the funerals of San Juan's most powerful people, he was buried in an unmarked grave. As Enríquez noted in his memoir—which he dictated to his nephew during his cloistered years—when he was free, Puerto Rico never lacked a thing.[54] He ensured the island had much-needed supplies and protection. But the white elite could not fathom that a man of color possessed such power.

Enríquez's life story highlights some of the contradictions that ensued during and after the consolidation of Spain's settler-colonial project. By the turn of the eighteenth century, official documents began referring to those born in Puerto Rico as *naturales* or *puertorriqueños*. A 1647 document is one of the earliest to describe the physical condition of naturales, or those born in Puerto Rico.[55] In 1705, some official documents referred to those born in Puerto Rico as puertorriqueños. That year, a military soldier complained to the Spanish Crown about the precarious situation in San Juan. He noted that there were 400 soldiers, but not even 250 were of use: "Many of them . . . are puertorriqueños, bastards of governors, of royal officers, and the army." The soldier said they were unworthy of the positions they had been granted while Spaniards were abandoned.[56]

While much research is still required, it seems that the category of criollo that began to be used in the 1700s in reference to those born in Puerto Rico was reserved for the white elite. "For Puerto Rican criollos," writes historian Mario R. Cancel-Sepúlveda, "being a *pardo*, as non-whites were defined at the end of the eighteenth century, made you not worthy of the title of criollo." For the elites, being "Black or mulatto was equivalent to an error or a lack of honor, dignity, and décor."[57]

As the social category of puertorriqueño was emerging, whiteness was zealously policed by colonial elites. Meanwhile, contraband was all but sanctioned by colonial authorities. This gave a person of color with the connections, will, and knowledge, like Enríquez, an opportunity for social mobility. Through contraband, he became a renowned shipowner with an impressive fleet that protected Spain's "key to the Indies" at a moment when the metropolis was too busy fighting other European powers. Merging the world of corsairs and contraband allowed Enríquez to acquire power and prestige. But the colonial elite never allowed him to forget that he was still a descendant of enslaved peoples.

Enríquez was not the only challenge colonial elites faced. In a society convinced that a person's race was inextricable from their value, Europeans were startled when, at the end of the eighteenth century, free and enslaved people of color in the French colony of Saint-Domingue took up arms and declared a revolution. The thirteen-year-long revolution led them to abolish slavery, end French colonialism, and create the republic of Haiti—the continent's second republic, after the United States, and, perhaps most important, the world's first Black republic. The winds of freedom that gusted from Haiti gave hope to many, but they also terrified the colonial authorities in Puerto Rico.

CHAPTER 3

REVOLUTIONARY WINDS: FROM REFORM TO REVOLUTION

During the first two centuries of Spanish colonization in the Americas, Puerto Rico was ruled with an iron fist. Spain created viceroys to control vast territories across the Americas that extended from modern-day Patagonia to Alaska. There were important exceptions, of course. Puerto Rico was not part of a viceroyalty. The Portuguese also claimed the territories of Brazil while European empires clashed in the Caribbean as they sought to expand their sugar-producing markets or their spheres of influence.

Puerto Rico was of military importance to the Spanish Crown, but the people who inhabited the archipelago were an afterthought. For those in the working classes, life in the colony was difficult. Contraband was officially banned as the state promoted trade through official channels, but reality was very different on the ground. People illegally traded with sailors on ships that flew different imperial flags—French, Dutch, or English. The ship flag's color didn't matter if its cargo brought much-needed provisions. Those ships carried supplies, but they also transported ideas—these were very dangerous to colonial administrators.[1]

The eighteenth century was a time of transformation for the Spanish Empire. After the War of Succession (1701–14), the House of Bourbon took over the Spanish Crown and issued a series of reforms meant to oil the imperial bureaucratic machine Spain had created in the Americas: the power of the Church was curtailed, contraband would be punished, and the state's administrative control centralized, among other things.[2] Social hierarchies anchored in race and gender were important for the functioning of the Spanish colonial apparatus. And when enslaved peoples got together and declared a revolution in the neighboring colony of Saint-Domingue, it set Puerto Rico's colonial authorities and planter class on edge.[3]

Saint-Domingue, later named Haiti, was the most profitable colony in the world by the late eighteenth century. A possession of the French empire, it produced enough sugar to satisfy the world. That enormous wealth, however, was produced on the backs and through the exploitation of Black peoples. In 1789, Saint-Domingue was inhabited by 32,000 white people, 55,000 people of color, and almost 450,000 enslaved people. The number of enslaved people may have been higher since they were considered chattel and often inaccurately counted in censuses by planters trying to evade taxes.[4]

What began as an enslaved insurrection in 1791 quickly became a revolution that produced the second independent nation of the Americas and the first Black republic in the world. For anthropologist Michel-Rolph Trouillot, the Haitian Revolution was "unthinkable" because Europeans could not fathom the idea that enslaved peoples had the capacity to organize a revolution.[5] But what took place in Haiti in 1791 occurred regardless of what Europeans thought, wanted, or desired. Perhaps that is why it remains powerful: the revolution may have happened on the fringes of Europe, but it reshaped Western modernity.[6] "Enslaved people who were considered chattel rather than human beings," writes historian Laurent Dubois, "successfully insisted that they had the right to be free and, secondly, that they had the right to govern themselves according to a new set of principles." In the process, they "propelled the Enlightenment principles of universalism forward in unexpected ways by insisting on the self-evident—but then largely denied—principle that no one should be a slave."[7]

After the revolution, Haiti came to signify different things to different people. It was a ghost that haunted white elites in the colonies and imperial metropoles. For those enslaved, Haiti became a glimmer of hope. Revolts proliferated throughout the Caribbean and it was not uncommon to find drawings of Haiti's revolutionary leaders like Henri Cristophe and Toussaint Louverture among the belongings of those captured.[8]

The Haitian Revolution was part of a broader revolutionary moment that swept the Atlantic world. In the United States, insurgents successfully created an independent country in their 1776 revolution. The people of France overthrew the monarchy and created a republican government in a revolution that began in 1789. Two years later, the first shots of the Haitian Revolution were fired. As Laurent Dubois has noted, the French and Haitian Revolutions "emerged symbiotically as news, ideologies, and people crisscrossed the Atlantic, as actors in the Caribbean deployed the ideals and symbols of republicanism and pushed the meaning of citizenship and national belonging in new directions."[9] These ideas posed an enormous threat to the Spanish Crown and its colonial possessions across the Americas. In less than two decades, revolution became inevitable in many Spanish colonial possessions. Because of its geographic location, Puerto Rico was at the center of the storm.

Between Colonial Reform and Imperial Crisis

In the eighteenth century, European wars created a ripple effect across the Atlantic world. During France's revolutionary wars, Napoleon Bonaparte excelled as a military strategist and politician. In 1799 he seized power and created a bureaucratic and dictatorial government. Shortly after, in 1803, he began a series of military attacks and conflicts later known as the Napoleonic Wars, which lasted until 1815. These had huge repercussions throughout the territories we know today as Latin America and the Caribbean. It was a time of revolutionary fervor and the expansion of Enlightenment ideas. The American and French Revolutions inspired fear in European monarchical systems. The call for *liberté, egalité, fraternité* was a powerful slogan that mobilized people to demand rights and to challenge monarchical systems of government by insisting on popular sovereignty.[10]

In 1807, Portugal went against France's wishes to close its ports and declare war on England, its old ally. Napoleon Bonaparte seized an opportunity to attack Portugal. Prince João fled to Brazil, along with the Portuguese Crown, moving the center of the empire's gravity from Lisbon to Rio de Janeiro. Napoleon sought to strike a deal with Charles IV and his son Prince Fernando to allow his army to cross Spain in order to invade Portugal. On May 2, 1808, as his forces marched to Madrid, Napoleon declared war on Spain, forcing the king and prince into exile in France. The Spanish courts moved from Madrid to Cádiz to resist the Napoleonic invasion. This created dueling seats of power in Spain between José Bonaparte, colloquially known as Pepe Botella (Pepe Bottle) because of his drinking habits, as the representative of the Napoleonic Empire, and the Regency, which became a symbol of Spanish monarchical resistance.[11]

While the Portuguese Crown held a strong grip on Brazil, these events immediately created a crisis of legitimacy for Spain in its colonies. Factions emerged in Spanish America that wanted to maintain their loyalty to the Crown, while others saw the moment as an opportunity to create new sovereign nations. From 1808 to 1826, revolutionary movements spread like wildfire in Spanish America, leading to the independence of Spain's former colonies—except for Cuba and Puerto Rico.

Both the Napoleonic government and the Spanish Regency sent emissaries to their American colonies to garner support. When the French arrived in Puerto Rico, Governor Toribio Montes arrested them and put them in the gallows at San Juan's Morro fortifications. He also sent a message of loyalty to Spain. Meanwhile, the Puerto Rican elite, then composed of white planters of European descent, were engaged in fiery debates about how to best proceed. Amid the political tensions between liberals and conservatives in the Cádiz courts, the Regency allowed representatives from its American colonies to join them in the royal courts.[12]

In May 1809, elections were called for the first time in Puerto Rico's history to select a representative. At that time, the archipelago was divided into five cabildos, or administrative councils: San Juan, San Germán, Aguada, Arecibo, and Coamo. Each cabildo chose five candidates, whose names were then forwarded to the provincial electoral board in San Juan. The board was composed of the governor, the bishop, and a member of the San Juan cabildo. After tense conversations, the cabildos elected a navy lieutenant educated in Spain and France, Ramón Power y Giralt.[13]

The cabildos oversaw the creation of a document containing *instrucciones* for Puerto Rico's first representative in the Spanish courts. All stated their loyalty to the monarchy and then proceeded to complain about Spain's "oppressive, arbitrary, and tyrannical" rule and suggest a series of reforms.[14] These included the creation of a University of Puerto Rico with campuses in San Juan and San Germán, more schools, the abolition of onerous taxes, and labor reforms.[15] The San Germán cabildo went further and proclaimed that if Spain fell into French hands, "this island shall be independent and free to choose the best way to conserve and to maintain the peace and Christian Religion of its inhabitants."[16] That Puerto Ricans understood their struggle as part of other independence movements is often minimized by historians. And, in the context of the wars for independence in Spanish America, the San Germán cabildo was echoing a sentiment perhaps more generalized than has been documented.

The town of San Germán had a long history of protesting the colonial government, stretching back to the eighteenth century. In addition, several members of the local criollo elite—as Puerto Ricans of European descent were called—were known to be separatists. In fact, the same year that Ramón Power y Giralt was elected to the Spanish courts, Francisco Antonio Ramírez de Arellano, a prominent member of the town's elite who had served as mayor, was secretly organizing an armed uprising to take place during the 1811 Christmas celebrations in San Germán.[17] The planned insurrection was halted a few days prior to its scheduled date because the rebels received information that a Spanish ship had arrived in Puerto Rico with four thousand troops. What they didn't know was that the ship carried just four hundred soldiers who were actually destined for Mexico and Venezuela to fight against *independentistas* there.[18]

News of the planned uprising eventually reached governor Salvador Meléndez Bruno, who launched an investigation on January 21, 1812. While charges were eventually dropped against those arrested or accused, the list of those involved included prominent members of San Germán's elite. The governor's fears about a possible rebellion were heightened by the appearance of leaflets and posters advocating for independence. Flyers arguing that no Puerto Rican would be sent to Venezuela to fight their brothers struggling for independence floated through the streets of San Germán. The authorities also believed that separatists in Puerto Rico were being protected by powerful people, including Ramón Power y Giralt and the first Puerto Rican–born bishop, Juan Alejo de Arizmendi.[19]

In 1823, when the Regency once again repealed the constitution and gave colonial governors absolute power to rule as they saw fit, the government's repressive apparatus was tightened. The move was heavily contested by colonial representatives in the courts and later abolished. In Puerto Rico, separatists were not the only group to be feared. The ghost of Haiti haunted government officials and a series of enslaved revolts heightened those fears.

Four years after the Haitian Revolution, enslaved peoples attempted an insurrection in the western town of Aguadilla. While the insurrection failed, it instilled panic about Haiti's influence in Puerto Rico.[20] Following the Peace of Basel in 1795, when Spain declared peace with the French and restarted commerce between the two countries, articles alluding to the French Revolution began circulating in Spanish America. Governor Ramón de Castro prohibited French imports to Puerto Rico. He also ordered local authorities to closely monitor foreigners, particularly those of French ancestry.[21]

Colonial fears once again came to the fore in 1805, when authorities reported that a Haitian agent named Chaulette was traveling through Puerto Rico. Governor Toribio Montes sent a notice to all of the island's lieutenants about his arrival and described him as an eighteen-to-twenty-year-old mulatto versed in English, French, and Spanish. He ended the notice by ordering his capture before "he spills his damn seed in this island that enjoys loyalty and calmness."[22] He was never captured, and it was later learned that he had been sent by Haitian general Jean-Jacques Dessalines to advocate for insurrection and revolution, not only in Puerto Rico but throughout the Caribbean.[23]

During the Napoleonic occupation of the Iberian Peninsula, Spain became, for the first time in its history, a constitutional monarchy. In 1812, the Cádiz courts approved its first constitution, colloquially known as La Pepa, which recognized for the first time in Spanish America's colonial history that Spaniards on both sides of the Atlantic were citizens of the Spanish nation, not subjects of the king. The constitution was revoked in 1814 when King Fernando VII returned to the throne after expelling Napoleon's forces. With political tensions running high, the Spanish Crown reestablished the constitution twice, only to abolish it again in 1823.[24]

The news of the constitution arrived in Puerto Rico on July 9, 1812. A year earlier, the courts had approved legislation known as the "Power Laws," in reference to Puerto Rico's colonial representative, Ramón Power y Giralt. These laws allowed the opening of ports in different coastal towns (thereby abolishing San Juan's port monopoly), authorized the free import of flour, and eased some taxes. Governor Meléndez disliked the politics that were beginning to operate in Spain but nonetheless declared the 1812 constitution in force. Great celebrations took place in different parts of the island.[25] Rumors circulated among the San Juan enslaved population that following the French and the British, the Spanish courts had also abolished slavery, but local officials were not complying. Authorities were informed about a planned insurrection that was never confirmed. The rumors gave the colonial government an excuse to accuse and arrest dozens. These events offered the government carte blanche to conduct state-sponsored terror, exploitation, and violence.[26]

Reform, Repression, and Revolution

After Fernando VII abolished the Spanish constitution in 1814, the situation in the Americas continued to worry his administration. It was in Spain's best interest to offer Puerto Rico reforms in hopes of keeping the colonial administration loyal to the Crown. Revolutionary winds were blowing through the creole elite, as the appearance of leaflets and posters made abundantly clear to authorities. In October 1814, King

Fernando asked the San Juan cabildo to send a list of potential reforms. The next year he issued the "Cédula de Gracias," a decree that granted a series of social and economic reforms to Puerto Rico for a period of fifteen years, unless extended by subsequent decrees.[27]

The Cédula de Gracias sought to move Puerto Rico from subsistence to a plantation economy, one capable of exporting its agricultural production. To that end, the decree alleviated taxes and restrictions on migration. The reforms worked. As historian Olga Jiménez de Wagenheim has noted, "Although there is no statistical breakdown of how many immigrants the Cédula attracted to Puerto Rico, there is evidence that between 1815–1834 the island's population grew by 38 percent, or 138,000."[28] The island's population also grew exponentially throughout the century, from 155,426 in 1800 to 953,243 in 1897. This demographic explosion was due to a higher natality rate, migration caused by the Haitian Revolution (1791–1804) and the Spanish American wars of independence (1808–33), and the slave trade.[29]

In 1819, the value per capita of exported products was 1,098,083 pesos and by 1844 it had reached 6,204,704. Puerto Rico began massively exporting coffee, tobacco, and sugar. In that triad, sugar became king. Its production, however, depended on the uninterrupted continuation of the system of chattel slavery.[30]

Under pressure from the British, the Spanish Crown signed the Anglo-Spanish Treaty in 1814 promising to limit the slave trade in their colonies. This treaty became a dead letter as Puerto Rico saw the growth of its enslaved population from 13,333 in 1802 to 51,265 in 1846.[31] During that same period there were at least twenty-five rebellions, insurrections, or conspiracies where enslaved peoples fought for their freedom. In some cases, they simply sought to escape their plantations while in others they advocated for a revolution. Maroon communities also existed at this time in places like Jamaica, Haiti, and elsewhere in the Caribbean. In all these cases, the struggle for liberation eluded archives and history books.[32]

Enslaved peoples' attempts to attain their freedom were not the only problem that troubled Spanish authorities. In the 1820s, separatists began organizing once again to advocate for the independence of Puerto

Rico through revolutionary means. The authorities always kept a watchful eye on a group, publicly known as liberals, which included María de las Mercedes Barbudo and her brother José Antonio de los Reyes, Juan Nepomuceno Otero, the priest Juan Abreu, the Spanish lieutenant Manuel Suárez del Solar, the deputy Demetrio O'Daly, and the Puerto Rican lieutenant Matías Escuté.[33] The liberals were members of the Puerto Rican elite, with contacts throughout the island and abroad. Some were arrested while María de las Mercedes Barbudo was exiled to Cuba and later spent time in Venezuela, where she is said to have known Simón Bolívar, later celebrated as the liberator of the Americas for his military role in the independence of various Latin American countries.[34] Barbudo's group were not the only Puerto Ricans agitating for revolution. In 1822, another liberal group from Puerto Rico's western district sent an invitation to Guillermo Lafayette Ducoudray Holstein, a veteran of Bolívar's army in Venezuela, asking him to organize an expedition to fight for Puerto Rico's independence.[35]

After a crushing defeat in Venezuela, Holstein had moved to the island of Curazao. He was studying French and piano when he received the invitation to liberate Puerto Rico, something Latin American revolutionaries had openly advocated for more than once. He accepted and moved to Philadelphia to garner financial support for the expedition. There, he recruited businessmen eager to begin trade with an independent Puerto Rico. He also assembled an army of two to four hundred men to fight. The plan was to invade through the town of Arecibo and then move to the city of Mayagüez, which would become the military headquarters for the Republic of Boricua.[36]

Preparations were cut short. In 1822 a new military governor, Miguel de la Torre, arrived on the island. Simón Bolívar's army had recently expelled Spanish troops from Venezuela and de la Torre had been one of those defeated in the Battle of Carobobo (1822). Haunted by this shameful defeat, the governor ruled Puerto Rico ruthlessly.[37] Shortly after his arrival, he ordered the persecution and arrest of those deemed subversives, among them the Barbudos, Escuté, and others. Deputy O'Daly was forced into exile in Saint Thomas.[38] The revolution's strategists were all imprisoned or exiled.

Rumors of Holstein's upcoming invasion, leaked by contacts in Philadelphia, also reached the governor's office. Spanish authorities moved forces to the town of Añasco, where the expedition was set to land. But Holstein never arrived in Puerto Rico. He set sail from the United States to the island of St. Bartholomew but the expedition was hit by a storm. When he arrived in Curazao, his ship was on the verge of sinking. Pressured by the Spanish Crown, Dutch authorities in Curazao arrested him before he could sail to Puerto Rico.[39]

Holstein's failed revolution was Governor Miguel de la Torre's welcome to the archipelago. His time in office (1822–37) was consumed with worry about Haiti, as had been the case with previous administrations. And after 1821 another specter began haunting the Spanish in the Caribbean: Simón Bolívar.

Puerto Rican authorities paid careful attention to a congress that took place in Panama in June 1826. There, Bolívar proposed the creation of a federation of nations, a plan that ultimately was not approved. The congress also discussed the possibility of creating a military expedition composed of forces from Gran Colombia and Mexico to fight for independence in Puerto Rico. Those plans were later abandoned. Meanwhile, in Mexico, independence generals José Antonio Paéz and José Antonio Valero were organizing an army of about twenty-five thousand men to fight in Cuba and Puerto Rico. This war did not materialize either but it nonetheless terrified colonial authorities. Rumors circulated about Bolívar's possible invasion in January 1827, March 1828, and February 1829. The fears of invasion dissipated after the Gran Colombia–Peru War (1828–29), the separation of Venezuela, Ecuador, and Panama from Gran Colombia, and Bolívar's death in 1830.[40]

In this tense atmosphere, the Spanish Crown once again suspended constitutional rights in 1823. Until then, Puerto Rico had been governed by two forces: a civilian governor and a military general. After that year, the position of civilian governor was abolished, giving way to rule by military men given dictatorial power by the Spanish Crown. Recognizing the powers bestowed on him, Miguel de la Torre passed the Bando de Policía y Buen Gobierno (The Police and Good Government Proclamation), which sought to shape, control, and dominate social relations in Puerto Rico.[41]

The bando was composed of dozens of ordinances regulating mobility, labor, and space. After it was approved on January 2, 1824, it was read aloud in the streets of every municipality.[42] Town mayors also received a copy and were instructed to implement it immediately. Some ordinances demanded that mayors inform authorities of any foreigners or strangers passing through their towns. It also forced them to create daily logs of information about everything that happened in their municipality. Residents could not admit strangers into their homes without the approval of the town's mayor. The island was put under an evening curfew and private meetings were banned. Lastly, the bando prohibited vagrancy, including young people who were unemployed. Those found guilty were arrested and sent to serve in the Spanish army.[43] The document was a response to Haiti and Bolívar as well as a testament to the circulation of separatist ideas in Puerto Rico.

Miguel de la Torre sought to surveil and control the laboring masses while also catering to planters and merchants. He granted special licenses to slaveholding planters to sell enslaved people even when the world markets were closed. In 1823 Spain signed the Anglo-Spanish Treaty with England to abolish the slave trade. But during de la Torre's administration, more enslaved people arrived in Puerto Rico than ever before.[44] "The state's repressive mechanism," notes historian Fernando Picó, also "made it possible for many [planters] to take out mortgages that were increased by interest rates which were, at least in theory, illegal."[45] The ports, recently opened in accordance with new reforms, received copious merchandise and de la Torre's government purged the Caribbean area of pirates.[46]

While some enjoyed the fleeting sense of prosperity, many suffered from de la Torre's harsh policies. Peasants who owned little or no property, salaried workers, and artisans were also targeted by his government. Despite his authoritarian rule, de la Torre is remembered for his policies around public celebrations—he is known to have ruled with the "three Bs": *baile, botella y baraja* (dancing, drinking, and gambling).

Hoping to quell revolutionary ideas from the Americas then circulating in Puerto Rico, he sought to entertain the masses.[47]

The apparent fiscal prosperity that Puerto Rico was enjoying depended on draconian labor laws and the exploitation of enslaved people. In response to a conspiracy by enslaved people discovered in Ponce in 1826, de la Torre passed new regulations. Building on a previous royal decree of 1789, the governor ordered the surveillance and monitoring of Black people traveling beyond their plantations. He also ordered enslaved people to be locked in at night. The government offered rewards to enslaved individuals who uncovered conspiracies or plans for insurrection. Ultimately, the regulations were meant to dissuade enslaved people from challenging their oppressive conditions. They didn't work. The following decade witnessed at least five other conspiracies in Puerto Rico.[48]

De la Torre established the foundations for other oppressive labor regulations enacted by governors Miguel López de Baños (1837–41), Juan Prim y Prats (1847–48), and Juan de la Pezuela (1848–51).[49] After the 1848 revolutions in Europe, the French government abolished slavery in Martinique and Guadalupe on April 29. The enslaved people of Martinique did not wait for official news to arrive and started an insurrection that eventually reached other Caribbean islands. Alarmed, Governor Prim y Prats sent a battalion to Santa Cruz with five hundred soldiers and two pieces of artillery. The insurrection was quelled, but he feared that it would spread in Puerto Rico. To that end, he passed the Bando contra la Raza Negra (Proclamation against the Black Race).[50] During these decades what we now call anti-Blackness became ensconced in laws that would have a lingering effect on Black people's livelihoods for centuries to come.

Prim y Prats's proclamation targeted Black people, freed or enslaved. According to Article I, if a Black person committed any crime, they would be tried and convicted by a military judge. The second article affirmed white people's superiority in the eyes of the law. If a Black man harmed a white person—even if it was justified and in self-defense—they would be found guilty. If a Black person insulted, threatened, or mistreated a white person, they would be condemned to five years in prison if they were enslaved and "judged accordingly" if they were free. Those who owned enslaved people were also given the power to kill them if they sought to revolt.[51]

Prim y Prats's dictatorial impulses, which also included extrajudicial executions of bandits, caused him to be removed from his charge by the Spanish Crown. His successor, Juan de la Pezuela, abolished the Bando contra la Raza Negra while exhorting enslaved Black people to be submissive and to submit to their condition.[52] The governor also moved to regulate labor by decreeing the Reglamento de Jornaleros (Day Laborer's Regulation) on June 11, 1849. It mandated that all young men be employed. Furthermore, workers were required to carry a logbook issued by the municipal judge. In that logbook, his employer noted information such as where the worker was employed and how much he was paid. If someone was stopped and surprised without their logbook, they were forced to pay a fine and work on public construction at half their usual salary.[53]

Known as the "logbook regime," the system was a way of controlling the island's labor population. It complemented Governor de la Pezuela's Police Proclamation, which curtailed mobility between towns, banned private meetings, and proscribed an evening curfew of ten o'clock. These proclamations and regulations made de la Pezuela highly unpopular among the laboring masses. He also won the distrust of the San Juan elite by publicly noting that "Puerto Rican society crawls clumsy and sluggishly, without more excitement than carnal appetites, with a vagabond generation, without faith, without religion and without thought" at the inauguration of the Royal Audience in 1849.[54] While de la Pezuela complained and looked down on Puerto Ricans, a new generation of intellectuals and revolutionaries were thinking hard about what it meant to be Puerto Rican in the first place.

The Seeds of Revolution

Spain opened Puerto Rico to foreign markets in the nineteenth century, but it failed to create an infrastructure for the colony to prosper economically. The U.S. Civil War had generated demand for sugar from foreign markets, particularly because of the blockade the North imposed on Southern states. When the war ended and those states rejoined the Atlantic markets, Puerto Rico's economy contracted severely. But that wasn't the only contraction that took place in the nineteenth century. As Salvador Brau, one of the leading historians of the period, has noted, the system of enslaved labor had produced enough wealth for planters to send their sons to study abroad. A generation of young men arrived in Paris, Madrid, and Michigan to study law or medicine. They also learned about liberalism, arriving back in the Caribbean with fervent abolitionist ideas, or in the words of historian Silvia Álvarez Curbelo, "Puerto Rico's first modernist discourse."[55]

In Puerto Rico, a sense of nationhood or belonging to something other than the Spanish Empire did not begin in the nineteenth century. As previously noted, the category of "puertorriqueño" had been used since the early 1700s.[56] The criollo category also emerged in the Americas to differentiate those who had been born in the Iberian Peninsula, referred to as *peninsulares*, from those born in Puerto Rico. These identity categories also carried power, as those in the upper echelons of the social structure were often peninsulares. Yet the multiple attempts of Puerto Ricans to become independent allow us to see the limits of Spanish loyalty in the colony.

Uncovering the origins of *puertorriqueñidad* might prove an impossible endeavor. It is important to note, however, that Puerto Rico began to be imagined and theorized through the world of letters. History also became a tool for affirming nationality in these years as scholars sought to locate the foundations of the society they were living in and trying to comprehend. Puerto Rico's indigenous peoples became a recurring theme in contemporaneous literary production, and intellectuals also began creating national canons that included the eighteenth-century painter José Campeche and Puerto Rico's first representative in the Spanish courts, Ramón Power y Giralt.

Two members of this intellectual and political generation were Ramón Emeterio Betances and Segundo Ruiz Belvis. They met in Paris, where Betances studied medicine and Ruiz Belvis finished his law studies. Weary of the colonial condition and with the sharpest of minds, they began working toward the independence of Puerto Rico. Both died in exile, but their work was not in vain. In 1868, the revolution they had helped organize took place in Lares, Puerto Rico. The Lares revolution failed in its objectives, but success cannot solely be measured through military and political rubrics. Lares became a symbol of national affirmation that is remembered and celebrated even today.

CHAPTER 4

IMAGINING THE GREAT PUERTO RICAN FAMILY

Different social worlds coexisted in nineteenth-century Puerto Rico: one was rural and the other urban, but colonial administrators were at the top of both. They were followed by plantation owners in the countryside and factory owners in cities and urban areas. Merchants bridged the two groups. As in the rest of Spanish America, criollos and peninsulares vied for status and control. Peninsulares held greater privileges and power in the social hierarchies that operated in Puerto Rico. In the towns of Lares, Yauco, San Germán, and Mayagüez, for example, the commerce and plantation systems were dominated by Corsican and Mallorcan immigrants. They hardly ever employed criollos, adding fuel to the already tense relationships among the elites.[1]

The planter class had amassed great wealth on the backs of enslaved people until the financial challenges of the 1860s. Sugar sweetened teas in England and coffee in Spain but it also depended on horrific forms of labor exploitation. When U.S. Southern states reentered the international markets after the Civil War (1861–65), Puerto Rico's economy contracted and another commodity began dominating production and exports: coffee. The coffee trade was less dependent on enslaved labor in part because unemployed, freed laborers lived in the mountainous regions where its production took place.[2] Sharecroppers, laborers tied to the hated logbook system, and poor peasants became a stagnant and floating group that was understood to be at the bottom of the social hierarchy.[3]

Some criollos dreamed of freedom and the creation of the sovereign Puerto Rican nation-state from within the archipelago, while others were doing the same in exile. One such criollo was Ramón Emeterio Betances. His mother had died when he was ten years old and his father, a wealthy plantation owner from the western town of Cabo Rojo, sent his son to study in France in the custody of family friends, a connection that was made possible through his Freemason contacts. Betances received his primary education in Toulouse, later making his way to Paris to study medicine as the city was shaken by the 1848 revolutions. It was his first lesson in political activism. Later in life he asserted with pride that when the Republic called, he became a soldier for the Republic of France. After finishing his studies, he returned to Puerto Rico just as a cholera epidemic spread through coastal towns, killing thousands of people. He quickly opened his doors to anyone in need, gaining the townspeople's respect and the nickname "Doctor of the Poor."[4]

Betances was part of a generation of young intellectuals who received their formal education in Europe. His experiences fighting for the French Republic fired his political imagination. Influenced by liberalism, he openly advocated for the abolition of slavery, individual rights, and democratic elections. These ideas were perceived as a threat by the Spanish government. Betances and his close friend Segundo Ruiz Belvis were expelled from Puerto Rico twice for their abolitionist activities; they were once accused of buying enslaved infants during baptism and immediately granting them their freedom. In 1867 the government ordered their arrest, but they escaped to the neighboring Dominican Republic and made their way to New York City where they joined a community of Latin American revolutionaries.[5]

These revolutionaries wrote a series of incendiary texts clandestinely or from exile calling for Puerto Ricans to take up arms. "Long Live the Revolution!" and "Long Live Borinquen!" punctuated their leaflets and manifestos, which were probably printed abroad and later put into circulation by the underground network organizing the forthcoming revolution. One can only imagine how it must have felt to carry a bag or briefcase full of such materials, to know those words were printed on paper. Words that called for another social order. Words that could send a person to the execution wall.[6]

In 1867, Betances drafted a document called the "Ten Commandments of Free Men." It was an ultimatum to the Spanish Crown. "If Spain feels capable of giving us, and gives these rights and liberties," wrote Betances, "then it can send us a captain general or governor . . . made of straw, which we will hang and burn on the days of Shrovetide to commemorate all the Judases that have sold us up to this day." The demands read as a quintessential liberal manifesto: the abolition of slavery was called for, as was the right to vote and freedom of association, the press, and commerce, among other things.[7]

Knowing that Spain would never consent to the demands, Betances used the Ten Commandments to document and promote liberal ideas. But the revolution was not just rooted in a call for more individual rights. For Betances, and possibly for some of those who risked their lives in the endeavor, the revolution would create the Puerto Rican republic. In many ways, the Puerto Rican nation was already a reality because there was a widespread sense of belonging distinct from affiliation with Spain. As one of the revolutionary leaflets noted, "Everything separates us from Spain." It continued, "The primitive race was destroyed; after that the African race was scarred, and with them the criollo was enslaved, dejected, despised, asking for justice to the godly skies. . . . And they still dare to scream at us: 'You don't want to be [a] Spaniard?' Well good, you'll be Indian or mulatto. So what? Since when has it not been more valuable to be the victim's son rather than the executioner's brother."[8]

The organizing was not limited to the Puerto Rican archipelago. Revolutionaries in New York, the Dominican Republic, and Saint Thomas created an impressive communications network. On October 27, 1867, as Betances worked to garner support and secure weapons in the Caribbean, Ruiz Belvis traveled to Chile in search of diplomatic allies. They were counting on the solidarity of their Spanish American brothers. As Simón Bolívar had noted decades prior, the liberation of the Americas would not be complete without the liberation of Cuba and Puerto Rico. Unfortunately, Ruiz Belvis died of natural causes four days after arriving in the port of Valparaiso. This was the revolution's first major setback.[9]

Despite the loss of Belvis and the failure of his mission, preparations for the armed insurrection continued. The revolution would begin on September 29, 1868, in the northern town of Camuy. Other towns were to follow Camuy's lead—it was expected that more than twenty secret societies would follow suit. Meanwhile, Betances planned to arrive with a shipload of weapons and ammunition from Saint Thomas. None of this happened. Rumors had been circulating about possible insurrections and Spanish authorities were on high alert. Their suspicions were confirmed on the night of September 20 when the nephew of one of the revolutionary leaders overheard a conversation between members of Camuy's Lanzador del Norte secret society and alerted the authorities. The repressive apparatus was immediately activated. Tense discussions and rapid decision making among the leaders ensued: after years of planning and organizing, the revolution now needed to happen in less than forty-eight hours and begin in an entirely different town: Lares. Since most of the secret societies were not aware of what had happened, those who did start to fight had to hope that their comrades would join them once they heard that the revolution had begun.[10] And in fact, some revolutionaries only found out about the change of plans when they were arrested by Spanish forces.

On the night of September 23, 1868, Lares was festive. A few hours prior, nearly six hundred freed and enslaved residents had gathered on Manuel Rojas's estate. Rojas was a plantation owner who had lost everything in the recent economic crisis. Some weeks before, he had declared bankruptcy after failing to pay back loans that he had struggled to service for years. Rojas was also president of the Junta Centro Bravo No. 2, one of the secret societies that had been organizing the Puerto Rican revolution for months.[11]

In a society where public gatherings made participants a target for the government and where publicly speaking about politics could lead to imprisonment, it would have been euphoric to hear hundreds of people shouting for the liberation of Puerto Rico that night at Manuel

Rojas's estate. There were people from all social classes in the crowd. Enslaved people were offered freedom for participating; day laborers who had been forced to work under the hated "libreta" system made a bonfire with their logbooks. While women took part in the conspiracy, they were not part of the military action.[12]

Passion was abundant even without weapons and military preparation. There were few horses and only a handful of rifles. The rest of the rebels armed themselves with knives, sticks, and machetes. When it was time to depart, Manuel Rojas gave a speech to rally the troops who shouted, "Death to Spain, long live liberty, long live free Puerto Rico, liberty or death!" as they marched toward Lares. The revolution had begun.[13]

In a few hours, they had taken the town and declared the Republic of Puerto Rico, along with a provisional government. Bernabé Pol, a mixed-race man recently expelled from his civilian job because of his skin color, was appointed secretary of state. The newly established government also drafted a "Declaration from Puerto Rico to the World." In its first official communication to the international community, Bernabe Pol wrote:

> Since the moment has arrived when arms need to be taken to sanctify the cause for rights, we are determined to die rather than to continue under Spanish domination; and in order for it not to be characterized as a riot or revolt of a bad type and to be considered a patriotic movement with tendencies to shake off the ominous yoke and create a free nation, and [we] state it for the whole world to know.[14]

Instead of marching on to the next town, San Sebastián del Pepino, the rebels decided to celebrate a Te Deum, a religious mass of gratitude—the first and last religious service to be celebrated in the brief existence of the Republic of Puerto Rico. Others looted the town's stores while a bonfire fueled by debt records lit up the night. These celebrations gave Spanish reinforcements time to arrive from different parts of the island.[15]

When the rebels arrived in San Sebastián after dawn on September 24, they had lost the element of surprise. After multiple attacks, they were unable to take the town's plaza. Better-equipped and more highly trained soldiers forced them to retreat into the mountains. Perhaps they could take cover until Betances arrived with reinforcements or wait for other secret societies to begin their attacks. The Spanish government ordered reinforcements from the nearby town of Mayagüez and began sweeping the area. In Saint Thomas, the Spanish pressured local authorities to confiscate Betances's boat, *El telégrafo*, along with the weapons and ammunitions he had been gathering over the previous year. Betances fled the island before authorities could catch him.[16] While historians often argue that the revolution only lasted about forty-eight hours, it seems that guerrilla tactics continued for at least two months. By December, 551 people had been arrested in connection with the insurrection; 3 of them were women and 49 were enslaved people. Of those, 7 were sentenced to death and 80 died in prison, victims of yellow fever caused by unsanitary prison conditions. Those who survived were set free in January 1869.[17]

The Lares rebels were not members of a single class or social group. They were a rowdy gathering for whom independence and liberation meant different things. There were planters like Manuel Rojas who had lost everything and perhaps wanted power. Others, like Bernabe Pol, who had been denied an administrative job because of his race, were disillusioned by the racist structures of Spanish colonialism. Enslaved people joined in hopes of attaining freedom and liberation, while day laborers sought better living conditions. There might have been a concerted class project from elites who wanted to topple the Spanish administration to establish their own, but solely focusing on elites would be an act of historical injustice to those who sacrificed their lives to imagine the possibilities of living otherwise.

Imagining the Nation

While the Lares revolutionaries failed in their military endeavors, they won a decisive symbolic battle. There had been separatist actions and attempts throughout the nineteenth century, but Lares marked a turning point. It made clear to the Spanish authorities what must have been obvious to many, that a unique sense of *puertorriqueñidad* had been built in opposition to Spain. The revolutionaries fought to build the nation's political apparatus.

The Spanish Crown faced other problems in late 1868. The Puerto Rican Revolution was part of a broader movement expanding through the Spanish Empire. Authorities were still chasing Puerto Rican revolutionaries in the mountainside when, on October 10, Cuban revolutionaries rose up in arms. The Grito de Yara proclaimed Cuba's independence and the establishment of a provisional government. While it started small, by the 1870s the movement for Cuban independence had attracted more than forty thousand volunteers from all social classes and races. Unlike Lares, which was immediately suppressed and limited to a few municipalities, the Cubans launched a ten-year war that set the foundations for three decades of struggle.[18]

In Spain, where liberals were discontented with the government of Queen Isabella II, another revolution was underway. In 1868, a rebellion led by none other than Juan Prim y Prats successfully overthrew the queen and created a regency. Prim y Prats had served as captain general of Puerto Rico in 1847, although his mandate only lasted a year before he was removed for his dictatorial tendencies. It was under Prim y Prats's rule that the Bando contra la Raza Negra was passed, giving slave owners unlimited power to exploit, punish, and legally murder enslaved peoples.[19] The so-called Glorious Revolution in Spain inaugurated years of political instability, including the assassination of Prim y Prats. Eventually, that revolution shaped the political conditions that led to the creation of the First Spanish Republic in 1873.

While the Republican government only lasted eleven months, it was a political experiment that sent shockwaves across the deteriorating Spanish Empire. New laws and regulations granted Puerto Ricans the freedom of the press and freedom of association and led to the creation of new political parties. A convergence of factors—including the agency of enslaved peoples, the proliferation of abolitionist politics among the intellectual elite, and recent events in the Spanish Peninsula—led to the approval and implementation of the Moret Law in 1870. This legislation, drafted by liberal intellectuals, was seen as a step toward abolition because it granted freedom to children born to enslaved mothers. The

Moret Law, the symbolic impact of Lares, and the unwavering insurgency in Cuba all signaled to Spain the threat of independence. And three years later, on March 22, 1873, the Spanish courts declared the abolition of slavery in Puerto Rico. Freedom, however, was not immediately granted to enslaved individuals. Instead, they needed to enter into contractual agreements with their former masters, or find new ones, for a period of three years.[20]

While the Moret Law promised freedom, Puerto Ricans remained trapped within decaying structures. As new technologies modernized the plantation system in the last three decades of the nineteenth century, the worlds of letters and politics operated within the scope and at the behest of the colonial government. Political parties could only advocate for full integration into the imperial orbit or, in the most radical case, some degree of autonomy. Separatist ideas were not allowed to be publicly professed or promoted; that does not mean such ideas did not exist. While coffee and tobacco were the main exports, sugar would make a comeback in the next century. Meanwhile, liberals, professionals, and the planter class all came together around a foundational myth that operates to the present day: the idea of the Great Puerto Rican Family.

The Great Puerto Rican Family

In November 1870, with just five days between their inaugural conventions, Puerto Rico's first political parties were created: the Liberal Reformist Party and the Conservative Party. Suffrage was limited to property-owning individuals who were wealthy and nearly all enfranchised voters were white. Elections were held to select deputies in the Spanish courts and a handful of local senators. In the first elections of 1871, liberals won fourteen out of Puerto Rico's fifteen districts. The liberal tide had changed by 1878 when conservatives won every single district.[21]

European progress and Enlightenment ideas animated and inspired Puerto Rican intellectual elites. The development of electoral politics was tied to the emergence of Puerto Rico's public sphere, a space outside the government where individuals and citizens sought to transform society and encourage political action.[22] Energized by the proliferation of print media in the form of newspapers, books, and plays, cities hosted traveling theatrical companies and housed bookstores while luxurious and modern architecture graced the avenues.[23]

Many of the country's leading intellectuals had studied and debated ideas in European classrooms, caroused through the streets of Madrid or Paris, and returned home with a desire to modernize Puerto Rico. World's fairs had given them a glimpse of the globe through a highly occidental and Western lens. Asia and Africa were imagined as barbarous, places and people to negate and move away from. The Puerto Rican elite, seen as lesser-than by the imperial metropolis, sought refuge in Western civilization even when they were not deemed worthy of it. For some, Spain no longer promised modernity, so they dreamed about Parisian luxury while envying London's capitalist ethos from their elegant colonial houses in Ponce, San Germán, or San Juan. Having absorbed ideas about progress and civilization, the Puerto Rican elite imagined themselves as capable leaders, masters, and teachers of those they considered to be the lazy, indolent, and uncivilized masses.[24]

Regardless of what the intellectual elite believed, the laboring masses also actively participated in political and intellectual exchanges. *El artesano*, the first artisan-led newspaper, was published in 1874, and it was soon followed by other publications whose titles document the emergence of an incipient working-class consciousness: *El obrero, Eco proletario, Justicia, El clamor obrero*, and *El criterio libre*. Makeshift libraries and night schools were established in these years as well as literary soirees, banquets, and mutual aid societies. The Sociedad Protectora de la Inteligencia del Obrero, an organization founded in the 1880s, was particularly explicit about their intellectual aspirations: it was "a project that will bring as its consequence intellectual uplift of the working class, making it stronger and respectable while guaranteeing its future."[25] Working-class people were actively self-fashioning their identities as intellectuals but were mostly ignored in conversations about the country's development.

Of chief importance to the intellectual elite—primarily young, criollo, and foreign-educated professionals—was the notion of the "Great Puerto Rican Family" as a racial democracy discourse that sought to create the illusion of consensus. Through the efforts of elites, who used politics, literature, and history to give shape and substance to the idea, everyone belonged to the Puerto Rican nation.[26] Given the patriarchal codes of the time, only men were allowed to speak in this imagined family. As the heads of the Great Puerto Rican Family, men from the upper classes spoke on behalf of the masses, who could join the family but only as accommodating, silenced, and, ultimately, whitened subjects. In fact, liberal intellectuals who led the abolitionist debates in the Spanish courts created a discourse of gratitude.[27] The formerly enslaved, elites thought, needed to be grateful for their freedom. Of course, this meant willfully ignoring the agency of those who led dozens of revolts, created maroon communities, and participated in subtle and undocumented acts of resistance.

The foundation of a unifying national myth also necessitated a creation of the past. In the 1850s a new generation of Puerto Rican students in Madrid began laying the foundation for the study of history. One of them was Alejandro Tapia y Rivera, a quintessential man of letters. Tapia y Rivera was born in 1826 to a well-off family descended on both sides from Spanish nobility; his father was also a military official. His family traveled between Madrid and Puerto Rico, so Tapia y Rivera played in Madrid as a child but received his education in San Juan. As a young man, he dueled with a military officer—for the wealthy elite in nineteenth-century Puerto Rico, honor was an important trait to defend at all costs—and while he survived, Governor de la Pezuela ordered his exile, which led him back to Madrid in 1849.[28]

Spain at that time was filled with young Puerto Rican intellectuals yearning for their idealized island, with Barcelona becoming an important intellectual hub. No less than three books documenting customs, songs, and poems from Puerto Rico were published in the 1840s. Around this time, Manuel Alonso Pacheco, a physicist and man of letters, also published *El gibaro*, one of the first attempts to portray puertorriqueñidad through literature. When Tapia y Rivera arrived in Madrid, Puerto

Rican students and intellectuals were busy imagining the nation through its past. On March 20, 1851, they created the Sociedad Recolectora de Documentos Históricos de San Juan Bautista de Puerto Rico (Society for the Recollection of Historical Documents Relating to San Juan Bautista of Puerto Rico).[29]

The group included men who would dominate Puerto Rican intellectual and political circles in the coming decades: Román Baldorioty de Castro, José Julián Acosta, Calixto Romero, Ramón Emeterio Betances, and Segundo Ruiz Belvis, among others. As young students, they spent their time browsing old libraries, sifting through archives, and reading moldy documents. This was not a mere intellectual exercise but an attempt to trace the historical coordinates of the Puerto Rican nation. Soaked in the positivist intellectual trends of their times, they imagined history not as an interpretation of the past but as something static that could be reached through primary documents. There was a particular fascination with the indigenous past, something that both Betances and Tapia y Rivera explored in literary novels as well.

In exile, they felt what it meant to be Puerto Rican. While some were forced to live in perpetual exile, most of the Sociedad Recolectora's members eventually made their way back to Puerto Rico. Tapia y Rivera, for example, edited multiple newspapers, joined the Liberal Reformist Party, and dictated courses on art and literature at the Puerto Rican Athenaeum, a hub for Puerto Rico's emergent world of letters and public sphere. In fact, Tapia y Rivera first proposed the Athenaeum's creation in 1855 although it was nearly twenty years before its doors opened to the public.[30] These men of letters were not all educated in literature; many of them were professionals from the worlds of law and medicine. Some advocated for women's participation in the country's intellectual life, but these spaces were male dominated. Women's intellectual pursuits were limited to their homes where they could hold soirees or *tertulias*. And while some newspapers included women's sections, periodicals too were mostly written by men.[31]

As these intellectuals imagined Puerto Rico's foundations, they also sought to reformulate the country's relationship to its imperial metropolis. The Liberal Reformist Party became a political battleground between two factions that held different views on the right relationship with their Spanish counterparts. A faction led by José Celso Barbosa, a Black, U.S.-educated physician, advocated holding out against conservative politicians in Madrid to gain autonomy.[32] They hoped that the situation in Cuba, which had been in an intermittent war for independence since 1868, would eventually grant Puerto Ricans greater freedoms. Luis Muñoz Rivera, a lawyer, poet, and journalist, disagreed. He led another faction willing to negotiate with Spain in order to secure political gains for Puerto Rico. Eventually, these tensions led to the creation of two different parties, the Autonomist Party and the Pure (Orthodox and Historical) Autonomist Party.[33] Both were fighting for an autonomous (self-ruled) Puerto Rico but they differed in their strategies.

Supporting autonomy could be dangerous. The year 1887 is known by Puerto Rican historians as "The Terrible Year." Spanish colonial authorities persecuted, and in some cases tortured, autonomists. After a tense election in 1886, conservatives began physically attacking autonomists and targeting their properties. In response, several secret societies, including La Torre del Viejo (The Old Man's Tower) and Los Secos (The Dry), in reference to those born in Puerto Rico, were formed to advocate a boycott of conservative-owned—meaning Spanish-owned—businesses.[34] Fearing that autonomists were behind these societies, Governor Romualdo Palacios González ordered the arrest of key autonomist leaders, including Román Baldorioty de Castro, through a system known as the *compontes* (pacifiers). The plan was to torture them into confession. The Civil Guard broke into dozens of autonomists' houses, arrested them, and dragged them to solitary places to torture them.[35]

These actions horrified Puerto Rico's political elite and had immediate ramifications in Madrid. Palacios González was accused of abusing his power and Spain's Council of Ministry agreed to his removal on November 9, 1887. Meanwhile, autonomists debated about calling for an end to their boycott on Spanish merchants and began considering which party they should negotiate with in Spain. Tensions among the autonomists came to the fore once again over whom to trust in Madrid. The faction led by

Luis Muñoz Rivera wanted nothing to do with local Spaniards but was willing to compromise with conservative factions in the metropole.[36]

In the neighboring island of Cuba, another war was declared in 1895. It had been years in the making, with committees organizing in Cuba, New York, and Florida. This time, Cuban revolutionaries brought the war to Havana. Victory, and with it independence, was seen as a possibility. In October 1895, in dialogue and collaboration with their Cuban counterparts, a group of Puerto Rican separatists created the Puerto Rican Revolutionary Committee in New York City.[37] Some Puerto Ricans, like the Arecibo poet Pachín Marín, joined the Cuban revolutionaries and died fighting in their ranks.[38]

Counting on the pressure generated by the war in Cuba, Luis Muñoz Rivera and a faction within the Autonomist Party revived a decades-old debate about creating strategic pacts with progressive parties in Spain. After several assemblies and internal debates, leading members of the Autonomist Party sailed to Madrid to meet with politicians including the prime minister, Antonio Cánovas del Castillo, and the main force within the Liberal Party and former prime minister, Práxedes Mateo Sagasta. The meetings were by and large successful: the prime minister timidly advocated for more autonomy for Puerto Rico and Sagasta signed a pact of collaboration with his Puerto Rican counterparts.[39]

While Puerto Rican autonomists were hard at work advancing their political project, the old revolutionary Ramón Emeterio Betances continued dreaming, scheming, and organizing from his exile in Paris. In the decades after El Grito de Lares, Betances served as a diplomat for the Dominican Republic, Haiti, and the Cuban revolutionaries. He also helped organize two failed insurrections in Puerto Rico. One of them, known as the Intentona de Yauco (Attempted Coup of Yauco) of 1897, was suppressed and the other never took place.[40]

Betances was entering his last decade of life but he remained a radical republican committed to Puerto Rico's independence. His office in Paris was a meeting place for agitators and activists from across the political spectrum, including internationally renowned anarchists like Charles Malato. Betances's contact with anarchists was probably facilitated by his friend Louis Bonafoux, who personally knew the internationally infamous Italian anarchist Ericco Malatesta.[41] Betances's fame and credentials preceded him and made his office an obligatory stop for many radicals. And then, in 1897, an Italian anarchist knocked on his door. His name was Michele Angiolillo Lombardi.[42]

Both had reasons to despise the Spanish government. Betances hated the government of Cánovas del Castillo because of the war it was waging in Cuba. Angiolillo had a vendetta against the Spanish Crown because they were known to torture and assassinate imprisoned anarchists. A few months prior to their meeting, Angiolillo had participated in a small gathering of "eight or nine comrades." The meeting included former Montjuich prisoners Juan Bautista Oller, Francisco Gana, and Fernando Tarrida del Mármol. Instead of the usual fiery speeches, Gana used his body as propaganda. He took off his clothes to show the scars, marks, and deformities inflicted by the brutal Spanish regime. It is said that Angiolillo left the event with only a terse good-bye.[43] His silence was fueled by anger and a desire to bring the perpetrators to justice.[44]

Not all anarchists agreed on tactics. Some favored organizing the laboring masses and disavowed the use of violence. For others, individual actions could advance larger social processes. In the latter group, some favored the use of revolutionary violence, which they named "propaganda by the deed."[45] It was a time when anarchist newspapers circulated throughout the world with instructions on how to build makeshift bombs. With the advent of photography, some carried pictures of anarchists (as they would pictures of Catholic saints) who had successfully murdered heads of state. Anarchists, real or imagined, were seen as a threat to Western governments.[46] It was likely Betances's revolutionary credentials that led Angiolillo to request a meeting with him.

What happened in that meeting can only be the source of speculation. It is known that Angiolillo confided his plan to assassinate young members of the Spanish royal family. Some scholars argue that Betances dissuaded Angiolillo from murdering members of the Spanish Crown but instead suggested the assassination of Cánovas del Castillo. After all, it was the prime minister who was responsible for the repression of the anarchist movement in Spain. He was also in charge of sending Valeriano Weyler—a general put in charge of the Spanish military forces against Cuban revolutionaries who quickly earned the nickname of "the butcher"—to Cuba.[47]

While certainty might be impossible, it seems that Betances did not formally agree with Angiolillo. However, a few days after their encounter, the amount of money Angiolillo had asked of Betances to finance his trip mysteriously arrived at his apartment. Perhaps that is why Betances would proudly tell his visitors during his last years of life, "in the chair you are sitting once sat Angiolillo."[48]

In August 1897, Cánovas del Castillo, prime minister and the best-known conservative politician in Spain, made a trip to the Santa Agueda de Mondragón spa. The warm baths were a treatment for his glycosuria. The prime minister was traveling with his wife, Joaquina de Osma, nine police officers, and twenty-five civil guards. A twenty-six-year-old by the name of Emilio Rinaldi also checked in to the spa. He was a bookseller and writer for the Italian newspaper *Il Popolo*. The name and profession were false, of course—this was Angiolillo's pseudonym and fake identity. Once there, Angiolillo studied the prime minister's every move. On August 8, 1897, he saw an opportunity and took it. Cánovas del Castillo was sitting on the patio by himself.[49]

Around noon, Angiolillo went upstairs to get his revolver and a pair of boots that would muffle the sound of his steps. He rushed to the patio and, without saying a word, shot the prime minister in the right temple and the neck. As the body felt to the ground, Angiolillo took his third and last shot, firing at the prime minister's back. Cánovas del Castillo had said he only needed three bullets to end the war in Cuba: one for José Martí, one for Máximo Gómez, and the last one for Antonio Maceo.[50] Ironically, Angiolillo ended Cánovas's life with three of the four bullets in his own revolver. When approached by Cánovas's wife and police officers, he surrendered calmly and said, "I have accomplished my duty and I am calmed; I have avenged my brothers in Montjuich."[51]

Perhaps unknowingly, Angiolillo's actions triggered a series of events that eventually shaped Puerto Rico's history. In the coming months, Práxedes Mateo Sagasta became the new prime minister and reconfigured the Spanish government. Soon after taking office, he released most of the Montjuich prisoners. He also granted amnesty to Puerto Rican and Cuban political prisoners and removed General Valeriano Weyler from his position. Most importantly for our story, on November 9, 1897, Queen Regent María Isabel II signed a series of decrees that extended the Spanish constitution to Puerto Rico, granted male suffrage to adults older than twenty-five, and allowed the creation of an autonomous government in Puerto Rico.[52] As historian Mark Bray has noted, "One could argue that Angiolillo's assassination was the most effective act of propaganda by the deed carried out by an anarchist during the era."[53]

Two weeks later, on November 25, 1897, an Autonomic Charter was approved for both Cuba and Puerto Rico. While the Cubans, on the verge of winning their three-decade struggle for independence, rejected the charter, autonomists celebrated it as a victory in Puerto Rico. The celebration, however, was brief. If three bullets consolidated Puerto Rico's autonomy, a bombing of its capital sealed its colonial future.

CHAPTER 5

CHRONICLE OF A WAR
FORETOLD

By 1897, there was not a single Puerto Rico but many. A census conducted that year by historian Cayetano Coll y Toste documented people of thirty-two different nationalities living in Puerto Rico. Coll y Toste also identified 869,681 people as Puerto Ricans—that is, born in the archipelago.[1] Two years later, another census noted that 69 percent of the population was illiterate.[2] For those writing its books and histories, being Puerto Rican meant something completely different to those who could not even spell their names. There was a Puerto Rico inhabited by the desperately poor, and one that was imagined and penned by those reminiscing about their bohemian lives in Paris or Madrid. Many endured long hours working in the fields for little pay, and some still carried memories of being enslaved themselves. Meanwhile, a small group of intellectuals discussed the most recent European literary trends at the Puerto Rican Athenaeum, the country's intellectual hub.[3]

Given such complex realities, not everyone favored autonomy or passively accepted colonialism. Separatist ideas were still being debated and imagined. In New York City, Puerto Ricans and Cubans came together to conspire for the independence of their Caribbean countries. In 1892, a revolutionary community of Cubans in exile created the Cuban Revolutionary Party along with their highly influential newspaper, *Patria*. In the first article of their platform, they noted, "The Cuban Revolutionary Party is created to achieve the absolute independence

for the island of Cuba and to aid and encourage that of Puerto Rico."[4]
The organization became a welcoming space for Puerto Ricans who
sought to end Spanish colonialism.

New York City became a node within the broader networks of the
revolutionary Caribbean.[5] Cubans launched their war in 1895 and
some Puerto Ricans not only conspired in solidarity from afar but
joined them to fight in the fields. In New York, this bond of solidarity
was commemorated by the creation of the Puerto Rican flag.[6] On
December 22, 1895, a group of Puerto Ricans created the Puerto Rico
Section of the Cuban Revolutionary Party and unveiled a new flag
that unified the national struggles of both Caribbean countries,
hence the similarities between the two flags.[7] Even among those who
participated in the Puerto Rico Section and shared anticolonial sentiments, there were factions and differing beliefs about Puerto Rico's
path. Some, like Ramón Emeterio Betances, believed in independence,
while others, like Julio J. Henna, who became the Section's president,
wanted to break from Spain to join the United States.[8] In the coming
years, New York became a destination for thousands of people from
different parts of the Caribbean, and for people who inhabited multiple Puerto Ricos.[9]

Separatist ideas were not limited to the Puerto Rican diaspora. Some
were still debating them in the archipelago. It is difficult to trace those
who supported independence because openly doing so could land anyone in prison or send them into exile. As Cubans gained ground in their
fight for independence and the shadow of the United States loomed
large over the region, Spanish authorities were wary of any form of rebellion or insurrection. Their fears were realized on March 24, 1897,
when a band of revolutionaries once again took up arms to declare the
Republic of Puerto Rico. This insurrection was led by Antonio Mattei
Lluveras in coordination with the Puerto Rico Section of the Cuban
Revolutionary Party in New York City. Mattei Lluveras was a landowner
who had bought and smuggled five thousand machetes to Puerto Rico.
The Section believed that once the rebellion was ignited, people both
in the archipelago and abroad would join their struggle.[10] This, once
again, did not happen.

As in the Lares revolution of 1868, someone alerted the authorities in Yauco about the uprising. When the rebels began their attack, colonial authorities were ready to repel it. The insurrection was unsuccessful and became a target of criticism by the autonomist elite.[11] Newspapers mocked and criticized the Yauco revolutionaries; some history books have ignored them altogether. While unsuccessful in military terms, Yauco succeeded in other ways. It demonstrated that separatist ideas were still circulating in Puerto Rico and that the autonomist hegemony was only one reality among many.

Two months after the Yauco uprising, San Juan's streets rang with the sound of dynamite. This was not another attempt at revolution but a government action. After two centuries, the city walls were being de-molished. On May 28, 1897, people from San Juan and its surrounding areas gathered to see the event, which turned into a massive celebration. Those workers who volunteered to be part of the demolition called themselves the Brigades of Honor.[12] Onlookers must have felt they were part of a historical moment: tearing down the walls would allow the winds of progress to blow freely through the city.

What authorities likely did not realize, however, was that socialist ideas arrived with those winds as well. In his pathbreaking study of the origins of socialism in Puerto Rico, sociologist Rubén Dávila Santiago has used the demolition to symbolize the proliferation of socialist ideas at the turn of the century.[13] Workers and artisans did not passively ob-serve the massive social changes of the last decades of the nineteenth century. Since the 1870s, they had been publishing their own newspa-pers, creating makeshift night schools to educate themselves, and organizing mutual aid societies. While the intellectual elites set the foundations of an imagined Puerto Rican nation, workers and artisans constructed different kinds of pillars in the margins.[14]

The proliferation of artisan and working-class organizations was an urban phenomenon, and their newspapers marked the emergence of a new working-class readership or audience. Reading, however, was not merely an individual practice. In a world where most of the laboring masses were illiterate, reading was a collective exercise. The practice of reading out loud in public spaces, for example, was common. But the artisans and working classes also often sought to emulate the codes and norms of the upper classes, reproducing hierarchies and exclusions among laborers. Reading and education, for example, became markers of prestige and social capital.[15]

These working-class intellectual experiments were the backdrop to Puerto Rico's first socialist ideas. In fact, Governor Sabás Marín explicitly, and incorrectly, linked the Yauco insurrection to socialism. The governor noted, "The movement showcased socialist characteristics as entire families of ignorant peasants headed to the town of Yauco that same night to take possession of the goods that they had been made to believe were theirs."[16] Similarly, the governor accused the newspaper *Ensayo obrero* of preparing the masses for the adoption of more radical strands of socialism like anarchism.[17]

As working-class newspapers began to be published in Puerto Rico, news arrived that the Spanish Crown had granted autonomy to its last two colonial outposts in the Caribbean. It was a desperate attempt to retain Cuba and Puerto Rico. While the Cuban revolutionaries did not accept Spain's benevolence, the news was joyously received in Puerto Rico. The first provisional government was organized in February 1898, and elections took place in March and April. Puerto Rico's first autonomous government officially took office on July 17, 1898.[18]

But the drums of war could be heard in San Juan. In igniting revolution across their entire island, Cubans accomplished what Puerto Ricans had only dreamed of. In addition, the United States was in the midst of an ongoing debate about whether the country should expand beyond its national borders, which were now secure after the displacement and genocide of Native American communities. U.S. interests in the region were not new. In fact, in 1854, a group of U.S. diplomats signed a document known as the Ostend Manifesto in which they argued it was necessary to acquire Cuba at any cost. Similarly, the United States' growing geopolitical interests in the region, particularly Panama, required that it bring Puerto Rico into its orbit.

It was no secret that the United States could intervene in the archipelago's affairs at any moment. The explosion of the USS *Maine* in Havana's harbor jump-started tensions between the two rival empires. On

April 20, 1898, the U.S. Congress declared war on Spain. In Puerto Rico, Governor Sabás Marín declared a state of emergency, canceling the upcoming first meeting of the autonomous government. Elected officials timidly offered loyalty to Spain but later changed their minds. Four days after the inauguration of the autonomous government, war arrived in Puerto Rico: the city of San Juan was bombed by U.S. Navy Rear Admiral William T. Sampson.

The War at Home

San Juan was on high alert. On May 11, 1898, Spanish officials spotted a vessel in the open sea. Some thought it was a spy ship, while others believed it was the USS *Yale*, a U.S. Navy auxiliary cruiser.[19] For weeks civilians had been living in a state of anxiety and military rule. The newly appointed governor, Manuel Macías Casado, announced a state of emergency following the U.S. declaration of war. Life went on as usual, but everyone knew it could change at any moment.

The following morning, the situation changed from one moment to the next. Roosters roaming the city, crowing at dawn, were interrupted by a loud explosion. San Juan's residents were rocked out of their beds. The blasts did not stop but multiplied. Many grabbed their children and the few possessions they could gather, desperately making their way out of the city as missiles and bombs seemed to rain over San Juan.[20] The fear was not limited to the capital. In the mountains of Corozal, washerwomen and workers screamed "¡Vienen los yankees!"[21]

Rear Admiral William T. Sampson led the attack on San Juan. He sailed from Cuba with orders to attack the city and destroy the Spanish fleet, which was considered primitive compared to the U.S. Navy's modern fleet.[22] Spanish authorities, however, had been preparing for the assault. They quickly mobilized soldiers and began their defense using the Morro Castle's cannons. In previous weeks, the governor had ordered more cannons installed. He also welcomed troops arriving from the battlefields in Cuba. While attempts to resist an invasion were made, both sides knew that Spain did not have the military capacity to properly defend the island. On the morning of May 12, 1898, Governor

Macías Casado led a defensive operation that repelled the attack and awed Sampson.[23] As Sampson got closer to the shore, it was clear that the Spanish fleet was not there and that San Juan would continue to resist. Three hours after the initial attack, Sampson retreated.[24] The governor's mansion, the Ballajá quarters, and the Morro fortress, symbols of Spanish power, endured heavy bombing. Other structures suffered minor damage.[25]

Live music and a festive atmosphere dominated the old city that night. Not only were there many Puerto Ricos, there were many San Juans as well. For some, the events had been a Spanish victory in a war against a more powerful enemy. But, as historian Francisco Scarano has noted, the event was highly traumatic for others. Many looked for shelter in the neighboring towns only to suffer in the coming days from hunger and heightened misery.[26] After May 12, however, one thing was clear: war was inevitable. The war waged by the United States in Cuba and the Philippines greatly affected the Puerto Rican economy. The United States had been one of the most important consumers of Puerto Rican sugar in the second half of the nineteenth century. War also affected exports to Spain.[27] But war did not arrive in Puerto Rico the next day, or the next week for that matter.

Two months after the attack on San Juan, and after securing Santiago de Cuba, U.S. officials began preparing for the invasion of Puerto Rico. Troops were gathered in Guantánamo Bay under the leadership of a seasoned military general, Nelson A. Miles. His name had become infamous among Native American communities in the United States. After serving during the U.S. Civil War (1861–65), Miles led multiple missions against Native American tribes in what became known as the Indian Wars, a euphemism for the U.S. government's settler-colonial wars of expansion. Miles's participation in these wars of aggression earned him the nickname "Indian Fighter." Before arriving in Cuba and Puerto Rico, he commanded the troops that violently and fatally suppressed the 1894 railroad workers' strike against Chicago's Pullman Company.[28]

The U.S. soldiers arriving in Cuba and Puerto Rico were part of an eclectic group that included career military men, thrill-seeking Ivy

League students, and veterans from the Confederate Army.[29] On the battlefield some white U.S. soldiers were shocked to discover that they were there to help the Black and Brown Cubans against white Spaniards.[30] According to historian Greg Grandin, the Spanish-American War of 1898 created a national pact in the United States whereby former Confederate soldiers could prove themselves worthy of fighting under the U.S. flag. For African Americans, the war offered the opportunity to join the nation but only if they understood their place at the bottom of the racial hierarchy. It was a pact that unified the country for the sake of white supremacy, although the integration of the army caused internal conflict at times.[31]

The president of the Puerto Rico Section of the Cuban Revolutionary Party, Julio Henna, and his secretary, Robert H. Todd, collaborated with Miles and other government officials, including President McKinley, to prepare for the invasion. The members of the Puerto Rico Section were unified in their hatred of Spanish colonialism, but they were divided as to what the future of Puerto Rico should look like. Some advocated for independence, but others, like Henna and Todd, preferred annexation by the United States.[32]

On July 21, 1898, General Miles sailed from Cuba with twenty-three thousand soldiers. Disembarking in San Juan—as the May attacks had demonstrated—was not an option. They had considered the eastern town of Fajardo but later decided on Guánica in the south. The port was ideal because it was not heavily patrolled and provided deep water close to shore. The invasion of Puerto Rico officially began on July 25, 1898.

Troops marched inland as one town after the other lowered their Spanish flags. General Miles wrote a short proclamation that was also translated into Spanish and distributed to anyone seeking to understand what was happening—or was simply intrigued. Miles's proclamation noted:

We have not come to make war upon the people of a country that for centuries has been oppressed, but, on the contrary, to bring you protection, not only to yourselves but to your property, to promote your prosperity, and to bestow upon you the immunities and blessings of the liberal institutions of our government. It is not our purpose to interfere with any existing laws and customs that are wholesome and beneficial to your people as long as they conform to the rules of military administration, or order and justice. This is not a war of devastation, but one to give to all within the control of its military and naval forces the advantages and blessings of enlightened civilization.[33]

On their way to San Juan, U.S. troops encountered resistance in the mountainous towns of Coamo and Aibonito.[34] But an armistice was reached on August 15, 1898, just a few weeks after U.S. troops disembarked at Guánica. Puerto Rican elites quickly aligned with the invaders.[35] On October 18, the U.S. flag was hoisted in San Juan after a ceremony in which military officials from both sides participated. Two months later, on December 11, 1898, the Treaty of Paris formally ended the war. Puerto Rico became a colonial possession of the nascent U.S. empire. But it wasn't just elites who sided with the occupiers.

Life Continues

When Sampson attacked San Juan, Santiago Iglesias Pantín heard the bombs fall on San Juan from his prison cell. La Princesa prison was built in 1837 and housed up to 240 inmates.[36] Iglesias Pantín was one of them. A Spanish carpenter who came to Puerto Rico in 1896 via Cuba, he had joined a group of socialists and radicals shortly after his arrival. Since early 1897, José Ferrer y Ferrer, Fernando Gómez Acosta, and Ramón Romero Rosa had been discussing the possibility of creating a newspaper and social center, something they eventually did. Iglesias Pantín was introduced to this group, and they all collaborated with the goal of organizing Puerto Rico's laboring masses.[37] Authorities took notice and began monitoring their activities. Repression soon followed. José Ferrer y Ferrer, a Black typesetter and cigar maker, was arrested for carrying a red flag at a public meeting. It was the first time that the red flag, as a symbol of socialism, had been publicly used in Puerto Rico.[38] Other labor leaders had suffered similar fates during the years of Spanish colonialism. The U.S. occupation did not break with this punitive logic against organized labor; instead, officials implemented new modes of surveillance and repression.[39]

One of Sampson's bombs landed on the prison, destroying a wall. According to Iglesias Pantín's larger-than-life memoir, he used the opportunity to escape. He was helped by his comrades in San Juan and made it to the eastern side of the island, using different disguises and safe houses, even dressing as a woman to escape authorities and leave the city.[40] Once in the island's eastern district, he joined the occupying U.S. forces. According to his own accounts, Iglesias Pantín delivered public speeches on makeshift soapboxes in the towns occupied by the U.S. Army.[41]

It is impossible to know whether Iglesias Pantín's story is true or the product of his imagination or both. Either way, his story confirms that U.S. forces were welcomed by unexpected factions. In later years, Iglesias Pantín became a famed labor leader, politician, and statesman. But in 1898 he was a carpenter. Even then, however, he enjoyed privileges that most of the laboring masses did not: he had traveled, he knew how to read and write, and, more importantly, he was a white European man. We should be careful not to equate the experiences of one man, or a handful of labor leaders, with those of the many more for whom the change from one imperial power to another would likely have meant very little.[42]

Artisans and skilled workers in urban centers like San Juan, Ponce, and Mayagüez dreamed of a new society, one that would solve what they identified as "the social problem," which consisted of poverty, lack of education, and unhealthy living conditions. These conversations, often held in small, damp apartments, led to the creation, in 1897, of Puerto Rico's first working-class Social Study Center, located in San Juan. It served as a space to socialize, theorize, and collectively educate each other. The group of workers that published the newspaper *Ensayo obrero* used its pages to discuss the possibility of creating labor unions and federations—which became a concrete reality on October 23, 1898, five days after the U.S. flag was hoisted. Labor unions were not the product of the U.S. occupation; workers had theorized about unions for years, but now there was a legal infrastructure to make them a possibility.[43]

The Federación Regional de Trabajadores (Regional Federation of Workers; FRT) served as a hub for urban skilled workers from different parts of Puerto Rico. The federation supported and promoted unions and the use of strikes as powerful tools to attain better living conditions. The FRT was presided over by Pedro Carlos Timothée, a Black lawyer and one of the most respected intellectuals of his time.[44] The FRT's leadership advocated for the annexation of Puerto Rico by the United States because they considered the United States to be the pinnacle of labor rights and democracy. This also led them to support the Puerto Rican Republican Party and to propose that the labor organization serve the interests of the party.[45]

The strategy of merging partisan politics with the newly created labor organization created tensions in the ranks. These came to a head in a heated assembly in Old San Juan on June 18, 1899. A group of labor leaders, including Santiago Iglesias Pantín, José Ferrer y Ferrer, and Ramón Romero Rosa, stood up and left the meeting in protest, only to reconvene a few blocks away. There, they created another labor federation, the Federación Libre de Trabajadores (Free Federation of Workers; FLT), and laid the foundations for a powerful labor movement that eventually saw its initial members assume positions of power in Puerto Rican and U.S. politics.

These labor federations emerged while Puerto Rico was ruled by a military government from December 1898 until May 1, 1900. Since the sugar industry was doing poorly and many residents could not afford to pay taxes, the military government passed a series of laws, two of which were of great importance. The first gave debtors a year to pay what they owed. As Fernando Picó noted, "this measure favored the farmers but was disadvantageous for the merchants," who were short of capital as U.S. corporations began arriving in the archipelago. The other measure devalued the local currency at an official exchange rate of 60 cents (US) per provincial peso.[46] Both laws proved detrimental to an economy that had contracted because of the war.

The majority of Puerto Ricans lived a precarious existence and the U.S. occupation only heightened their insecurity. While some intellectuals, including those from the working classes, hoped to profit from allying themselves with the invaders from "the land of Washington," many Puerto Ricans simply wanted to have food for their next meal. Historians have dedicated countless pages to debating whether the occupation was traumatic or not. Many Puerto Ricans had been living in trauma for centuries.

Some U.S. soldiers were impressed by the warm reception they received from Puerto Rican peasants. Others used their military power to take advantage of local people. In the town of Caguas, for example, Private John Burke was murdered seven months after the occupation by a civilian, Rafael Ortiz. It was not a patriotic action. Ortiz was avenging his honor after being insulted and beaten in front of his girlfriend by Burke in a drunken outburst. Ortiz was sentenced to death, which was changed to life imprisonment after intervention from Governor Guy V. Henry and President McKinley, and his sentence was eventually commuted after five years. He was the first Puerto Rican to be incarcerated in a U.S. military prison.[47]

During and after the occupation, the poor continued to live in misery. On August 8, 1899, Puerto Rico was hit by Hurricane San Ciriaco. The people of Puerto Rico had learned to live with natural disasters throughout their history; in the years from 1851 to 1899 ten major storms or hurricanes battered the archipelago.[48] San Ciriaco was the deadliest. Approximately 3,400 people lost their lives and more than 2,000 were injured. Many victims succumbed to floods from twenty-four hours of heavy rains. Some towns recorded as much as twenty-five inches of water. The recently established military government estimated damages to be more than $50 million, a hefty sum for an island undergoing a financial crisis. The agricultural industry was also badly hurt.[49]

The most gruesome and detailed descriptions of the days after the hurricane were recorded in the pages of the only Puerto Rican novel published in 1899, *Estercolero* (Muckheap). Drawing on the naturalist tradition, author José Elías Levis Bernard painted a dire picture, carefully detailing the misery in which most Puerto Ricans lived at the time. In the novel, members of the elegantly dressed upper classes stroll through streets inhabited by starving children playing in dirty water.[50] Unlike many of the literary elite, Levis Bernard was born into a humble family and knew the poverty he described firsthand. For him, the problem of misery "grows like a wave, becomes giant, roars like a hurricane. . . . Now we have a boiling need to think of a way to conjure the hurricane that roars in over our heads."[51] Ramón Juliá Marín, a contemporary of Levis Bernard, wrote, "hunger had started its empire."[52]

Disruptions and Continuities

San Ciriaco proved to be an enormous challenge to the occupying forces. The U.S. federal government approved emergency funds to alleviate the hurricane's impact but Puerto Rico's poor road system made some towns and sectors inaccessible, and the government failed to quickly distribute relief to those who needed it most. In total, Washington sent about $200,000 in relief supplies, while sponsoring a program of private donations from cities with populations over 150,000.[53]

The U.S. military did not help Puerto Rico out of a sense of altruism. As historian Stuart Schwartz has noted, "both General Davis in San Juan and President McKinley in Washington understood that the disaster was an opportunity to demonstrate to the Puerto Ricans the efficiency and charity of the new government."[54] This went hand in hand with the notion that Puerto Ricans were an alien race and inferior people, an opinion shared by many in the United States and codified in legislation, academic publications, and newspaper articles.

While the United States had experience with territorial expansion from waging a violent war of aggression against Native Americans, the acquisition of vastly different countries with distinct cultures proved a legal challenge to the empire. The United States became, in the words of anthropologist Lanny Thompson, an imperial republic.[55]

Many among the Puerto Rican elite saw the occupation as a steppingstone toward annexation and statehood. Racist and xenophobic ideas in the United States about the lesser nature of Puerto Ricans—ideas that were shared by local elites—did not seem to promise such outcomes.[56] After much discussion, and attentive to the reports from colonial administrators, the U.S. Congress moved to end the military government in Puerto Rico. The Foraker Act established a seemingly democratic civil government in Puerto Rico. It also created a legally ambiguous Puerto Rican citizenship that was not recognized in international forums.

While there was much debate about possible next steps, Washington reached a consensus that Puerto Ricans were not fit to rule themselves. They needed to be civilized, enlightened, and educated. Of course, all these notions and ideas rested on racist and xenophobic attitudes toward peoples in the newly acquired territories, even as specific regions and areas were all deemed different. This is why the United States created different legal formulas for each territory; it was not one-size-fits-all imperialism. As Lanny Thompson noted, "Hawai'i was the only territory to be incorporated into the United States and eventually (1959) to be admitted as a state." Meanwhile, Puerto Rico and the Philippines "were not incorporated; rather they belonged to, but were not part of, the body politic of the [U.S.] republic," while "a military government was established and maintained" in Guam.[57]

As these changes were taking place in Puerto Rico, Betances watched from afar.[58] He began corresponding with another disillusioned separatist, Eugenio María de Hostos, about the situation in the Caribbean. Hostos was a Puerto Rican–born intellectual who had received his higher education in Spain and traveled the Americas working for Panamericanism, an Antillean federation, and the independence of Cuba and Puerto Rico from Spain. He was also a brilliant educator. His pedagogical ideas transformed the educational systems in the Dominican Republic and Chile, influencing many others.[59] Betances and Hostos kept each other company through their correspondence. Betances also wrote to Estrada Palma, who a few years later would become the first president of the Cuban republic, asking him not to forget about Puerto Rico's unwavering support of their independence cause. Betances died on September 16, 1898, in exile. He died dreaming of returning to the Cabo Rojo of his childhood.[60]

Hostos, on the other hand, lived long enough to see the U.S. occupation fail to bring either annexation or independence. Instead, the United

States kept perpetuating colonialism. As a firm believer in Antillean solidarity, Hostos left Puerto Rico in 1900 to continue his work reforming the education system in the Dominican Republic, where he is still considered one of the country's most illustrious figures. He died on August 11, 1903. His wishes were for his body to be returned to Puerto Rico only after its independence. His remains rest in the Dominican Republic awaiting that day.

CHAPTER 6

FOUNDATIONS OF U.S. COLONIALISM IN PUERTO RICO

As the United States acquired new territories after the war of 1898, a debate ensued in Washington about how to deal with the people living in those territories. The so-called white man's burden was to educate Puerto Ricans in Anglo-Saxon traditions, which was part of a broader colonial project. Native communities had been forcefully and violently assimilated through a system of boarding schools; Hawai'i, the Philippines, and Cuba also proved to be testing grounds for formulas to promote and enforce Americanization.[1] In Puerto Rico, a new educational project began with the occupation. On July 1, 1899, the military government reorganized the public school system by centralizing it, creating local boards, and making education free. The occupying force copied the Massachusetts Department of Education model, which generated resistance from locals because it was deemed incongruent with Puerto Rican realities.[2]

Education was considered an instrument for the assimilation and Americanization of Puerto Ricans. In her in-depth study of the education system in Puerto Rico after the occupation, historian Aida Negrón de Montilla identified fifteen concrete ways in which the educational system was used to assimilate children. These included the celebration of U.S. holidays, ways of life, and history. English also became the language of instruction. In fact, in the 1920s and 1930s, classroom language issues generated a fiery debate within academic circles.[3] The decision to use English also impacted the archipelago's name: shortly after the occupation, the country became "Porto Rico" because, as geologist Robert T. Hill noted in an 1899 article published in *National Geographic*, "Puerto" was unpronounceable in English.[4]

Schools needed qualified teachers. Although efforts were made to bring teachers from the United States to Puerto Rico, the demand for educators outstripped the supply. As a result, Puerto Rico's Department of Education recruited those who had served as teachers during the Spanish regime but had been decertified by the military government. Even with these efforts, schools still lacked enough qualified teachers.[5] In 1903, the University of Puerto Rico (UPR) was created through the U.S. federal government's land grant program. Originally, the UPR was established as a teacher's college to advance Puerto Rico's educational system and, with it, Americanization.[6] But history is never so simple; while the UPR was initially formed to advance U.S. interests, it eventually became a laboratory for Puerto Rico's liberation in the late twentieth century.

Nineteenth-century Puerto Rican liberal intellectual traditions that understood the nation as racially harmonious dominated classroom discussions at this time. According to historian Solsiree del Moral, such understandings shaped and redefined the Great Puerto Rican Family narrative that presented Puerto Rico as a racial democracy. This imagined nation could exist within the U.S. empire but remained culturally distinct from it.[7] Since teachers, students, parents, and administrators had different class and racial backgrounds, school classrooms became spaces of negotiation. Although they were forced to sing "The Star-Spangled Banner," students and teachers also forged unique ideas of the nation that were not always in line with Americanization. Teachers in particular took pride in their language, heritage, and culture, affirming that they were Puerto Ricans and not Americans. Some teachers continued their classes in Spanish in opposition to the mandate of administrators and with the complicity of students and parents.[8]

Education was not the only arena in which Puerto Ricans negotiated colonialism. Medicine became a marker of modernity and enlightenment. The efforts of Dr. Bailey K. Ashford, for example, to diagnose and treat hookworm were seen as a great success and were portrayed in the media as an illustration of progress.[9] Imbued with the era's social Darwinism, scientific determinism, and eugenics, the United States used Puerto Rico as a testing ground to control tropical diseases through "medicina tropical."[10] U.S. public health policies were also imported, often with little attention to local realities. In the process, the opinions and voices of Puerto Ricans were ignored and their dietary and health practices portrayed as backward or primitive at best.[11]

Religion was another contested sphere. Four hundred years of Spanish colonialism had made Puerto Rico a deeply Catholic country. The Catholic Church's hegemony, however, was broken by the U.S. invasion. In fact, a group of Protestant denominations came together and divided the island into zones to evangelize. While the United States advocated the separation of church and state, the lines were often blurry. One of the first reports on Puerto Rico, for example, was written by Henry K. Carroll, a Protestant minister sent by President McKinley to study the conditions in the archipelago.[12]

Sexuality and gender norms were carefully surveilled and controlled through legislation and strict social codes. The 1902 Civil Code legalized divorce, which empowered women and garnered support for the U.S. regime from the working classes. This was not an altruistic moral measure but a strategy to make marriage more appealing. U.S. officials were surprised to find that while nineteenth-century elites jealously protected patriarchal codes of honor, many Puerto Ricans lived in concubinage or entered into other forms of sexual and moral agreements. U.S. officials saw marriage as a tool to civilize Puerto Rican society, beginning at home.[13]

Sex work, which was both legalized and regulated during Spanish rule, was once again banned.[14] Homosexuality was socially looked down upon, and sodomy was made illegal in 1902.[15] Those who engaged in these illicit practices were pushed to the margins, but they did not disappear. Sex work continued to proliferate and, while much is unknown, it seems that a gay scene also thrived, particularly in urban centers.[16] Queerness and sex work took place in intimate spaces behind closed doors or under the moonlight deep in the sugarcane fields—the same fields, it's worth noting, that burned with fire during strikes.

The World of Labor and Their Struggle for Political Participation

While labor leaders sided with the U.S. occupation and promoted Americanization, working-class militancy worried colonial administrators. One of the largest labor actions took place seven years after the invasion. The strike was the product of anger, hunger, and disillusionment with unions and the political elite. In April 1905, at the peak of the sugar harvest, workers demanded "a raise in their daily salaries to 75 cents for men and women, the abolition of child labor, and a nine-hour workday."[17] For weeks they had been organizing a strike in Puerto Rico's southern district, mobilizing as many as twenty thousand people at times. Tired, angry, and hopeless, workers were willing to go against not only the landowning sugar barons but also their own labor leaders if needed. Santiago Iglesias Pantín wrote in his memoirs that he led these massive strikes, but that was not the case. In fact, his labor federation wanted workers to wait to negotiate with bosses and administrators before declaring a strike. Workers ignored this and staged perhaps the most significant strike in Puerto Rico's history up to that moment.

The strike was the result of the tireless organizing of many anonymous working men and women who led makeshift night schools where they taught reading and writing as well as how to form and sustain a union. Children joined the strike-organizing efforts by raising funds in their neighborhoods. Women, erased from the archival records because their contributions were rarely remunerated, also worked in the fields and did essential domestic and care labor that sustained the entire sugar-harvesting enterprise.[18]

The U.S. colonial government used the recently created Insular Police to suppress the strike. The force had been established in 1899 but Governor Charles Allen officially sanctioned its creation in 1901 to centralize police power. One of its mandates was to suppress any social agitation—which they did with both force and violence.[19]

On April 16, 1905, a labor meeting took place in the city of Ponce's main plaza in support of the striking workers. It was common for police officials to stand next to labor leaders as they delivered speeches. If the speech was too fiery, the police would order speakers to modify their tone. On that night, as labor leader Eugenio Sánchez López gave a passionate speech to over six thousand peasants, workers, and onlookers, Detective Gutiérrez from the Insular Police began hitting someone in the crowd with a club. In a matter of seconds, chaos ensued. Police officers began shooting their guns and attacking anyone in sight. More than forty people were wounded and several labor leaders arrested.[20]

The violence that took place in Ponce only added fuel to the fire. After several weeks, workers continued their strike and eventually succeeded. Most of their demands were met. The Free Federation of Workers (FLT) also joined the strike and provided crucial support in the form of funds, political networks, and seasoned negotiators. Those who successfully organized to "storm heaven," to borrow a phrase from Karl Marx, remain anonymous.[21] Their names do not appear in history books, but they greatly shaped the lives of many through their agency, *desafío y solidaridad* (defiance and solidarity).[22]

As had happened before the occupation, women were excluded from the country's political and cultural spheres. They did not stand to the side passively, however. Women from different social classes became active thinkers, theorists, and political organizers.[23] Middle-class women created a powerful and influential suffrage movement in the first two decades of the twentieth century. Those who led the movement had been educated abroad and held professional jobs as nurses or teachers. The Liga Femínea, founded in 1917, became the Liga Sufragista (Suffragist League) in 1921. It was created and led by women such as Ana Roqué de Duprey, Mercedes Solá, Carlota Matienzo, Ángela Negrón Muñoz, and Olivia Paoli, among others.[24] The Liga Sufragista joined other suffragist organizations created in the 1920s to successfully push conversations about voting rights into Puerto Rico's mainstream.[25] While most of the women involved came from the middle classes, the suffragist movement was not a homogeneous group. When the Puerto Rican legislature approved women's right to vote in 1929, only literate women were included. In a country with soaring illiteracy levels, this meant most Puerto Rican women were denied the right to vote. The universal suffrage law was finally passed in 1935.[26]

While middle-class women made strides, working-class women also organized unions and demanded more rights, as they had since the labor movement's early days. For example, working women urged labor leaders to advocate for universal suffrage in a labor congress organized by the FLT in 1908. This was not a one-time demand as working women continued to call for representation within the labor movement.[27]

In June 1919, the same month that the Paris Peace Conference ended World War I, the U.S. Congress passed the Nineteenth Amendment, granting women the right to vote. Puerto Rico was excluded because it was (and is) considered a territory *belonging to* but not *part of* the United States. Working women wrote letters to the colonial governor asking for equality with their U.S. counterparts. They were also attentive to events unfolding in the international sphere.[28]

Four months after the passage of the Nineteenth Amendment, working women from around the world gathered in Washington, D.C., for the inaugural International Congress of Working Women. Working women in Puerto Rico sought to emulate their peers by creating a similar conference to advocate for women's suffrage and more labor rights. For unionized Puerto Rican working women, the struggle was not only against the state as they were also ready to go up against the recently created Socialist Party if needed.[29]

The Insular Labor Party, created a few years prior by members of the FLT, had shocked the country by winning the municipality of Arecibo in the 1914 elections. The moment seemed ripe for the creation of a true Socialist party. Sugarcane workers set fire to fields throughout the island in militant strikes. Founded in Cayey by fifty-six labor delegates in March 1915, the Socialist Party became an important force in Puerto Rico's polity. But, just as in the broader labor movement, women were not allowed to occupy positions of power within its ranks. Some working women who had been organizing around suffrage were left without the right to vote. The political coalition between Socialists and Republicans passed legislation that made universal suffrage a reality that helped them secure a victory in the 1936 elections.[30]

While working women were often denied participation in the labor movement's highest echelons, the anarcho-feminist Luisa Capetillo fought for space within the male-dominated world of unions. Her father was from Spain and her mother from France. They traveled to Puerto Rico seeking better job opportunities. He was to run an amusement park and she was to be a governess for a wealthy family. Things did not go as planned, however. They experienced downward social mobility although their European heritage granted them access to certain spaces, like literary soirees, that not every Puerto Rican enjoyed.[31]

Luisa Capetillo was born in the northern town of Arecibo on October 28, 1882. Her parents, both avid readers of the European romantics, made sure to provide her with an education. She attended a private school in her hometown, where she excelled in all her classes. Her parents' precarious economic condition did not allow her to pursue higher education, something she addressed in her writings. Nonetheless, Capetillo demonstrated a deep understanding of writers ranging from Leo Tolstoy to Piotr Kropotkin to John Stuart Mill and Victor Hugo.[32] Not content with merely studying the era's social problems, she devoted her life to changing those conditions. In the 1905 strikes that burned through the sugarcane fields, Luisa Capetillo saw an opportunity to test her ideas. She participated in the organization of the strikes of Arecibo, an experience that profoundly influenced the rest of her life.[33]

In a highly illiterate society, Capetillo began working as a *lectora* (reader) in a tobacco factory. These were people who read out loud to cigar makers as they worked. Lectores were paid out of workers' own pockets and played a pivotal role in the education of the working classes. Mornings were dedicated to reading local and international newspapers while literature readings took place in the afternoons. Workshops became, as one tobacco rover described them, their universities. It was not uncommon, then, for impromptu *tertulias* to take place after work hours, where a worker who did not know how to read or write could engage in debates about Victor Hugo's *Les Misérables* or what had triggered the recent strikes in Belgium.[34]

Writing and printing a book in the early twentieth century was an impressive feat; for a working-class woman to do so was especially noteworthy. Capetillo was able to publish not one but four books. She also published a newspaper titled *La mujer*. While no copies have survived, the newspaper circulated well beyond the confines of San Juan. She had newspaper exchanges with comrades across Europe, the United States, the Caribbean, and Latin America.[35]

Capetillo advocated for free love, a society without prisons, and the emancipation of women. She is remembered as one of the first women to wear men's pantsuits, which led to clashes with authorities in both Cuba and Puerto Rico. She challenged gender codes imposed by the state and the upper classes as well as by her comrades in the labor movement. She was accepted by her labor peers if she did not intrude into men's business, as one labor newspaper warned.[36] An obituary upon her death in 1922 demonstrated male labor leaders' contempt toward her. They cynically wrote that she had not really comprehended the socialist theories she advocated.[37]

Not content to simply write about labor issues, she participated in sugarcane strikes in the island-municipality of Vieques (and was subsequently arrested), traveled throughout the archipelago to spread her ideas in town plazas, and became one of the strongest advocates of universal suffrage. She was one of the few working women who actively participated in the FLT's labor congresses. In a world where women's bodies were highly monitored and surveilled, Capetillo defiantly traveled across different national borders. She organized alongside Cuban anarchists, sold her books, and spoke at public meetings in the Dominican Republic. She spent time with radicals in Ybor City and opened a vegetarian restaurant and hostel in New York City.[38]

While in New York, Capetillo joined a growing community of Puerto Ricans who were shaping and transforming the city's landscape during the first two decades of the twentieth century. Some, like Arturo Alfonso Schomburg, impacted not only Puerto Rican communities but the fabric of U.S. culture as a whole. Schomburg, the son of a Black

West Indian mother and a German-descended father, was born in Puerto Rico but migrated to New York in 1891 at the age of seventeen. He advocated for the independence of Puerto Rico and Cuba and later became a passionate bibliophile. His archival collection and curatorial practices became foundational for Black Studies and were one of the major influences of the Harlem Renaissance, a cultural moment guided by the proliferation of Black art, dance, music, literature, and intellectual production.[39]

The diaries of working-class intellectuals like Jesús Colón and Bernardo Vega also provide a window into the worlds of those who left Puerto Rico for a better life in the big city.[40] Contract laborers and job-seeking workers were the "pioneers" who established the first Puerto Rican communities in the United States.[41] Over time, small enclaves led to complex communities. But the migration patterns were also marked by a series of political turning points that transformed Puerto Ricans from foreigners into (second-class) citizens.[42]

From Colonial Subjects to Colonial Citizens

On May 1, 1899, the military government in Puerto Rico officially ended with the Foraker Act. This legislation, drafted by Senator Joseph Benson Foraker, created a civic government for Puerto Rico in which the governor, his cabinet, and the upper house would all be appointed by the U.S. president. The legislation's final form, however, took shape after a series of heated debates about the future of the recently acquired territory. The occupation provided fertile ground to discuss the limits of the U.S. Constitution, conversations that arose from different interpretations of the future of the United States as an empire. Politicians debated, for example, whether the newly acquired territories should be incorporated into the nation as had been the case with Louisiana, Hawai'i, Indigenous Nations, and the territories that formerly belonged to Mexico.[43]

As the War of 1898 raged, Democrats in Congress pushed through the Teller Amendment, which guaranteed that the United States would not incorporate Cuba. The next question, then, was what to do with the

Philippines, Guam, and Puerto Rico. Here, the era's xenophobic and racist ethos guided ubiquitous depictions of Puerto Ricans as ignorant, lazy, and incapable of self-rule.[44] These discourses were perpetuated by Ivy League professors, politicians, colonial administrators, and the president of the United States.[45] The press also took part in generating images, articles, and books depicting Puerto Ricans as inferior. During the occupation and in the first decades of the twentieth century there were dozens, if not hundreds, of books, cartoons, and films that reproduced these stereotypes.[46] One of the many photo books published in the United States during and after the invasion of Puerto Rico was *Our Islands and Their People*. It provided visual referents to the U.S. reading public about the newly acquired colonies.[47] As the title suggested, however, the Caribbean islands of Puerto Rico, imagined as idyllic tropical paradises, now belonged to the United States—but its people did not. In the pages of the book, Puerto Ricans were imagined and portrayed as inferior, alien, and savages.[48]

Some members of the Puerto Rican elite also reproduced these ideas. For them, the laboring masses were rowdy, lazy, and too Black. The nineteenth-century "Great Puerto Rican Family" trope reproduced in the literature of the elites sought to address just this. Workers and laborers would be incorporated into the nation (conceptualized as one big family) but needed to be docile and follow the patriarch, embodied by the liberal, white, male elite.[49]

While extending U.S. citizenship to Puerto Ricans had been discussed in Congress, it was later eliminated from the Foraker Act; Puerto Ricans were not deemed fit for it. This again spurred debate about the limits of the U.S. Constitution and how "the supreme law of the land" should operate in new territories. The United States was grappling with the fact that it was now an empire with colonial possessions. For Puerto Ricans, the Foraker Act provided citizenship that was legally ambiguous and not formally recognized in international forums. Puerto Ricans were in limbo as the United States created a legal borderline.[50]

The legal dimensions of the Foraker Act and the ambiguity of Puerto Rico's relationship to the United States were put to the test through a series of Supreme Court cases during the first decades of the twentieth century known as the Insular Cases. In one case, in 1901, Samuel Downes sued George R. Bidwell, the U.S. customs inspector in the port of New York. Downes, the owner of S.B. Downes & Company, claimed that he had been unfairly charged import duties for oranges imported from Puerto Rico, which, according to him, was a territory of the United States because of the War of 1898.[51]

The case made it all the way to the Supreme Court, which ultimately defined Puerto Rico as an unincorporated territory of the United States. According to historian Robert McGreevey, U.S. intellectuals and states-men equated Puerto Ricans to Native and Black communities in the United States. "If ideas of how [to] best train southern [B]lack [people]s in citizenship helped shape and justify colonial policy in Puerto Rico," Mc-Greevey noted, "the experience also shaped attitudes towards [B]lack [people]s in the United States." In fact, eight of the nine justices who ruled in the case had also decided *Plessy v. Ferguson*, which legally segregated the U.S. South. The Supreme Court ruled that Congress had plenary power over Puerto Rico, which was a possession of the United States.[52]

Two years later, in 1903, the Supreme Court heard another case involv-ing Puerto Rico, this time testing the limits of Puerto Rican citizenship. Isabel González had traveled to New York to find her fiancé, who had left the archipelago to work in a factory. As a young mother expecting an-other child, she was deemed an "alien" and a potential public burden. To resolve the case, the Court created a new category, "nationals." These were "neither aliens nor citizens" but "owed allegiance to the United States and were granted freedom of movement within US borders." Most basic citizenship rights, however, were denied.[53]

The question of citizenship was debated by different social sectors in Puerto Rico, from the middle classes to leaders in the organized labor movement. For many, U.S. citizenship would be a logical step toward annexation, which would grant Puerto Rico all the rights enjoyed by the states of the union. In 1917, the Jones-Shafroth Act was signed by Presi-dent Woodrow Wilson. The product of years of debate and tireless organizing from different sectors of the middle and working classes, the act granted Puerto Ricans U.S. citizenship. Many Puerto Ricans migrat-ing to the United States had no way to prove that they had been born in

Puerto Rico, however, and were often denied documents that would confirm their legal status. As later events would demonstrate, Puerto Ricans remained second-class citizens.

The Jones-Shafroth Act also restructured the government along the lines of the three-branch U.S. model: executive, legislative, and judicial. While the U.S. president still appointed the governor, some cabinet members would now be appointed by the recently created Insular Senate. The legislative branch was divided into two bodies: the House of Representatives, composed of thirty-nine seats, and the Insular Senate, which had nineteen. All would be democratically elected.

Three years later, the Merchant Marine Act was approved, establishing what have become known as the cabotage laws, whereby all imports to Puerto Rico had to be shipped in a U.S. vessel, disrupting the price of goods and products on the archipelago. In addition, any import had to be transported by the U.S. merchant marine in U.S.-made ships, flying the U.S. flag, with an all-U.S. crew. This nativist legislation, which served to promote the U.S. merchant marine, hindered Puerto Rico's economic development. Over one hundred years later, it is still enforced.

Racist attitudes and a precarious labor market effectively made Puerto Ricans a colonial labor reserve. In New York, for example, academics, charity boards, and the Bureau of Insular Affairs "defined Puerto Ricans as foreign for the purposes of restricting immigration, reducing relief tolls, or denying free government transport."[54] Denied equal treatment, Puerto Ricans also had limited access to benefits enjoyed by U.S. citizens. In another Supreme Court case, the relationship between the empire and its Caribbean colony was once again put to the test. This time, the case involved a working-class intellectual from Mayagüez named Jesús María Balzac.

Balzac was a typesetter, long-time member of the FLT, and writer who published three books in the first decade of the twentieth century: *Revolución* (Revolution, 1900), *Apuntes históricos* (Historical notes, 1904), and *Unión y fuerza* (Union and strength, 1910). In these works, Balzac outlined and defended his socialist ideas and promoted the FLT's agenda in Puerto Rico. Balzac was one of many self-educated workers who were creating a vibrant intellectual community at the turn of the century. He was charged with libel for an article criticizing Governor Arthur Yager (in office, 1913–21) in his newspaper *El baluarte*. The case was known as *Balzac v. People of Porto Rico* (1922).[55]

A former history professor and president of Georgetown University, Arthur Yager was appointed colonial governor of "Porto Rico" in 1913 by his friend President Woodrow Wilson, whom he met during doctoral studies at Johns Hopkins University. When Yager arrived in Puerto Rico he declared war on the organized labor movement—which also declared war on him. From 1915 to 1920, a record-breaking 335 strikes occurred across all sectors.[56] Yager responded by persecuting labor leaders and repressing strikes, actions that resulted in the death of multiple striking workers. Yager went so far as to secretly plot the creation of a government-sponsored labor federation to downplay the power of the FLT and its political arm, the Socialist Party.[57]

Balzac was charged with libel, a misdemeanor. The Code of Criminal Procedure of Porto Rico only granted a jury for felony cases but Balzac argued that the U.S. Constitution's Sixth Amendment granted him the right to a jury trial. He further argued "that the language of the alleged libels was only fair comment, and their publication was protected by the First Amendment."[58] Balzac was sentenced to nine months in prison. He appealed to Puerto Rico's Supreme Court and the charges were affirmed. He then appealed to the U.S. Supreme Court.

What this self-educated typesetter did not know—though he might have guessed—was that his case would redefine Puerto Rico's colonial relationship to the United States. Echoing the racist and xenophobic ethos of the times as well as previous Insular Cases, Chief Justice William Howard Taft argued that Puerto Ricans could only enjoy the full benefits of U.S. citizenship if they moved to one of the states of the union.[59]

Puerto Rico was considered, as noted in *Downes v. Bidwell*, foreign in a domestic sense; it belonged to the United States but was not part of it. Balzac's case added another colonial layer. Puerto Ricans had been U.S. citizens since 1917, but because the archipelago had not been incorporated into the union, the Bill of Rights invoked by Balzac did not apply to them. Only the U.S. Congress could decide which parts of the Constitution applied to Puerto Ricans. The precedents from these three cases continue to shape the colonial relationship between Puerto Rico and the United States. Puerto Rico is still considered an unincorporated territory and only parts of the Constitution apply to those who live in the archipelago.

The 1920s were marked by deepening inequality. The sugar industry, dominated by absentee corporations, prospered. Meanwhile, the economy increasingly centralized around exports, including sugar, tobacco, coffee, fruits, and manufactured products. The working classes, as expected, did not reap the benefits. Because of the large number of unemployed workers, salaries stagnated and precarity once again dominated. Politically, the Socialist Party became a force to be reckoned with and transformed the electoral landscape. Traditional parties created alliances and coalitions to limit a possible socialist victory. And then, in 1928, Hurricane San Felipe made landfall in Puerto Rico. While the official death toll paled in comparison to that of Hurricane San Ciriaco in 1899, the impact on the island's agricultural sector was massive. And then, in 1929, the Great Depression began in the United States.

The 1930s promised to be a turbulent decade. And it was.

CHAPTER 7

A TURBULENT DECADE

The 1930s are often portrayed in Puerto Rico's official history as a decade of crisis. And they were turbulent times indeed. By the 1930s, the archipelago had become, in the words of historian Fernando Picó, "a vast sugar plantation."[1] Meanwhile, the Great Depression wreaked havoc on a population for whom trauma had become part of their everyday experience. But the 1930s were also a moment of political effervescence—a time when various groups and individuals began testing out other ways to live. The nation, or at least the essence of what it meant to be Puerto Rican, was once again theorized and reimagined by intellectuals. And while old hegemonies shattered and gave way to new orthodoxies, nineteenth-century national myths continued to hold power.

In the southern region of Puerto Rico, a Black physician named José Lanauze Rolón was thinking about ways to construct those other possibilities. Born in 1893, Lanauze Rolón was educated in his hometown of Coamo and became a teacher there. He later traveled to Washington, D.C., received his medical degree from Howard University, and returned to Puerto Rico, where he opened a medical office in the city of Ponce.[2]

As a doctor, Lanauze Rolón was a distinguished member of Ponce's middle class. He was also a prominent writer and essayist who penned numerous articles in the local press and published his first book, a *poemario* titled *Momentos: Poesías y cuentos fantásticos* (Moments: Poetry and fantastic stories), shortly after returning from Howard University.[3] From 1925 to 1928, he also organized a group that advocated for birth control. He was influenced by neo-Malthusian ideas about population control then popular in certain working-class circles. In fact, these ideas had been discussed in Puerto Rico since the early 1900s and had advocates that included the anarcho-feminist Luisa Capetillo.[4] For Lanauze Rolón, Puerto Rico was overpopulated. Nonetheless, he opposed abortion and extramarital sex; he believed education and access to information would help women—men were exempt—make decisions about their life and health. Sex, on the other hand, did not have to solely be practiced for the sake of reproduction. These ideas, which he published in newspapers and promoted at public events, were compiled in his second book, *El mal de los muchos hijos: Polémica sobre el neo-malthusianismo* (The harm of many children: Arguments about neo-Malthusianism).[5]

By the 1930s, however, Lanauze Rolón had been radicalized in a different way. In 1932 he published a book that gave a glimpse of the author's fiery and combative ideas, *Por los caminos de la violencia: La idea comunista* (On the paths of violence: The Communist idea). For Lanauze Rolón, Russia was an example to follow, a beacon of hope. Russians had shown how revolutionary struggle could not be achieved solely through books and writings; instead, overthrowing the capitalist order also entailed violence.[6] The 1917 Russian Revolution had influenced many radicals in Puerto Rico, including members of the FLT and the Socialist Party. In their congresses, they saluted their Russian comrades and sought to emulate their example. This discourse, however, was quickly toned down because the leaders of both groups were affiliated with the more conservative American Federation of Labor. Both the Socialist Party and the FLT were not homogeneous institutions. Deep divides existed between the leadership and the rank and file, something that caused major splits and tensions in the 1930s.[7]

Communist ideas like those promoted by Lanauze Rolón began circulating in Puerto Rico in the 1920s. Many intellectuals flirted with them, including Luis Muñoz Marín, the future governor of Puerto Rico. In the 1930s, however, communists were one of the many groups that imagined Puerto Rico otherwise, even if it meant giving their lives to the fight against capitalism or U.S. imperialism. Others used their pens.

Others the classroom podium. Others theorized about all of this with wine-stained lips during their evening *tertulias*.

Lanauze Rolón was part of a broader Black radical tradition in Puerto Rico that took an active part in shaping the lives of many and the history of the archipelago itself. It is a Black radical tradition that can be traced back to the actions of maroon communities resisting Spanish colonialism and the revolts of enslaved peoples that haunted colonial administrators in the nineteenth century.[8] The erasure of this tradition from historical narratives, however, is not accidental; as anthropologist Michel-Rolph Trouillot has noted, silences are always actively produced.[9] Puerto Rican historians have often reproduced, without questioning, the agreed-upon norms and dominant codes of their times. Yet Lanauze Rolón and others like him challenged the elite's patriarchal ideas of who belonged to the nation by incorporating class discourse attentive to the working masses. The following pages trace the ways the idea of the nation was negotiated by working-class intellectuals, revolutionary nationalists, and elite intellectuals.

A Social and Political Storm

Puerto Rico's economy depended on its agricultural exports. In the 1920s, however, Puerto Rico did not reap the benefits of the post–World War I era. Sugar continued its steady growth and production, but other crops such as tobacco, fruit, and coffee suffered greatly. Behind the economic statistics, people's livelihoods were badly affected as inflation drove up the cost of food and other necessities while unemployment grew and salaries stagnated.[10]

Because of its geographic location, the archipelago's history has also been marked by storms and hurricanes. In the early morning hours of Wednesday, September 12, 1928, the winds began howling, carrying with them torrential rain and pieces of zinc roof that sliced through the night like projectiles. San Felipe was a category 5 hurricane with wind gusts estimated at 160 miles per hour or more. It stormed Puerto Rico for about sixteen gruesome hours, leaving behind a path of destruction. Some compared the hurricane to the four horsemen of the apocalypse.[11]

The colonial administration's experience and recent advancements in technology meant a catastrophe like what had happened in San Ciriaco in 1899 was avoided. San Felipe's death toll was estimated at 312, in comparison to San Ciriaco's more than 3,000. With approximately $50 million in property and infrastructural damages, Hurricane San Felipe only added to the average Puerto Rican's daily misery.[12] The empire of hunger colonized the empty stomachs of Puerto Rico's laboring masses, and Puerto Rico's dependence on the United States created a fatal recipe. The year following San Felipe, the New York Stock Exchange collapsed, giving way to the Great Depression. Three years later, in 1932, at one of the most difficult moments of the Depression, Puerto Rico was hit again by another hurricane, San Ciprián. It left 225 people dead in its wake and caused $30 million in damages.[13]

Conditions only worsened for the laboring masses. For example, from 1931 to 1932, the daily wage of a sugarcane worker went from 90 cents to 50 or 60 cents, an amount similar to that of the turn of the century.[14] Meanwhile workers in the tobacco sector earned about $1.27 weekly for thirty hours of work. In the needlework industry, which was dominated by women, workers received about $3.32 per week if they worked in a factory. Most, however, did not work in factories but in their own houses, where they earned even less.[15]

The local government's reaction to the situation in Puerto Rico was underwhelming; meanwhile, the U.S. government sought merely to protect their economic interests in the archipelago. Alleviating poverty and rampant social ills was not seen as a priority. As the Depression took its toll, the United States sent a new governor to Puerto Rico. Theodore Roosevelt Jr., son of former president Theodore "Teddy" Roosevelt, arrived in early 1929 and sought to understand Puerto Rican culture, something that previous governors had not done. He prided himself on the rustic Spanish he learned while in office and even nicknamed himself the *jíbaro de la Fortaleza* (peasant in the governor's mansion).[16] Roosevelt Jr. went to work fundraising among private donors, founding a hospital for tuberculosis patients, and creating Puerto Rico's Department of Labor, led by Prudencio Rivera Martínez, one of the founding members of the FLT and the Socialist Party.

In 1930 the U.S. government ordered a study from the Brookings Institution, which eventually became titled *Porto Rico & Its Problems*. The report documented the precarious existence of the majority of Puerto Ricans. The median annual income for peasant families was $250. Further, malnutrition caused 43.9 percent of deaths due to diarrhea, enteritis, and tuberculosis. Education, however, had improved. By 1930, 97 percent of urban school-age children and 40 percent of those in the countryside attended school.[17] Lack of clothing and families' need for child labor to offset the cost of living were two of the main reasons some did not attend school. A decade later, this was still the case, as my grandmother would often tell me. She only made it to the fourth grade because by then she needed to take care of her younger siblings. In a household of thirteen children, they had only one pair of shoes for two children. My grandmother went to school in the morning, met her brother at noon to give him her shoes, and he attended class in the afternoon.

Before leaving office in 1932 to become the governor of the Philippines—transferred from one U.S. colonial post in the Caribbean to another in the Pacific—Roosevelt Jr. and Commissioner of Education José Padín successfully lobbied to include Puerto Rico within the Smith-Hughes Act. This legislation assigned $105,000 for the creation of vocational schools in Puerto Rico. The Puerto Rican legislature matched it and approved $108,000 for the project. By 1932, there were twenty-three agricultural vocational centers, twenty-two domestic economy schools, and a school of arts and trades.[18]

A coalition between the Republicans and Socialist Party, the Coalición, claimed victory in the 1932 elections. The highly bureaucratized Socialist Party and the creation of alliances with those they had considered their "class enemies" were unsustainable. The Coalición won the 1936 elections, but internal tensions ripped the Socialist Party apart and factions within the Coalición also created severe obstacles to passing legislation.[19]

In the United States, the election of Franklin Delano Roosevelt and his New Deal program inevitably impacted Puerto Rico as well. While the Coalición won the electoral ticket, the political panorama was vastly more complex. It had different nodes: the colonial governor, elected officials, and federal New Deal programs. In 1933 the Puerto Rico Emergency Relief Administration (PRERA) was created to distribute food and promote construction projects to ease unemployment. As expected, there was a struggle between the Coalición and the Liberal Party (formerly the Union Party) as to how to distribute funds and manage the program. Furthermore, although the Liberals had lost the elections, they won enough votes to secure key positions, including a Senate seat for Luis Muñoz Marín, the future governor whose political star was rising fast in the 1930s. Through his contacts in Washington and political networks in Puerto Rico, including those he made as editor of *La democracia*, one of the most influential newspapers of the era, Muñoz Marín unofficially became a New Deal emissary to the dismay of Coalitionists.[20]

Since the War of 1898, Puerto Rico had been put under the War Department's Bureau of Insular Affairs. Now, in 1933, its jurisdiction was transferred to the newly created Division of Insular Territories and Possessions in the Department of Interior, directed by Ernest Gruening.[21] His appointment was seen as a victory for the members of the Puerto Rican Liberal Party.[22]

In 1935, the Puerto Rican government created a commission to study the archipelago's challenges. It was led by Carlos Chardón, provost at the University of Puerto Rico. Chardón wrote a detailed report about the conditions in the archipelago along with a plan to address them. The plan identified three main problems: large estates, absentee corporations, and monoculture. It also sought to industrialize Puerto Rico, centralize the public school system, and tend to other developmental needs. After much debate along partisan lines, the plan was not approved; instead, the U.S. government created the Puerto Rico Reconstruction Administration (PRRA). The PRRA sought to boost the economy through the creation of public programs and enterprises, including new hydroelectric works, new roads, and an electric infrastructure in the country along with educational programs. The PRRA also invested in a cement company, cooperatives, and two sugar mills.[23]

While these programs were not entirely successful, by seeking to transform the economy through direct state intervention they created the ideological and administrative infrastructure that proliferated in the following decade. These ideas were incorporated into the program of the Popular Democratic Party (PPD), the topic of the next chapter.

As these changes were taking place, there were large mobilizations among the organized labor movement. The widespread misery of the laboring masses pushed them to demand better living conditions and salaries, not only of the government and their bosses but also of their labor unions. By the 1930s, the FLT dominated the world of unions, acquiring political power that would have been unimaginable to those who created it in 1899. While often unacknowledged in traditional historical narratives, the actions of the FLT directly challenged the colonial administration of Puerto Rico. Strikes and militant labor actions provided a space for working-class individuals to enact new forms of solidarity and to think about different forms of liberation, even if only briefly.

In the first five years of the 1930s there were dozens of strikes in which more than sixty thousand workers demanded better salaries and living conditions. Unionized and nonunionized workers from different sectors went on strike and closed their workshops and factories or stood up in their living-room workspaces. Needleworkers, sugarcane workers, taxi drivers, and tobacco workers were some of those who defied their employers and made the elite tremble with signs that demonstrated the simplicity of their demands: "we are not asking for the sky."[24]

These mobilizations not only demonstrated workers' militancy but were a testament to the fragility of the FLT's control over the organized labor movement. By the 1930s, there was clear discontent over the divide between labor leaders and the rank and file. This was accentuated by the coalitions and alliances the Socialist Party made with Republicans. In the 1920s, some aging labor leaders warned against bureaucratization and the infiltration of white-collar workers into their ranks. Labor leader Prudencio Rivera Martínez, who became Puerto Rico's first commissioner of labor in 1932, complained that one rank-and-file worker wrote to him angry because instead of receiving a warm response from Rivera Martínez with the language of comradery and solidarity, he had received a letter where he was addressed as "usted."[25]

But these tensions went beyond formalities and came to a head in two major strikes that took place in 1933 and 1934, both of which publicly challenged the FLT and the Socialist Party and delivered blows from which they would never recover. The first was a strike against Rafael Alonso Torres, a self-educated worker who had become one of the labor movement's most important leaders. In 1933, for example, he held eleven official positions between the FLT and Socialist Party, including as their interim president. He was appointed to the University of Puerto Rico's board of trustees by Governor Robert H. Gore, as a political favor to the Coalición, with whom he sided.[26]

As a result of Alonso Torres's appointment, students at the University of Puerto Rico declared an unprecedented strike that extended to the Mayagüez campus as well as to several high schools across the archipelago. While the government and the Socialist Party first dismissed the students, their cause generated enormous public sympathy, as documented in surveys in the press. For the students, having an "ignorant ox," as they often described Alonso Torres, as board member would mean the death of the university. Socialists, by contrast, believed that it was a way of democratizing higher learning. Political parties also capitalized on the strike. For Liberals like Luis Muñoz Marín, the moment was ripe to attack the image of the Socialist Party.[27]

Rafael Alonso Torres was pressured to resign from the university's board of trustees by the governor and his party. Some of its members argued that they had ceded to the students their most powerful weapon, the strike. But the working classes were not ceding anything. In fact, the following year another powerful strike took place in the sugarcane fields and challenged not only hacendados but also the FLT's leadership.

The FLT's rank and file was growing disillusioned with its leadership's bureaucratization. In 1933, a series of sugarcane strikes led to the creation of a one-year collective bargaining agreement between the FLT's Agricultural Workers' Union and the sugar corporations' Association of Puerto Rico's Sugar Producers. This agreement, however, had been made behind closed doors and was not discussed or ratified by the rank and file. Further, some of the wages agreed upon were even lower than what workers were currently paid.[28]

On Three Kings Day, January 6, 1934, a day after the collective agreement was signed, sugarcane workers in Salinas's Central Aguirre declared a strike; twenty-nine of the forty sugar *centrales* in Puerto Rico followed suit.[29] Demoralized by hunger and the lack of support from their labor leaders, they demanded better salaries and working conditions for both men and women, something quite unusual at the time. Although their strike was unsuccessful, their actions dealt a decisive blow to an already fragmented labor federation.[30]

While the FLT and the Socialist Party's leadership openly advocated for the annexation of Puerto Rico to the United States, this did not necessarily resonate with their rank and file. On January 11, 1934, for example, striking workers sent a telegram to a nontraditional ally. They asked Pedro Albizu Campos, a Harvard-educated lawyer and leader of the Nationalist Party, to help them lead the strike. While the alliance between organized labor and the Nationalists was short-lived, it demonstrated the enormous influence of Albizu Campos and deepened the rupture between the laboring masses and the traditional labor movement.[31]

Winds of Resistance, Storms of Defiance

In 1932, a member of the Nationalist Party handed Pedro Albizu Campos a letter from Cornelius P. Rhoads, a U.S. oncologist residing in Puerto Rico, to one of his colleagues. In the letter, Rhoads echoed the era's typical xenophobia and racism. He was in Puerto Rico with funding from the Rockefeller Foundation. In the letter Rhoads argued,

> They are beyond doubt the dirtiest, laziest, most degenerate and thievish race of men ever inhabiting this sphere. It makes you sick to inhabit the same island with them. They are even lower than Italians. What the island needs is not public health work but a tidal wave or something to totally exterminate the population. It might then be livable. I have done my best to further the process of extermination by killing off 8 and transplanting cancer into several more. The latter has not resulted in any fatalities so far. . . . The matter of consideration

for the patients' welfare plays no role here—in fact all physicians take delight in the abuse and torture of the unfortunate subjects.[32]

Albizu Campos circulated the letter, which caused immediate public outrage. Its veracity was never confirmed; Rhoads argued that he was joking. His sentiments, however, were familiar to Puerto Ricans. Most knew that they were despised by U.S. officials. Now, they could read that they were seen as something to exterminate. Rhoads was removed from his position at the Ashford Hospital but continued to have a thriving medical career, during which he conducted experiments on human subjects.[33] Albizu Campos became a larger-than-life figure in Puerto Rico. If Bolívar and Haiti had haunted Puerto Rico in the nineteenth century, Albizu Campos and the Nationalist Party tormented the U.S. government in the 1930s and 1940s.

The Nationalist Party had been founded a decade earlier, in 1922. It was created as a response to the Union Party's decision to remove independence from their platform. Its leadership was composed of members of Puerto Rico's cultural and political elite, including José Coll y Cuchi, Vicente Geigel Polanco, and José S. Alegría.[34] José S. Alegría's son, Ricardo, became one of the main architects of the 1950s vision of the Puerto Rican nation.[35]

Albizu Campos joined the Nationalist Party in 1924; just over a decade earlier, he had received a scholarship to study at the University of Vermont but transferred the following year to Harvard University where he not only finished his undergraduate degree but also pursued a law degree, which he received in 1921. It was at Harvard that he met his Peruvian wife, Laura Meneses del Carpio.[36] When World War I began, he joined the army, serving until 1919. After joining the Nationalist Party, he was sent on a solidarity mission to Latin America. He spent time in the Dominican Republic, Haiti, Venezuela, Peru, Mexico, and Panama—a formative experience for the young man.[37]

Five months after returning to Puerto Rico from his solidarity tour, Albizu Campos was named the Nationalist Party's president. This appointment transformed the party and Puerto Rican politics. The party had been essentially dormant before it joined the electoral race in the

1932 elections. The results were disastrous: the Nationalist Party received just 5,257 votes, or 1.38 percent of all ballots cast.[38]

After the elections, the Nationalist Party's leadership decided that independence could not be asked for politely through the ballot box and they abandoned the electoral process altogether. The party instead sought to organize actions that would call international attention to the ways that U.S. colonialism impacted Puerto Ricans. After 1932, Albizu Campos's discourse became fierier. Unlike traditional politicians, he believed that Puerto Ricans had the right to independence, whether the United States was willing to grant it or not.[39] Federal agencies immediately took notice and began surveilling members of the Nationalist Party and other so-called subversives.[40]

Tensions between the Nationalist Party and the government came to boil from 1935 to 1939. Albizu Campos had never abandoned the idea of using arms in defense of independence. In 1935, however, a series of events pushed the party to oblige its members to participate in military service.[41]

In a congress that took place on December 8, 1935, the Nationalist Party officially advocated for armed struggle to achieve their objectives, a policy decision stemming from the repression and persecution that Nationalists then faced. Earlier that year, four Nationalists traveling to the University of Puerto Rico had been accused of plotting to detonate a bomb. They were intercepted by the police and gunned down. Three of them died immediately and another was badly wounded. A few blocks away, José Santiago Barea, another Nationalist, was ambushed by the police. Santiago Barea did throw a bomb before he was arrested and executed.[42]

The incident became known as the Río Piedras massacre. Albizu Campos blamed police chief Francis Riggs for the men's deaths. To avenge the murders, two Nationalists, Hiram Rosado and Elías Beauchamp, fatally shot Riggs. They were arrested, taken to the police station, and executed in cold blood.

It was war.

Governor Blanton Winship instructed police officers to shoot to kill when dealing with Nationalists. Albizu Campos warned that Nationalist blood would be avenged with the same violence. This marked a turning point in the struggle for Puerto Rico's national liberation. While intellectuals had theorized the nation and Dr. Lanauze Rolón had written about the necessity of violence, the Nationalist movement was ready take up arms to attain Puerto Rico's independence.[43]

After these events, the Nationalist Party's leadership was arrested and sentenced to federal prison. Calling for the release of their leaders, party members planned to march through the city of Ponce on Palm Sunday, March 21, 1937.[44] Although their permits were denied at the last moment, the Nationalists began a peaceful protest. Suddenly, a loud bang was heard—to this day its origin is unknown—and the police proceeded to shoot at the crowd. Twenty-one people died, including men, women, children, and two police officers caught in their own crossfire. Hundreds more were wounded. That day has gone down in Puerto Rican history as the Ponce Massacre. The American Civil Liberties Union and the Bar Association of Puerto Rico conducted investigations that ultimately blamed the governor for the massacre.[45]

The situation in Puerto Rico became so tense that a bill was drafted in the U.S. Congress by a former friend of Riggs that would have granted Puerto Rico independence. Known as the Tydings Bill (1936), it proposed a referendum to give Puerto Rico independence but at an unfavorable financial cost to the archipelago, which would have had to pay high tariff rates. It was a measure to punish those who had advocated for independence.[46]

The Tydings Bill caused great debate among the political elite. Nationalists supported it, but others like Luis Muñoz Marín did not. In fact, in 1936 no less than three bills advocating for Puerto Rico's independence were circulating. The Tydings Bill was followed by the Wilbur Cartwright Bill, presented on February 18, 1936, written and drafted by Luis Muñoz Marín. Another bill was presented by Vito Marcantonio, a friend of the Puerto Rican Nationalists and a progressive congressman from New York. These bills were largely ignored by the U.S. Congress.[47]

The Nationalists were not the only radical group causing trouble for the U.S. government in the 1930s. On September 23, 1934—the anniversary of the Grito de Lares—another party was formed: the Communist Party of Puerto Rico. Among its members were José Lanauze Rolón, the Black oncologist from Ponce. The leadership also included lawyers and working-class people like Miguel Bahamonde, Julio Camacho, Estanislao Soler, and Manuel Cofresí Ramírez. The Communist Party's general secretary, Alberto Sánchez, had spent time in the Soviet Union.[48]

The Communist Party immediately allied itself with the Communist International, which meant it had connections to the Soviet government and the USSR. There were some communists in Puerto Rico who disagreed and sought to operate autonomously. While much research is still required, there seems to have been two different Communist parties operating in the mid-1930s. One was the Communist Party formed by Lanauze Rolón and Sánchez, and the other was the Independent Communist Party led by Luis Vergne Ortiz, a former Nationalist Party member. These two factions would eventually merge.[49]

The Communist Party did not seek to participate in electoral processes. Instead, they focused their attention on organizing workers. They also excelled in propaganda activities, such as publishing newspapers and books and hosting social events. Their newspaper, *Verdad* (Truth), documented their activities and actions with traditional industrial workers as well as their work organizing unemployed workers, tenants, and other activists. *Verdad* was also a translation of *Pravda*, the name of the Communist Party of the Soviet Union's official newspaper.

Another radical group that reconfigured the 1930s political arena was Afirmación Socialista (Socialist Affirmation), a splinter group from the Socialist Party that called for Puerto Rico's independence and for a return to the Socialist ideas that had led to the party's creation. While small, the group was able to mobilize thousands of workers for political meetings before dissolving.[50]

By the end of the 1930s, the Socialist Party was divided. Another party emerged under the leadership of those who had been expelled from the Socialist Party, including Prudencio Rivera Martínez. The Pure Labor Party, as it was called, did not last long and joined two other parties to form the Tripartite Union.[51] The final blow to traditional politics came with the creation of a new party that emerged from the Liberal

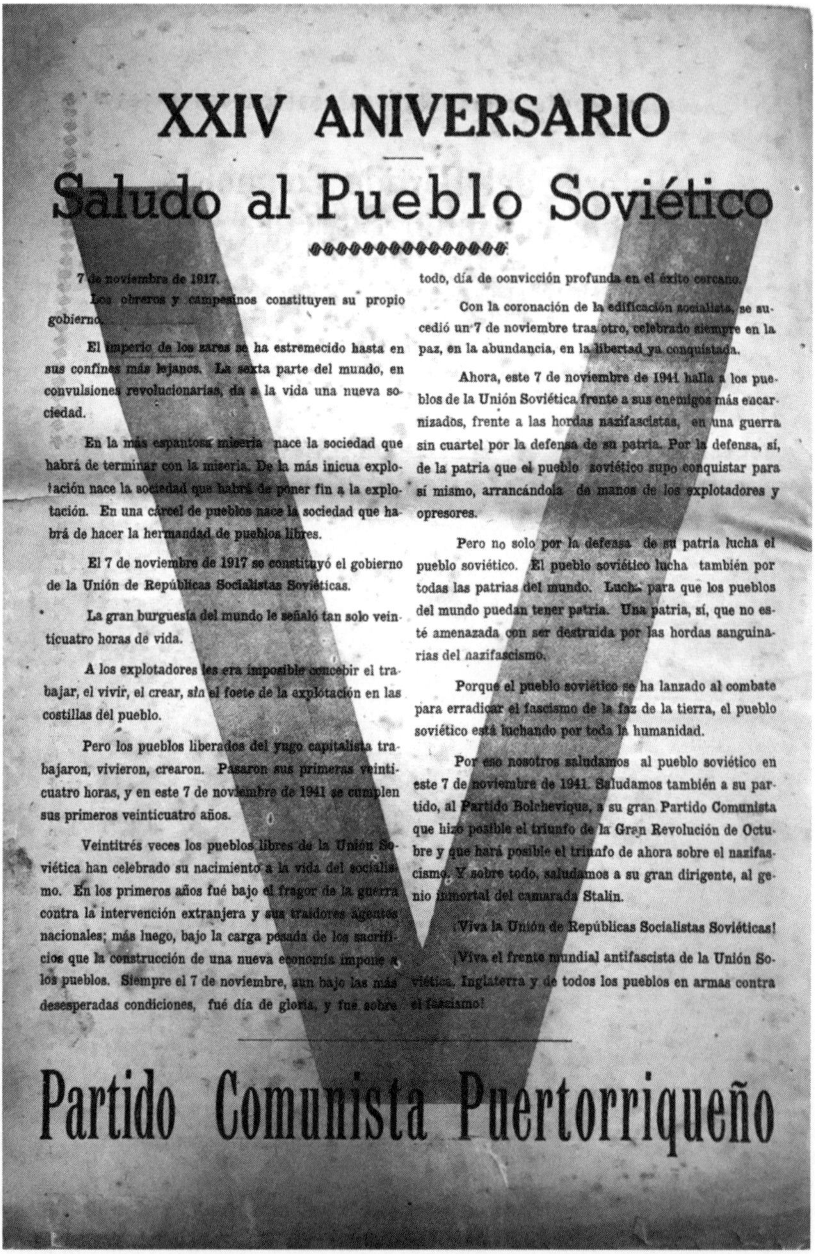

XXIV ANIVERSARIO

Saludo al Pueblo Soviético

7 de noviembre de 1917.

Los obreros y campesinos constituyen su propio gobierno.

El imperio de los zares se ha estremecido hasta en sus confines más lejanos. La sexta parte del mundo, en convulsiones revolucionarias, da a la vida una nueva sociedad.

En la más espantosa miseria nace la sociedad que habrá de terminar con la miseria. De la más inicua explotación nace la sociedad que habrá de poner fin a la explotación. En una cárcel de pueblos nace la sociedad que habrá de hacer la hermandad de pueblos libres.

El 7 de noviembre de 1917 se constituyó el gobierno de la Unión de Repúblicas Socialistas Soviéticas.

La gran burguesía del mundo le señaló tan solo veinticuatro horas de vida.

A los explotadores les era imposible concebir el trabajar, el vivir, el crear, sin el foete de la explotación en las costillas del pueblo.

Pero los pueblos liberados del yugo capitalista trabajaron, vivieron, crearon. Pasaron sus primeras veinticuatro horas, y en este 7 de noviembre de 1941 se cumplen sus primeros veinticuatro años.

Veintitrés veces los pueblos libres de la Unión Soviética han celebrado su nacimiento a la vida del socialismo. En los primeros años fué bajo el fragor de la guerra contra la intervención extranjera y sus traidores agentes nacionales; más luego, bajo la carga pesada de los sacrificios que la construcción de una nueva economía impone a los pueblos. Siempre el 7 de noviembre, aun bajo las más desesperadas condiciones, fué día de gloria, y fue sobre todo, día de convicción profunda en el éxito cercano.

Con la coronación de la edificación socialista, se sucedió un 7 de noviembre tras otro, celebrado siempre en la paz, en la abundancia, en la libertad ya conquistada.

Ahora, este 7 de noviembre de 1941 halla a los pueblos de la Unión Soviética frente a sus enemigos más encarnizados, frente a las hordas nazifascistas, en una guerra sin cuartel por la defensa de su patria. Por la defensa, sí, de la patria que el pueblo soviético supo conquistar para sí mismo, arrancándola de manos de los explotadores y opresores.

Pero no solo por la defensa de su patria lucha el pueblo soviético. El pueblo soviético lucha también por todas las patrias del mundo. Lucha para que los pueblos del mundo puedan tener patria. Una patria, sí, que no esté amenazada con ser destruida por las hordas sanguinarias del nazifascismo.

Porque el pueblo soviético se ha lanzado al combate para erradicar el fascismo de la faz de la tierra, el pueblo soviético está luchando por toda la humanidad.

Por eso nosotros saludamos al pueblo soviético en este 7 de noviembre de 1941. Saludamos también a su partido, al Partido Bolchevique, a su gran Partido Comunista que hizo posible el triunfo de la Gran Revolución de Octubre y que hará posible el triunfo de ahora sobre el nazifascismo. Y sobre todo, saludamos a su gran dirigente, al genio inmortal del camarada Stalin.

¡Viva la Unión de Repúblicas Socialistas Soviéticas!

¡Viva el frente mundial antifascista de la Unión Soviética, Inglaterra y de todos los pueblos en armas contra el fascismo!

Partido Comunista Puertorriqueño

FIGURE 7.1. Note saluting the Soviet Union on its twenty-fourth anniversary published in *Verdad*, the official newspaper of the Communist Party of Puerto Rico. Source: Centro de Investigaciones Históricas at the Universidad de Puerto Rico, Río Piedras.

Party, the Partido Liberal Neto, Auténtico y Completo (Net, Authentic, and Complete Liberal Party). Its name was soon shortened to the catchier Partido Popular Democrático (PPD). It dominated electoral politics for the next two decades.

The Nation and Its Intellectuals

By the 1930s, the University of Puerto Rico was a bustling intellectual hub. It served as the center of San Juan and a bridge between the Americas. Intellectuals from the United States, Latin America, and Europe visited the Río Piedras campus. The press carefully documented lectures, publications, and any other university-related events.[52]

The foundation of the Hispanic Studies Department in 1927 was fundamental to the university's transformation during its first two decades of existence. Collaborative exchanges with other centers of higher learning also contributed to its development. José Vasconcelos, for example, Mexico's minister of education and one of the most respected Latin American intellectuals of his time, visited the university and toured Puerto Rico. In his book *Indología* he wrote about his trip and, particularly, how impressed he was by Albizu Campos.[53]

As the 1933 strike against the nomination of Rafael Alonso Torres to the university's board of trustees demonstrated, the university was an important extension of Puerto Rico's political sphere. Intellectuals played a crucial role in shaping discourses that eventually transformed the idea of Puerto Rico itself. In the nineteenth century, the intellectual elite was dominated by professionals—doctors and lawyers, for example—who also dabbled in intellectual matters. Now, there was a new generation of writers, professors, and scholars who began discussing and debating the essence of Puerto Ricanness.

When the 1898 occupation took place, many intellectuals sided with the invaders because they understood the United States to be a land of democratic rights and liberties. This allegiance would soon fray as political and intellectual elites understood they were seen as second-class citizens at best. By the 1930s, then, a new ideology began circulating in cafés, university classrooms, and soirees. Hispanismo, an ideology that took pride in Puerto Rico's Hispanic heritage, began to dominate intellectual conversations.[54]

Colloquially known as "the thirties' generation," scholars and writers began seeking answers to the enigma of the Puerto Rican identity. One of the towering figures of this literary generation was Antonio S. Pedreira. He received his undergraduate education in Puerto Rico, his master of arts from Columbia University, and his doctoral degree from the University of Madrid. A student of Federico de Onís, who created the Hispanic Studies Department at the UPR, Pedreira reshaped the conversation about Puerto Ricanness.[55]

Before his death in 1939 at the age of forty, Pedreira helped create the highly influential *Índice* magazine and published several books that were obligatory reading for anyone seeking to understand Puerto Rican culture in these decades. The most influential of these books, *Insularismo*, also exemplified the racist and xenophobic tendencies that were prevalent in some of Puerto Rico's intellectual circles.[56]

Insularismo's premise was that Puerto Ricans had inherited certain traits from the past and Puerto Rico was now *al garete*, or sailing without a destination. For Pedreira, Puerto Ricans inherited docility and backwardness from their Black African ancestors. And while he described the Taínos as brave, he also highlighted their fragility.[57] In this racist conceptualization, the only ancestral traits to celebrate were those from white Spaniards and Anglo-Saxon culture. The book was highly influential for a generation of scholars who wanted to construct a Puerto Rican identity in contrast to the United States. In this case, Pedreira located Puerto Ricanness in Spanish heritage.[58]

Pedreira's project to identify and understand the essence of Puerto Ricanness was not too distant or different from that of the nineteenth century, when the intellectual elite crafted the racial democracy myth of the Great Puerto Rican Family as a unifying trope for the Puerto Rican nation. Pedreira, in the 1930s, instructed Puerto Ricans to recognize that their identity was grounded in a historical triad, and he encouraged them to foster their European heritage. By downplaying Blackness and indigeneity, his proposal was not a rupture but a continuation of the tenets of nineteenth-century nation-building discourses.[59]

Pedreira, however influential, was not the only intellectual of the 1930s. Others also took part in these conversations and produced books that became landmarks. One of them was Tomás Blanco's *Prontuario histórico de Puerto Rico* (Puerto Rico's history handbook). Others, like Eugenio S. Belaval and Margot Arce de Vásquez, also made important contributions.[60]

These books shared an ethos as well as an understanding of historical development. In all, there was a desire to steer the ship that Pedreira condemned for being *al garete*. Perhaps the past could provide coordinates for a better future. Historical books from this era, for example, sought to uncover a fixed past through primary sources. Understanding the past's shortcomings could help steer Pedreira's ship in the right direction. That is, it could help move society toward progress, civilization, and enlightenment. Of course, all those aspirations were coded in the racist and xenophobic interpretations of the Puerto Rican essence, or lack thereof.

As these developments were taking place in the world of letters, the University of Puerto Rico—particularly after the University Reform of 1942—began creating new departments and programs. The emerging national discourse, which eventually absorbed the populism of the moment, needed to be legitimized academically as well. The formalization of social sciences and historical studies, for example, took place at the same moment that nationhood was once again being reimagined. The educational system expanded, private universities opened their doors, and a new political movement overtook the electoral landscape. If the intellectual elite was consumed by hispanismo in the 1930s, it turned to populism in the war years.[61]

CHAPTER 8

THE POPULIST MOMENT

The political and economic transformations that took place in the 1940s altered Puerto Rico's social fiber. Its agricultural economy was slowly industrializing. Those who had never before left the countryside now ventured into cities with their recently built avenues, parks, and stores. The advent of air travel also facilitated the movement of people from the archipelago to Puerto Rican enclaves in New York, Philadelphia, and New Jersey.

A massive literacy and cultural campaign distributed movies, posters, and books in the mountainous communities. The government created cultural organizations that promoted a new conception of history. They sought to break with the past because they thought of themselves as creating a new future. And with the population growth also came a renewed interest in child development.[1]

By the 1950s, anything seemed possible. In 1952, the same year that the commonwealth was created, children experienced a white Christmas. It was imagined to be just like New England but in the warmest of Caribbean weathers.

Doña Felisa Gautier de Benítez, popularly known as Doña Fela, had been one of the architects of the Partido Popular Democrático (PPD). She rose through the party's ranks and was elected mayor of San Juan in 1946 and served until 1969. Her initial victory was particularly important because it was the first time a woman was elected mayor of any major Latin American city. Her wigs, opulent taste, and somewhat eccentric manners became her trademarks.[2]

In 1951, Eastern Airlines inaugurated a flight to Puerto Rico, breaking Pan Am's monopoly on air travel. To best promote their flights, Eastern Airlines joined forces with San Juan's mayor in an unprecedented campaign: they would use one of their planes to bring snow from Vermont and New Hampshire to Puerto Rico. The event took place for the first time in 1952. It was repeated on the same date—January 6, Three Kings Day—over the next two years. The event was part of a series of celebrations, including the giving of gifts to working-class children, that took place all over the city commemorating Three Kings Day. According to Doña Fela, it was an opportunity for poor children to experience snow at least once in their lifetime.[3]

As was to be expected, things did not go as planned. Nature immediately broke the illusion. The first scheduled snow fight took place in the Luis Muñoz Rivera Park in San Juan. As children were impatiently waiting, snow began to melt. When the snow fight began, it was difficult to distinguish snow from mud. The following year, 1953, the crowd grew weary of waiting for the snow fight to begin. Hundreds of children took the oranges that had been provided as snacks and began a massive, unplanned food fight. Doña Fela and a police officer were both hit in the orange crossfire.[4] The last year the event took place, 1954, the snow was distributed in small cardboard boxes. Frustrated by the melting snow, children began tearing apart the boxes and using them as projectiles in their imaginary war.[5]

The melting snow became a fitting metaphor for the historical moment. The illusion that anything was possible was just that, an illusion. For many who lived through the 1940s and 1950s, however, it seemed as if they were part of a historical transformation. Meanwhile, populism took the political landscape by storm. Political scientists Carlos de la Torre and Cynthia Arnson define populism as "a form of governance between 'the people' and 'the oligarchy.' The role of charismatic, personalistic leadership is central, such that the direct or quasi-direct relationship between the leader and the masses preempts and at times overrides the role of institutions in the day-to-day functioning of the government."[6] Puerto Rico was no exception. Similar processes took place in Brazil under Getúlio Vargas and Argentina during Juan Domingo Perón's rule.

In Puerto Rico, Luis Muñoz Marín and the PPD incorporated common people into the political sphere while embarking on massive industrialization projects, the promise of which remained unfulfilled.

The Rise of the Popular Democratic Party

The same year that snow arrived in Puerto Rico, the country became a commonwealth with its own constitution. These transformations did not happen overnight. They had been brewing since the late 1930s when the PPD reshaped Puerto Rican politics.

After two members of the Nationalist Party assassinated Puerto Rico's chief of police Francis Riggs in 1936, there was growing concern in Washington about the future of Puerto Rico. Ernest Gruening, the former editor of the *Nation* turned administrator of the Puerto Rico Reconstruction Administration, demanded a reaction from Luis Muñoz Marín. Muñoz Marín was quickly climbing the Liberal Party's ranks and becoming a force in local politics. He was also seen as a New Deal emissary in Puerto Rico and had close ties with Roosevelt's administration. It was important for Gruening to have Muñoz Marín on record condemning the attack. He declined to do so.[7]

Enraged, Gruening told him: "I'm afraid you are just another politician. I thought you were something different." Muñoz Marín replied, "Many lives may have to be lost in the liberation of Puerto Rico. I take the long-range view contemplating the destiny of our country." When Gruening retorted that he was just contemplating his own destiny, Muñoz Marín answered, "The destiny of Muñoz Marín and the destiny of Puerto Rico are inseparable."[8]

Muñoz Marín's words can be interpreted in multiple ways. Perhaps it was cockiness or youthful bravado. It could have been the product of his ambition and the confidence his last name, Muñoz, inspired; he was the son of Luis Muñoz Rivera, one of the best-known politicians at the turn of the century. However his words are interpreted, they proved prophetic. The political party that he helped create and the movement it started shaped contemporaneous political realities and created Puerto Rico's political status, which persists today.

As Muñoz Marín's influence grew, tensions emerged and began to create ruptures within the Liberal Party. Some believed that the party should abstain from participating in the 1936 elections because the Nationalist attacks would hurt their chances, more so because the party officially advocated for independence. The Tydings Bill, proposed that same year, also created a split within the party. While he eventually changed his mind, back then Muñoz Marín favored independence but argued that the bill was a death sentence for Puerto Rico. Antonio Barceló, the Liberal Party's leader, said that he would accept independence even if they had to starve. Amid these debates, Muñoz Marín and other pro-independence Liberals created a group called Acción Social Independentista (Pro-Independence Social Action) two months before the 1936 elections. The Liberals decided to go to the ballot box, only to be defeated by the Republican-Socialist Coalition.[9]

The frictions within the Liberal Party were irreparable. In May 1937, the party's Executive Committee expelled Luis Muñoz Marín from its ranks and declared that *La democracia*, the newspaper he edited, was no longer the party's print organ. The following month, Muñoz Marín and a group of collaborators created the Partido Liberal Neto, Auténtico y Completo, which made independence the focus of their platform. By 1938, they had changed their name to Partido Popular Democrático (PPD).[10]

In its origins the PPD incorporated a social justice rhetoric and declared war on absentee corporations. It borrowed a slogan from the Communist Party, "Pan, Tierra y Libertad" (Bread, Land, and Liberty). One of its centerpiece demands was the need to expropriate corporations that had not followed the five-hundred-acre law, a piece of early twentieth-century legislation that sought to limit absentee corporations' power but was a dead letter. The party attracted people from various social classes: rural peasants, urban professionals, and intellectuals, among others. This, in turn, presented Muñoz Marín and the party's leadership with their first challenge: creating consensus.[11] The organized labor movement provided its first testing ground.

Puerto Rico's premier labor federation, the FLT, lost ground in the 1930s. The strikes that took place in 1933 and 1934 damaged their legitimacy.

Internal tensions within the Socialist Party also gave way to several splits that led to the creation of the Pure Labor Party. New international labor organizations like the Congress of Industrial Organizations (CIO) and the International Ladies Garment Workers Union (ILGWU) also had members in Puerto Rico.[12] Labor militancy increased; there were at least forty-five recorded strikes in 1939.[13]

The PPD leadership understood the need to attract the labor movement and to take advantage of the tensions within both the FLT and the Socialist Party. As they geared up for the 1940 elections, two of the PPD's founding members, lawyers Ernesto Ramos Antonini and Victor Gutiérrez Franqui, represented workers in various court cases. When the Confederación General de Trabajadores (CGT) was founded in March 1940, they had strong bonds with both the Communist Party and the PPD. Unlike previous labor federations, the CGT understood the question of Puerto Rico's colonial status as intrinsic to their class struggle. This later led to divisions and, eventually, its dissolution.[14]

The PPD had an impressive run in the 1940 elections. While the Coalición party won key positions like the seat for resident commissioner—a position that had been created in 1902 and had a voice but no vote in the U.S. Congress—the PPD won ten seats in the Senate, eighteen seats in the legislature, and twenty-nine municipalities. The Liberal Party was all but defeated. The gains also gave the PPD legislative power to begin crafting a host of social reforms that launched the party's political hegemony for the next two decades.[15] The 1940 elections demonstrated that Muñoz Marín could succeed in attracting various social groups and generate consensus. The challenge was now to do the same within the party's ranks. The PPD, like any political party, was not a monolithic institution and various political ideologies coexisted within its ranks.

In the party's early days, the unifying trope had been independence. In fact, independence was what animated the party's creation. In the early 1940s, however, Muñoz Marín began shifting the discourse. He began focusing on social justice and ameliorating the pressing social ills that affected Puerto Ricans: poverty, lack of education, and landlessness, among others. To advance this agenda, and gradually move away from focusing solely on independence, Muñoz Marín needed to consolidate his hegemony within the party.

The PPD was founded by a host of politicians and professionals such as Doña Fela, Vicente Geigel Polanco, and Ernesto Ramos Antonini, people who were well known and excelled in their professions or public appointments. However, to be part of the party, Muñoz Marín demanded loyalty.[16]

While Muñoz Marín succeeded in generating consensus within the party, it was not without tensions. Ernesto Ramos Antonini's trajectory is perhaps the best example. He was the only person to preside over the party, albeit briefly, during Muñoz Marín's time. Ramos Antonini was a Black lawyer with an artistic spirit and a labor-oriented ethos. In 1940, he became officially involved with the labor movement. When the newly created CGT split between those who favored independence and those who sided with the Communist Party, Ramos Antonini led the competing faction that became loyal to the PPD. He also represented Puerto Rican unions in international congresses. But when he referred to himself as Puerto Rico's main labor leader, Muñoz Marín was not pleased. Muñoz Marín, by then governor of Puerto Rico, noted that Puerto Rico's premier labor leader lived in Fortaleza, the governor's mansion.[17]

Tensions only increased within the party's leadership after Muñoz Marín began moving away from independence as the party's goal. With this ideological shift, he abandoned the ideas that had gotten him expelled from the Liberal Party. Instead, he articulated a program reminiscent of his father's early twentieth-century autonomist ideas. In 1944, another party that championed independence was created by disillusioned PPD members. The Partido Independentista Puertorriqueño (PIP) was led by Gilberto Concepción de Gracia and became the PPD's main opponent during its first years.[18]

Social justice now became the unifying theme of the PPD. While some of its prominent members, like Vicente Geigel Polanco, openly disagreed with Muñoz Marín, they remained loyal after he publicly noted that independence and the PPD's program were incompatible. The 1944 elections also marked a turning point in the PPD's history. The party dominated the legislative branch and won every single election until 1968.

Now in power, the PPD began promoting an industrialization program that sought to improve the country's economy and ameliorate its social ills. The New Deal programs had laid the foundations for these transformations. This was facilitated by the appointment of Rexford G. Tugwell as governor of Puerto Rico.

Tugwell was a scholar and a planner. A graduate of the University of Pennsylvania, he was a New Dealer who had been appointed to several positions within President Franklin D. Roosevelt's administration. Some considered him to be too left leaning and gave him the nickname of Red Rex. His ideas, however, were not that radical. He believed that private industries and individuals had a responsibility to respond to societal needs.[19]

Before being appointed governor, Tugwell served as the University of Puerto Rico's provost. Once in office, he aligned with Muñoz Marín and the PPD in its mission to industrialize Puerto Rico. According to geographer Joaquín Villanueva, "Tugwell had a vision of a Planning Board that worked as the fourth power—a theory he developed that suggested that planning was the fourth power alongside the executive, legislative, and judicial branches."[20] The PPD's industrialization program, organized through the Planning Board and the new Banco de Fomento (Development Bank), became known as Operación Manos a la Obra, often translated as Operation Bootstrap. It was an ambitious idea. It sought to promote foreign investment through tax incentives. In practice, however, it heightened Puerto Rico's dependence on the United States.[21]

Tugwell advocated for the appointment of a Puerto Rican to hold the governor's office. Similar to what had happened at the turn of the twentieth century, Washington officials debated whether Puerto Ricans were capable of governing themselves. While many agreed that a Puerto Rican should become governor, such a measure was seen as a lukewarm reform by the members of the PPD. The conversations that took place in the U.S. Congress laid the foundation for later debates about Puerto Rico's political status.[22]

In 1946, President Harry S. Truman appointed Jesús T. Piñero as the archipelago's first Puerto Rican governor. At the time he was serving as Puerto Rico's resident commissioner in Washington, D.C., a position he gave up to take the governor's seat. Congress also passed legislation allowing Puerto Ricans to vote for their governor in the upcoming 1948 elections. Until then, Puerto Ricans could only vote for their legislators, senators, and the resident commissioner. Governors had been hand-picked in turn by U.S. presidents.[23]

It was not a surprise that Luis Muñoz Marín ran and won by a land-slide in 1948. He had served as Senate president in 1941, where he was able to help pass a comprehensive land reform bill that became a pillar of the PPD's populist policies.[24] Muñoz Marín's electoral victory secured his power in the governor's mansion, where he resided for sixteen years. By then, Muñoz Marín and the PPD's ideologues had devised an autonomist formula that would maintain Puerto Rico's relation to the United States while expanding self-governing rights. Muñoz Marín succeeded, historian Eileen Findlay has noted, because he understood how to communicate with different groups of people.[25]

After World War II, Puerto Rico's colonial status was problematic in terms of the image the United States wanted to project abroad. Social unrest in the archipelago was also seen as a real threat in Washington. The recently created United Nations had a mandate to push for the de-colonization of countries throughout what became known as the Third World. Further, Luis Muñoz Marín played the Cold War card early on. He told his contacts in Washington that discontent could make people gravitate toward the Soviet Union. It was in this context that conversations about Puerto Rico's political status began taking place.[26]

The PPD advocated for a referendum that would allow Puerto Rican voters to decide whether they wanted to have their own constitution without altering their relationship with the United States. That is, Puerto Rico would be taken off the UN's list of colonies.

On July 3, 1950, President Truman signed Law 600. It allowed the Puerto Rican government to hold the referendum to create a new form of self-government. The bill passed with 76 percent of the votes. The PPD then organized a constitutional assembly composed of seventy

members of the PPD, fifteen from the Republican Party, and seven Socialists. The PIP abstained. While a minority, the Socialists were crucial
in incorporating some of their decades-old labor demands into the constitution. María Libertad Gómez Garriga was the only woman who
participated in the constitutional assembly.[27]

Once Puerto Rico's constitution was drafted, it was sent to the U.S.
Congress for approval. After much deliberation, Congress eliminated
the constitution's Bill of Rights. Modeled after the UN's Universal Declaration of Human Rights, the Puerto Rican Bill of Rights sought to
protect and guarantee free education, secure housing, and employment
for everyone. It was one of the most advanced constitutions the international community had ever seen. The U.S. Congress also added a
clause retaining the right to revoke any legislation and to approve any
amendment.

The people of Puerto Rico voted again and ratified the constitution
on March 3, 1952. Four months later, on July 25, 1952, Puerto Rico's constitution went into effect. And with it, Puerto Rico officially became a
commonwealth of the United States. While some officials announced
the end of colonialism, Congress still held absolute power over the
country. The PPD had succeeded in generating a political hegemony.
They also created a new political status. Now they needed to craft a new
idea of the nation.

The Cultural Nation

The idea of the nation that the PPD articulated was detached from the
country's actual political status. Instead, the PPD promoted a shared
sense of culture and belonging while romanticizing and idealizing
Puerto Rico's rural life. The party's emblem became the *jíbaro* (rural
peasant) wearing a *pava* (straw hat). This appropriation of the jíbaro was
not new. It was built on liberal ideas circulated by elite intellectuals since
the nineteenth century. In this fantasy, the jíbaro was whitened, erasing
the Black and Brown realities of many inland Puerto Ricans.[28]

This idea of the nation also reproduced racial democracy myths
rooted in the nineteenth century. During that time, intellectuals honed

the idea of the "Great Puerto Rican Family." Now, the state appropriated the 1930s intellectuals' racial triad. Officially, Puerto Ricans were recognized as the product of racial mixture between Spaniards, Taíno Indians, and Africans. These discourses, however, highlighted the Spanish ancestry while folklorizing Blackness and presenting Taínos as biologically fragile.

The racial triad became the emblem of the Instituto de Cultura Puertorriqueña (Institute of Puerto Rican Culture; ICP), founded on June 21, 1955. The ICP became the PPD's cultural cornerstone. It was presided over by a moderate pro-independence intellectual, Ricardo Alegría. The ICP sought to promote new ideas of the nation while also seeking to preserve the past through the creation of museums and archives.[29]

It was the first time that Puerto Rico, as literary scholar Catherine Marsh Kennerly notes, had a nation-building process like other Latin American countries.[30] In a lecture delivered at Harvard University, Governor Luis Muñoz Marín outlined what he referred to as Operación Serenidad (Serenity Operation). For Muñoz Marín, industrialization could not succeed without also changing or impacting people's essence. Thus, for any industrial process to be successful, it needed to include a cultural counterpart. To accomplish this, the state needed to create more than museums and archives.[31]

Law 372 of 1949 created, among other things, one of the populist government's most ambitious projects: the División de Educación de la Comunidad (Division of Community Education; DIVEDCO). It was a multilayered grassroots educational program that sought to impact communities. Beyond a massive literacy program, it also promoted the government's new ethos and national ideals. The program consisted of the creation of posters, books, and movies that were distributed throughout Puerto Rico. It aspired to empower communities to generate discussions about multiple topics ranging from hygiene to labor rights to proper etiquette.[32]

DIVEDCO's cultural production was created by the generation's brightest artists and intellectuals. New Dealers like Jack and Irene Delano captured Puerto Rico's realities through photograph and plastic arts. Meanwhile, local writers and artists, such as René Marqués and Lorenzo Homar, produced books and paintings. They felt as if they were part of a moment of transformation. Just like Doña Fela's snow, anything seemed possible.[33]

A social transformation of such magnitude also needed technocrats to lead the government. If most nineteenth-century intellectuals had been educated in Europe, now the majority of PPD leaders studied in the United States. They understood, however, the need to transform the UPR to serve Puerto Rico's needs. The University Law of 1942, then, consolidated the transformation of the UPR as the premier center of higher learning in Puerto Rico.[34]

Jaime Benítez, chancellor of the UPR's main campus in Río Piedras, was a close ally of Muñoz Marín. During his tenure as chancellor, the UPR system was consolidated into a "house of learning." The UPR system also gradually expanded throughout Puerto Rico. Ideologically, however, Benítez understood any interest in the nation as parochial and limiting. Instead, he promoted a Western and Eurocentric approach to the curriculum, emulating the education he had received at the University of Chicago.[35]

The UPR became a marker of class mobility for many Puerto Ricans. It afforded students a window to other worlds and possibilities. In 1948, for example, a protest on the Río Piedras campus shattered the illusion of the PPD's hegemony. After being imprisoned in exile, Pedro Albizu Campos arrived back in Puerto Rico. His presence reinvigorated the Nationalist Party. Students at the UPR were eager to hear Albizu Campos and invited him to campus in 1948. To receive him, a group of students lowered the U.S. flag.[36]

Enraged, Jaime Benítez expelled some of the student leaders. He argued that politics had no space in the "House of Studies." Students responded with a massive strike against Benítez, forcing him to decree an academic recess. The strike also signaled the beginning of a new period of Nationalist mobilizations and renewed militancy.[37]

Since nationalism was resurging as a political force in the archipelago, the Puerto Rican congress approved Law 53 on May 21, 1948. The law made it a felony to encourage or attempt to overthrow, destroy, or paralyze the Insular Government through force. Known as the "Gag Law," it was signed by the governor but not put into action until two years later when the Nationalists attempted to overthrow the Puerto Rican government through an insurrection.[38]

It was clear to members of the Nationalist Party that electoral politics would not solve the status question. They also believed that the constitutional assembly would only solidify and consolidate Puerto Rico's colonial condition. In 1950, the Nationalists clandestinely organized a military action that was to take place in different parts of the archipelago. On October 30, after a group of Nationalists was stopped by the police and caught with weapons and ammunitions, the Nationalist Party decided that it was time to act. Much like what had happened in Lares, there was much passion but not enough weapons or ammunitions. After all, Pedro Albizu Campos had famously stated that the motherland required valor and sacrifice.

The insurrection took place in different municipalities of the island but one of the most active points was the inland town of Jayuya where a group led by Nationalist leader Blanca Canales attempted to take the town and burned down the police headquarters. In San Juan, a group of Nationalists who were supposed to take over the police headquarters in the capital instead decided to drive straight into the governor's mansion. They were planning to take Luis Muñoz Marín hostage, but the police knew they were coming and ambushed them.

Puerto Rico was undergoing a revolutionary moment. To quell the insurrection, the National Guard was activated, and the following day U.S. air forces bombed the town of Utuado. But the bullets were not only felt in Puerto Rico. Two Nationalists, Griselio Torresola and Oscar Collazo, attempted to take over the Blair House in Washington where President Truman was staying—and were killed in the attempt. At the end of the insurrection, which only lasted a few days, there were twenty-seven deaths and ninety gunshot injuries.[39] Many Nationalists were arrested, including Pedro Albizu Campos.

Neither repression nor the approval of the Puerto Rican Constitution stopped Nationalists from attempting to demonstrate against the colonial status of Puerto Rico to the international community. On

March 2, 1954, four Nationalists made their way to the U.S. Congress. At 2:20 p.m. the House was discussing a bill to continue the Mexican farm labor program. As the "ayes" and "noes" were being counted, Dolores "Lolita" Lebrón unfurled a Puerto Rican flag and shouted "Viva Puerto Rico Libre!" Immediately afterward several gunshots were fired by the other Nationalists, Rafael Cancel Miranda, Irving Flores, and Andrés Figueroa Cordero. Five congressmen were wounded, but all survived.

The Nationalists were taken into custody and said that they had planned the attack on George Washington's birthday. According to the *Washington Post*, the police found a note in Lolita Lebrón's bag indicating that she was solely responsible for the incident:

> Before God and the world, my blood claims for the independence of Puerto Rico. My life I give for the freedom of my country. This is a cry for victory in our struggle for independence which for more than half a century has tried to conquer the land that belongs to Puerto Rico.
>
>   I state forever that the United States of America are betraying the sacred principles of mankind in their continuous subjugation of my country, violating their rights to be a free nation and a free people, in their barbarous torture of our apostle of independence, Don Pedro Albizu Campos.[40]

All of the Nationalists spent twenty-five years in prison except for Andrés Figueroa Cordero, who was released early due to a terminal cancer diagnosis. None of them ever disavowed their actions and, in fact, said that they would do it again if necessary.

The PPD used the gag law and the Nationalists' actions to repress the independence movement. Meanwhile, the PPD leadership sought to industrialize the country. They believed that for the industrialization project to be successful, the state could not support everyone; some people in the government considered Puerto Rico "overpopulated." They advocated for the migration of Puerto Ricans to different parts of the Americas, but the scheme was seen as too complicated. The state, then, promoted the migration of Puerto Ricans to the United States. Colloquially known as Operación Válvula de Escape (Operation Escape Valve), the Puerto Rican government sponsored migration programs and opened offices abroad to help Puerto Ricans migrate north. The government also used the DIVEDCO program to produce pamphlets to educate potential migrants about racism in the United States.[41]

The industrialization project also triggered internal migration. Thousands of families moved from the countryside to urban centers in search of a better life. Lack of infrastructure pushed many of these migrants into urban slums. Overcrowded communities on the margins of cities such as El Fanguito and La Perla were a testament to the government's failure in housing people. Around this time, the state also sponsored the creation of public housing units known as *caseríos*. These spaces were also fertile ground for the government's educational program. The PPD administration even created a newspaper by the same name, *El caserío*, targeting its residents.[42]

Many decided to join the growing diaspora and try their luck abroad. Hundreds of thousands of people migrated without knowing that they were being socially and collectively ejected as part of a calculated government move. In the process, enclaves and communities formed in the Puerto Rican diaspora began to rethink the idea of the nation and, more importantly, who belonged to it.

CHAPTER 9

THE GREAT MIGRATION

Those who left the archipelago to try their luck in the United States during the middle of the twentieth century had different experiences depending on which Puerto Rico they inhabited. An urban middle-class family could migrate via steamships while drinking wine and eating crabmeat cocktail and fried filet of sole *à la meunière* while a working-class youngster might have saved just enough money for his tickets doing *chivos* here and there.[1] Just as there was no single Puerto Rico, there was no universal migration experience. Around 835,000 left the archipelago from 1940 to 1970, and their migration impacted both their communities back home and where they arrived.

Each migration story was different, but there were also commonalities. While the Puerto Rican government created the infrastructure that made possible what became known as the Great Migration, many felt that migrating was a difficult and entirely personal decision. Such was the case of Doña Gabriela, an older woman with two sons, Luis and Chaguito, and a daughter, Juanita, all of whom struggled financially in San Juan's countryside.

While Puerto Rico experienced great transformations during the 1940s and 1950s, those who lived in the countryside felt outside the modernizing project even when the PPD's target electorate was the peasantry. After much debate, Luis, Doña Gabriela's eldest son and the family's main breadwinner, convinced them to try their luck in the city.

The city, however, was not what they expected. San Juan, like Puerto Rico as a whole, was segregated according to social and class status. Luis and his family did not live in the elegant colonial houses near the city's bustling plazas; they could only afford a modest house in the extramural working-class neighborhood of La Perla, which began as a community of formerly enslaved workers and eventually became associated with poverty and the lower classes. Its location—outside the city walls— only added to its notoriety.

After moving to La Perla, things did not change for the better for Luis and his family. His younger brother, Chaguito, was arrested on multiple occasions for petty theft. Steady work was hard to come by. And Luis felt that his sister, Juanita, challenged his authority by dating multiple men. For Doña Gabriela, life in San Juan felt like punishment. The sounds of waves crashing and airplanes overhead were a constant reminder of the possibility of leaving for *allá 'fuera*.

The family eventually made the trip abroad, joining hundreds of thousands of Puerto Ricans seeking better opportunities in the northeastern cities of the United States. But Luis and the family did not find much happiness in New York either. He now could afford a radio, fake jewelry, and a jacket for his mother. But Chaguito was behind prison bars in Puerto Rico, his mother longed for the countryside in her homeland, and his sister continued challenging his position as patriarch, this time by becoming a sex worker.

Yet Luis and Juanita worked. They joined thousands of others like Juan, Miguel, Milagros, Olga, and Manuel. They worked and were always on time. They were never late, never spoke back when they were insulted, never took days off; Luis never went on strike. Much like Bernardo, a worker from the town of Las Marías, Luis had hopes of one day returning to Puerto Rico. They never did. Bernardo worked in a factory and died from exhaustion. Luis died after his body was trapped in a pot-making machine. Juan died dreaming about a new car. Miguel died dreaming of new anti-poverty programs. Milagros died dreaming of a trip to Puerto Rico. Olga died dreaming of real jewelry. Manuel died dreaming about the Irish sweepstakes.

These stories never happened. They are fictional characters in the play *La carreta* by René Marqués and in the poems "Boricua en la luna" (Boricua in the moon) by Juan Antonio Corretjer and "Puerto Rican

Obituary" by Pedro Pietri.[2] The stories, however, serve as a powerful invitation to remember the hundreds of thousands of people whose lives and histories never made it into the history books. They are similar to stories I heard from my grandparents about racism, classism, heartbreak, and the pain of winters.

Yet Puerto Ricans did create community; they created a sense of belonging on the Lower East Side of Manhattan and in Philadelphia, Hartford, and Chicago. They brought with them ancestral knowledges, culture, and culinary traditions. In the process, Puerto Ricans created a diaspora that forces us to once again rethink what constitutes the Puerto Rican nation.

Modernization and Migration

The migration of almost a million people did not happen by accident. Their lives were impacted by structural factors that pushed them to look for opportunities abroad. The Great Migration reconfigured social relations and disrupted communities in Puerto Rico. Many left the archipelago in tears. They prayed and hoped for a speedy return. Some never did. Their families eventually joined them in the United States where they created vibrant communities and bonds of solidarity. But many did return. In the 1970s, a circular migration began to take place and has continued ever since.[3]

Puerto Rican migration, however, did not begin in the 1950s. Puerto Ricans had been making their way to U.S. cities since the late nineteenth century. Pro-independence revolutionaries like Ramón Emeterio Betances and Eugenio María de Hostos, for example, spent time in New York City.[4] They organized alongside Cubans who were fighting for their independence and navigated the city's racial dynamics.[5] As previously mentioned, the Puerto Rican flag was a result of these interactions with members of the Cuban Revolutionary Party. Businessmen and members of the middle classes also migrated in search of better opportunities.[6]

The number of Puerto Ricans in the United States at the turn of the twentieth century was not staggering. Shortly after the U.S. occupation

and Hurricane San Ciriaco in 1899, about 5,000 Puerto Rican workers
were recruited as agricultural workers in Hawai'i. Puerto Ricans were
seen as a displaceable labor force.[7] By 1910, however, 1,513 Puerto Ricans
were scattered across the mainland United States. These numbers grew
exponentially in the following decades. By 1940, there were 69,967
Puerto Ricans in the United States. The passing of the Jones Act, which
made Puerto Ricans citizens, was crucial in facilitating migration.[8]

These migrants did not come from the middle classes, nor were they
swayed by revolutionary fervor. Most came from the working classes
and migrated in search of opportunities in the United States' post–
World War II economy. The new transportation routes provided by
steamships also facilitated the process.[9] Bernardo Vega and Jesús Colón,
two working-class intellectuals who were part of that wave of migration
and who are often referred to as *pioneros* (pioneers), left their impres-
sions in the form of memoirs. Both were socialist militants, and their
writings offer a window into the difficulties they faced. However, their
memoirs also recall the joys of community, the beauty of the diasporic
culture that was emerging, and the grassroots political organizing they
participated in.[10] From a few urban enclaves, Puerto Ricans began creating a community. Bodegas (small markets) became spaces for socialization while civic and cultural associations offered an opportunity to meet
other recently arrived migrants.[11]

By the mid-1940s, the migration process accelerated and became an
exodus. This was due, in part, to the economic situation in both countries. Puerto Rico had been badly hit by the Great Depression and jobs
were scarce. The PPD's industrialization project triggered an internal
migration from the countryside to urban centers, which in turn impacted the agricultural sector. The United States, on the other hand,
was understood as a land of opportunity. After the end of World War
II, the booming postwar economy created jobs and there was a labor
shortage.[12]

Since the very first days of the U.S. occupation, government officials
had complained about the archipelago's "surplus population." In 1901,
for example, Governor Charles Allen noted, "Porto Rico has plenty of
laborers and poor people generally. What the island needs is men with

capital, energy, and enterprise." In 1915, another colonial governor, Arthur Yager, described the "wretchedness and poverty among the masses," and explained, "I do not hesitate to express my belief that the only really effective remedy is the transfer of large numbers of Porto Ricans to some other region."[13]

While promoting a populist discourse focusing on the poor, the PPD's economic policies paradoxically reproduced earlier themes and conversations around population density. Operation Bootstrap relied on foreign manufacturing companies that had been lured to the archipelago with tax exemptions. Thousands needed to migrate for industrialization to succeed. And while the government never officially promoted migration, it was seen as a necessary step toward modernization.

On May 12, 1947, Puerto Rico's legislature approved Public Law 25. It created the Employment and Migration Bureau and clearly articulated the government's official stance on migration: "The Government of Puerto Rico does not stimulate or discourage the migration of Puerto Rican workers to the United States or any foreign country; but it deems its duty to duly orient [them] regarding the occupational opportunities and adjustment problems in ethnologically strange settings."[14] Although he was one of its main proponents, this law did not stem solely from Luis Muñoz Marín's will and power. The PPD's cadre of intellectuals had closed ranks around the necessity of migration for the modernization of Puerto Rico.[15]

The University of Puerto Rico (UPR) also played a role in fostering these conversations and giving them an aura of intellectual legitimacy. When the UPR's Social Science Research Center (SSRC) was being organized, chancellor Jaime Benítez invited a University of Kansas and Columbia University graduate to help organize it.[16] This young intellectual was Clarence Senior, a former member of the Socialist Party of America, known for being part of its "militant" faction.[17] He befriended many people within the PPD, including Luis Muñoz Marín. In 1947 he published *Puerto Rican Emigration*, a book that set the tone for conversations within the archipelago's intelligentsia. Senior argued for the migration of Puerto Ricans to Latin America, but this proved too costly. His main thesis about the necessity of emigration echoed other conversations taking place in the Puerto Rican government.[18]

These conversations were driven by the same narrative that colonial governors had been articulating since the beginning of the twentieth century. That is, they were framed as solutions to Puerto Rico's over-population. For example, a 1938 study by UPR sociologist Lawrence Chenault noted, "One important factor which can cause migration from a country as crowded as Puerto Rico is the lack of natural resources to support its growing population." But most migrants traveled to New York City, which, as Edna Acosta-Belén and Carlos E. Santiago have noted, "had a population density almost 150 times higher than that of Puerto Rico at the time."[19] Puerto Rico was no more populated than the cold northern cities that would receive these migrants.

"Aquí me muero de frío" (I am dying of cold here)

In 1916, the Puerto Rican modernist poet Virgilio Dávila published the poem "Nostalgia" in his book *Aromas del terruño*. While his words struck patriotic and nationalist tones they also read like a warning, pre-saging the experience of hundreds of thousands of Puerto Ricans in the coming decades.

¡Mamá, borinquen me llama!
¡Este país no es el mío!
¡Borinquen es pura flama,
y aquí me muero de frío.

Mama, borinquen is calling!
This country is not mine!
Borinquen is pure flame,
and I am dying of cold here![20]

Puerto Ricans migrated to urban enclaves in the Northeast with the help of government agencies and "sponsored migrations," to borrow a phrase from Puerto Rican Studies scholar Edgardo Meléndez.[21] But migrants also depended on extended networks within the enclaves and communities already there. Correspondence, phone conversations, and photographs all created a feeling of proximity and, in a sense, acted as a lure to those back in the archipelago. The handwritten notes that accompanied the photographs sent back home, for example, described a life of happiness, success, and stability, even when these pictures were staged.[22]

The Puerto Rican government also sought to soften the culture clash many felt upon arrival in the United States. In fact, as anthropologist Jorge Duany has noted, "the Migration Division distributed millions of copies of publications orienting Puerto Ricans about American 'life and laws,' as well as Americans about Puerto Rican culture."[23] One such book was *Emigración* published by the PPD's Division of Community Education (DIVEDCO). The book was part of the Libros del Pueblo (The people's books) series, which were central to the PPD's cultural project.[24] Their topics ranged from hygiene to proper etiquette, from history to migration.

Emigración began with a global history of migration and then moved on to explain the history of the United States. The idea was for migrants to understand the broader historical context they navigated while also offering them an introduction to the histories of the places they were arriving at. One of the book's main arguments was that those who migrated needed to be prepared. While many used government programs in the Migration Division or the Department of Labor's Farm Labor Program, others simply migrated without any support, savings, or preparation. The book advised caution when making the decision to move abroad. In its pages, potential migrants could also read about weather in the United States, life in metropolitan cities, and xenophobia. Following the government line, the book argued that Puerto Ricans needed to work hard, adapt, and be loyal to the United States to challenge prejudices against them, portraying prejudice as the product of ignorance rather than structural inequality and systemic racism.

While migrants arrived in different contexts depending on the city or state, there was also a shared experience of navigating racism, xenophobia, and prejudice. The Puerto Rican Migration Division Office in Chicago warned against the creation of Puerto Rican enclaves in the city, even developing a campaign for Puerto Ricans to learn English to be able to fully navigate the city. Officials feared that if they settled in

FIGURE 9.1. Front cover of *Emigración*. Author's personal collection.

enclaves, as had happened in New York, they would never integrate into the city.[25] What these officials failed to acknowledge was that Chicago was already racially segregated.

Puerto Ricans occupied a liminal space within U.S. society. Not only had they received U.S. citizenship in 1917, but in 1940 Puerto Ricans were retroactively given birthright citizenship, which meant, according to legal scholar Charles Venator-Santiago, "birth in Puerto Rico was tantamount to birth in the United States."[26] This did not mean much when dealing with landlords, municipal officials, and neighbors. In the 1970s, sociologist Samuel Betances noted, "Blacks see Latinos as honorary whites and whites see Latinos as honorary blacks, and that leaves Latinos in a racial no man's land."[27] While ethnic and racial tensions created contention between Puerto Ricans and other migrant groups like Mexicans, their shared experiences navigating faulty school systems, broken-down housing markets, and the brunt of U.S. racism also allowed them to create bonds of community and solidarity.[28]

The experience of Puerto Ricans arriving in Philadelphia was in many ways similar to that of other major urban enclaves. Puerto Rican migrants arrived expecting an abundance of work only to find what historian Carmen Teresa Whalen has called "a plethora of limited opportunities": Puerto Ricans "were confined to the secondary labor market, in jobs that paid poorly, required few skills, and offered poor working conditions, little security, and few avenues for economic mobility."[29] *Bulletin*, a local Philadelphia newspaper, documented in 1957 how a "host of outsiders descend on the city. They are poverty-stricken, and foreign (not necessarily alien but strange)." Such passages highlight the anxiety around Puerto Ricans and the lack of real understanding about their relationship to the United States. The reporter interviewed an "obviously decent woman . . . that [said] she didn't want Puerto Ricans as next-door neighbors; they were noisy, unclean and—much as she hated to say it—dangerous."[30]

Such conditions also pushed Puerto Ricans to organize at a community level to change their immediate conditions.[31] A younger generation of Puerto Ricans radicalized by the Cuban Revolution created militant groups like the Young Lords, the U.S. branches of the Puerto

Rican Socialist Party, and armed organizations like the Frente Armado de Liberación Nacional. But revolutionary rhetoric was not the only organizing tool used by Puerto Ricans. Many Puerto Ricans joined civic organizations and sought to become part of their city's social fabric. From 1970 to 1972, Puerto Ricans led anywhere from 217 to 469 different civic organizations in New York City.[32] They also participated in electoral politics through grassroots activism. In 1937, for example, Puerto Ricans successfully organized to elect Felipe Torres, the first Puerto Rican in New York's legislature. This was followed by many council members and other officials, leading to the election of Herman Badillo to Congress in 1970.[33]

Music and the arts were other important avenues through which Puerto Ricans created a sense of belonging.[34] In the world of letters, poets created spaces to share and theorize their realities and liminal existences. The term *Nuyorican*, often used as a derogatory word for Puerto Ricans who had settled in the United States, was resignified. For example, the Nuyorican Poets Café became a central point of encounter for those in the diaspora. It also offered a safe space for queer folks navigating the hostility of the city and Puerto Rican machismo. As performance scholar Karen Jaime has noted, "the Café since its inception functioned as a space for artistic *and* sexual exploration, experimentation, and the challenging of identarian fixity."[35]

The queer community is an important element of Puerto Rican realities in New York City yet it is often ignored in mainstream histories.[36] One of the most revered and remembered activists, although she was ostracized in life and died in extreme poverty, was Sylvia Rivera, a trans organizer, sex worker, and revolutionary. Rivera's father was Puerto Rican and her mother was Venezuelan, but she was raised by her grandmother in a mostly diasporic Puerto Rican environment. Along with her African American friend Marsha P. Johnson, Rivera claimed to be part of the famous Stonewall Riots, an event that became a turning point for queer communities in the United States. Rivera excelled at organizing, helping to found multiple organizations, and she was vocal about trans rights. In the early 1970s, she was also in dialogue with the Black Panther Party and the

FIGURE 9.2. Sylvia Rivera and the Street Transvestites Action Revolutionaries (STAR). Creative Commons Attribution-Share Alike 4.0 International License.

Young Lords Party. She was able to accomplish all of this while navigating a violent and poverty-stricken environment that did not accept her gender identity.[37]

While the situation was dire for many Puerto Ricans, others created a sense of home. They began to plant roots, fostering a sense of community within their neighborhoods. The phrase "aquí me quedo" (I am staying here) became an important affirmation that later graced restaurants in Hartford and became the title of a history of Puerto Ricans in Connecticut.[38] This sense of belonging was facilitated by the ever-changing idea of Puerto Rico itself. Puerto Ricans brought with them their traditions, customs, and values. While most lived in small, substandard apartments, it was there that they created a cultural microcosm. When asked about how they kept customs alive, an interviewee in a 1950 migration report responded: "Today is the last day of Christmas, it is the Three Kings Day. My wife and I are expecting a gang from Utuado coming to play the guitar, cuatro, guacharo, and the maracas. The neighbors probably are coming as soon as they hear the music."[39]

Not all Puerto Ricans arrived and settled in urban enclaves. Through the Puerto Rican government's Farm Labor Program thousands were recruited to work in the fields of New York, Connecticut, Michigan, Wisconsin, and Florida, among other places. The well-oiled migration machine created by the government provided some guarantees that eased the process for those who wanted to migrate but did not have any savings, networks abroad, or English-speaking skills. Unlike other seasonal farm laborers such as the braceros, Puerto Ricans possessed U.S. citizenship. But as anthropologist Ismael García-Colón has noted, "Puerto Rican farmworkers are both expendable and disposable: expendable because they can be replaced with guest and undocumented workers and disposable because their U.S. citizenship does not protect them from discrimination in an industry that takes advantage of immigrants."[40]

Once they arrived, most farmworkers were confronted with the harsh reality of precarious labor conditions. They worked long hours in the fields only to sleep in barracks that resembled prisons. In addition, they were often not paid what they were owed for their labor. Some were able to save enough money to send back home; others made their way to the closest city. They wrote letters to government officials and even to Luis Muñoz Marín, Puerto Rico's governor, about how they had been abandoned and left behind.[41] Notwithstanding the hardships faced by many, these migrations also set the foundations for Puerto Rican enclaves in states along the East Coast and across the Midwest.

By the 1970s the modernization project launched in Puerto Rico was showing signs of fatigue. In the United States, economic crises triggered a rise in unemployment. The "plethora of limited opportunities" offered by migration had also waned. It was more difficult for Puerto Ricans to find steady jobs or sources of income. And yet many stayed. They planted roots and gave birth to generations of Puerto Ricans in the diaspora. While some may never have visited the archipelago or even spoken Spanish, they carried with them a sense of pride and belonging to the Puerto Rican nation. Thousands, however, decided to return.

Returning

In 1972, Luis Muñoz Marín returned to Puerto Rico. The leader of the PPD had left Puerto Rico in 1968 after his party's first major defeat in that year's election. The Partido Nuevo Progresista (New Progressive Party; PNP) won the ballot box after a major split within the PPD. Tensions came to the fore after a plebiscite regarding Puerto Rico's political status held on July 23, 1967. Those who favored independence abstained and received 1 percent of the vote while those who supported annexation received 30 percent; the commonwealth emerged victorious with 60 percent of the vote.[42]

Governor Roberto Sánchez Vilella had won the 1964 election with the endorsement of Luis Muñoz Marín. Both leaders broke off their collaborative relationship when Sánchez Vilella joined the party's leftist faction, which became critical of the 1965 U.S. occupation of Santo Domingo and the military draft of Puerto Ricans. This faction eventually boycotted the plebiscite and created a new political party, Partido del Pueblo (People's Party). These divisions led the PPD to lose the 1968 ticket to the PNP, the new party that had also split from the Statehood Party due to differing views on the plebiscite.[43]

Muñoz Marín referred to his time abroad as "voluntary exile." Unlike the hundreds of thousands of people who decided to migrate back to Puerto Rico given the difficult economic situation they faced in the United States, Muñoz Marín spent his time in Rome thinking about the future of his party and of Puerto Rico, which he considered inseparable.[44]

When Muñoz Marín left the country, he did not know when or even if he would return. The PNP's victory in 1968 caused him great concern. These elections marked the beginning of Puerto Rico's two-party system, which continues to the present day. Until then, the PPD's party structure had not been formally institutionalized as it revolved around the figure of Muñoz Marín himself. The party needed to be reinvigorated if it was to win the elections in 1972; it needed to continue without its charismatic but aging leader. The commonwealth status the party had created in the 1950s was now threatened by the possibility of U.S.

annexation of Puerto Rico. The PNP's platform was based on Puerto Rico obtaining statehood. Hawai'i and Alaska had been incorporated in 1959. Two years later, a constitutional amendment granted Washington, D.C., voting rights. The PNP leaders were hopeful that Puerto Rico would become a state in the span of a decade, as its leader Luis A. Ferré predicted would happen.[45]

A month before the elections, in October 1972, the PPD announced Luis Muñoz Marín's return. A massive political rally to celebrate was planned in the parking lot of San Juan's Plaza las Américas, the Caribbean's largest shopping mall. Approximately 150,000 rank-and-file members of the PPD showed up, eager to hear their leader. Upon his return he gave a speech and threw his support behind the party's electoral candidate, Rafael Hernández Colón, securing Colón's victory the following month. Historian Silvia Álvarez Curbelo called this event the PPD's "coup de gracia."[46]

The rally can also be understood symbolically, and in this way it was a historical turning point. While the PPD had presented itself from its beginnings as the party of the poor, this event took place in the quintessential symbol of Puerto Rico's emerging consumerist culture, Plaza las Américas. The event also marked Muñoz Marín's return just as hundreds of thousands of Puerto Rican migrants were also returning to the archipelago. These anonymous workers had not spent their time in the United States pondering the muses. Rather, they had worked in factories, hustled in the streets, or committed themselves to grassroots community and political organizing.

When Muñoz Marín gave his speech, it was clear that the modernization project had failed. Heralded as an economic miracle by many or as "democracy's laboratory in Latin America" in *Time* magazine's second cover article dedicated to Luis Muñoz Marín, modernization was nonetheless a bust.[47] Although Muñoz Marín argued that neither independence nor statehood was realistic, the commonwealth was beginning to collapse.

Puerto Rico was hit hard by the 1973 oil crisis and ensuing U.S. recession. The local agricultural industry all but disappeared, leaving thousands of people without steady income. Unemployment reached

17 percent while the country's gross national product fell from 7 percent in 1960 to 3.3 percent in the following decade. Poverty was rampant, forcing the Puerto Rican government to lobby for an extension of the Nutritional Assistance Plan and federal food stamps to the archipelago to assist low-income families. Instead of fostering the expansion of local agricultural production, these funds were spent on imports from the United States.[48]

In the United States, Puerto Ricans faced a decline in manufacturing and the expansion of a service economy that displaced many of them. Given the limited opportunities available during an economic recession and the restructuring of urban areas in the Northeast and Midwest, many Puerto Ricans decided to return to the archipelago.[49] Between 1975 and 1980, 137,000 Puerto Ricans went back to their homeland while migration to the United States dwindled to 65,817 during those years.[50] Many traveled with children and adolescents who had been born abroad and now returned to live in the nostalgic land of their parents.

Those who participated in the circular migration that began in the 1970s cannot be reduced to numbers and data. Flights arriving in San Juan were loaded with Puerto Ricans who had a new understanding of what being Puerto Rican meant. The returning migrants also created new understandings of the nation that included those who had decided to stay behind and celebrate Three Kings Day with the warmth of family and community as an escape from the cold. Some were coming back home. Others stayed home in New York, Milwaukee, Hartford, or Worcester. All of these urban enclaves were extensions of a nation that was not defined by geographic boundaries and that existed notwith-standing colonial erasures and imperial violence.

CHAPTER 10

THE COLD WAR AND
THE NEW PUSH
FOR INDEPENDENCE

In the late 1930s, Luis Muñoz Marín traveled Puerto Rico's country-side gathering votes and attracting people to the recently formed Popular Democratic Party (PPD). One of the party's catchphrases, which became part of its anthem, was *jalda arriba* (up the hillside).[1] On his visits to the western town of Mayagüez, Muñoz Marín stopped in Ricardo Trabal's *gallera* (cockpit). Cockfighting was an important social event in rural Puerto Rico. Trabal, one of the founding members of Mayagüez's PPD branch, was also an ardent believer in Puerto Rico's independence. Muñoz Marín's visits were an event and Francisca Rivera, Ricardo's wife, made sure to cook her famous rice and chicken for him.[2]

During one such visit, Ricardo and Francisca's daughter, Providencia Trabal, met her political hero, Muñoz Marín. Providencia, known as Pupa, had been born into extreme poverty on May 1, 1926. Wanting a better life for their child, her birth parents gave her to her godparents, Ricardo and Francisca, who raised her like their own. Pupa recounts that she had a humble and happy life. In grade school she met a shy boy who "was raised as a bourgeois" and excelled in all his classes. His name was Juan Mari Brás. He later became a prominent lawyer, an important figure in

Puerto Rico's pro-independence movement, and one of Pupa's lifelong friends.[3]

Pupa was a young girl the day she met Muñoz Marín. She sat in his lap and Muñoz Marín told her "the *patria* [fatherland] is always first, and the first thing that you need to love in your life is the patria."[4] When the PPD won the 1940 elections, there was a huge celebration in Pupa's household. They supported the party until Muñoz Marín, as Pupa later described, "became a coward" and declared independence incongruent with being a *popular*. It was then that she broke away from the PPD and dedicated her life to the struggle for Puerto Rico's independence.[5] She eventually married Néstor Nazario Grillo, a pharmacist from a middle-class family who shared her political commitments.[6]

Pupa was an avid organizer and a dedicated worker, involved in any activity that could advance her ideals. She was also a medium and opened a Spiritist center in her house, located in Mayagüez's #11 San Vicente Street. Pupa's practice granted her the respect and love of her community. She also used the Spiritist center as a space to host pro-independence meetings.[7]

Pupa's activism caught the attention of the archipelago's police department. They began surveilling her activities in 1956, the same year that a group of university students created the Federación Universitaria Pro Independencia (Pro-Independence University Federation; FUPI).[8] Pupa was eventually expelled from the Partido Independentista Puertorriqueño (PIP) along with other dissident members who criticized the party's bureaucratization and its sole focus on electoral politics. Many of those dissatisfied with the PIP began meeting to talk about creating other alternatives.[9]

On January 11, 1959, a group of *independentistas* gave a televised speech advocating for the advancement of Puerto Rico's liberation. That same evening, a meeting took place in Pupa's house. It included her former classmate Juan Mari Brás, along with other comrade independentistas. So many people joined the meeting that it had to be moved outdoors to the patio. There they created a new organization, the Movimiento Pro-Independencia (Pro-Independence Movement; MPI).[10]

Pupa's life was the embodiment of sacrifice to a higher ideal, that of independence. A founding member of both the MPI and the Puerto Rican Socialist Party (PSP), she collaborated actively with their newspaper *Claridad* and founded a women's Masonic lodge. She even met with Latin American revolutionaries like the Chilean poet Pablo Neruda, future Chilean president Salvador Allende, and the Cuban revolutionary Fidel Castro. Pupa always bragged about her cooking and recalled the time she made *almojábanas* (cheese-flavored roll made with corn flour) for the Cuban leader. Constantly harassed by authorities—who even planted bombs in a pharmacy she owned with her husband—she was arrested on several occasions on fabricated accusations. Pupa lived a revolutionary life in revolutionary times.[11]

Being an independentista in Puerto Rico during the 1960s and 1970s could be dangerous. Those who carried the Puerto Rican flag were targeted as potential subversives. Pupa Trabal's life is an example of the hardships faced by so many. She was harassed and framed for crimes she did not commit. As a woman, she also faced discrimination within her own ranks.

When Pupa met Salvador Allende in Chile, they had a brief but powerful exchange. She referred to him as the next president of the country, but he laughed and said that would not happen. She insisted, perhaps confident in her Spiritist sense. He said that if he did become president, she would be the first person invited to his inauguration. When the invitation arrived from President Allende, she excitedly told her old friend Juan Mari Brás, by then the MPI's undisputed leader. He dissuaded Pupa from going, saying that it would be more appropriate for a member of the PIP to attend such an occasion.[12] This might have also been an example of the misogyny and machismo that so many women denounced from their ranks.[13]

While people had been advocating and fighting for independence throughout the twentieth century, new and different forms of understanding, repertoires of struggles, and cross-class collaborations marked the period known as the "new struggle for independence."[14] Revolutionary winds were again blowing in Puerto Rico but with them came debris in the form of colonial violence and state repression.

The Turbulent 1960s and 1970s

The creation of new pro-independence organizations in the 1950s marked a turning point for Puerto Rico's anticolonial movements. National liberation struggles were claiming victories in Asia, Africa, and Latin America, and these new organizations were highly influenced by unraveling events in the Third World. The MPI, for example, was originally imagined as a multiclass coalition that centered their agenda around the independence of Puerto Rico but later became a working-class party. Even after it morphed into a Marxist-Leninist group, it retained its national liberation ethos. In the process, the MPI became one of the most important organizations of the period, able to attract students, workers, and professionals to its ranks. This also made the MPI a target of the Puerto Rican Police Department, the Federal Bureau of Investigation (FBI), and its counterintelligence program, COINTELPRO.[15]

Since its inception, the MPI had wanted to gain influence on a national scale. They created a far-reaching grassroots project through cells known as *misiones* (missions). According to César Andreu Iglesias, a founding member and influential Marxist intellectual of the time, the struggle should not be led by a single organization but by various groups united in the same goal of independence. To do so, the MPI needed to create various fronts within the working classes, cultural institutions, and electoral politics. While not included in Andreu Iglesias's conceptualizations, students later became central political figures in the movement.[16]

Ten days before the MPI's founding meeting on Pupa's patio, a group of revolutionaries one thousand miles away had triumphantly marched in Havana. Fidel Castro's revolution had succeeded in toppling Fulgencio Batista's government in Cuba. The Cuban revolutionaries had accomplished what seemed impossible: they were able to overthrow Batista's dictatorship and, later, declare the revolution communist. All this a mere ninety miles from the United States. Their success, and the defiant anti-imperialist discourse of the Cuban Revolution, was appealing to a generation of Latin American radicals who felt disenfranchised and left behind by the promises of modernization. Ernesto "Che" Guevara's guerrilla handbook—published and widely distributed by the Cuban government—also added fuel to an already flammable moment. Armed guerrilla movements sought to emulate the Cuban experience. Guevara's *foco* theory was particularly popular. Unlike traditional Marxism, he argued that a small band of committed rural guerrilla fighters could create the conditions for revolution. Many groups also experimented with the foco theory in urban settings with various degrees of success.

The Cuban Revolution sent shockwaves across the Americas. Puerto Rico was no exception. The MPI's first resolution, formulated that night in Pupa's house, was to send a fraternal salute and congratulations to commander Fidel Castro. The second was to formally create a fifteen-member organizing committee.[17] As expected, the MPI began collaborating with the Cuban cause almost immediately. In the MPI's foundational assembly, which took place in November 1959, Che Guevara himself sent a letter saluting the newly established organization.[18]

The bonds of solidarity and collaboration only intensified during the 1960s. The MPI was invited to participate in the Tricontinental Conference that took place in Havana and included hundreds of delegates from Asia, Africa, and Latin America.[19] It was there, for example, that the Puerto Rican revolutionary leader Filiberto Ojeda Ríos met with people like Salvador Allende from Chile, Amílcar Cabral from Guinea-Bissau, and Hoàng Bích Sơn from Vietnam.[20] The MPI opened a mission in Havana that became the Misión de Puerto Rico in Cuba, an organization that survived the MPI and still operates today. A former MPI member noted that Cuba also provided tactical support to the Puerto Rican revolutionary struggle via funding, weapons, and military training.[21]

Members of the MPI, then, saw themselves as the defenders and promoters of the Cuban Revolution in Puerto Rico. This made them the target of right-wing Cuban exiles' paramilitary groups. Immediately after the Cuban Revolution succeeded, right-wing groups began organizing across the Caribbean basin with the support of federal agencies like the FBI and the CIA. Some of them had legitimate fronts and were registered as nonprofit organizations in Puerto Rico's Department of State. Their names are quite telling: Frente de Liberación Nacional Cubano (Cuban National Liberation Front), Ejército Latinoamericano Anti-Comunista (Anti-Communist Latin American Army), and Omega 7.[22] Beyond advocacy, these groups used armed tactics to advance their objectives. There were at least 303 acts of terrorism perpetrated by Cuban exiles and other right-wing organizations in Puerto Rico from 1960 to 1990.[23] These included kidnapping attempts, assassinations, and bombings. The MPI headquarters, its newspaper *Claridad*, and their printing press were recurrent targets.

The Cuban government also championed the cause of Puerto Rico's independence on an international scale. Shortly after the creation of the Commonwealth of Puerto Rico, the United States advocated its elimination from the UN's list of colonies. The UN's General Assembly decided in a 1960 resolution that there were three ways of achieving self-government: independence, free association with an independent state, or integration into an independent nation-state. Another resolution also called for the unconditional end of colonialism across the world.[24] In 1965, as decolonization movements proliferated in Africa and new nations joined the UN, Cuba asked that Puerto Rico to be added to the UN Decolonization Committee's agenda.[25]

The discussion about Puerto Rico's colonial status was postponed until 1972. Cuba presented another motion to include Puerto Rico on the General Assembly's agenda. George H. W. Bush, the U.S. ambassador who later became U.S. president, objected and was able to garner the votes to block Puerto Rico's inclusion. The next year, the Decolonization Committee took up Puerto Rico's case again and invited members of Puerto Rican organizations to testify at the UN. Members of various pro-independence organizations like the MPI, the PIP, and the Puerto Rican Communist Party gave their testimony. In 1978, members of all the major political parties in Puerto Rico delivered speeches condemning the archipelago's colonial situation.[26]

UN debates about Puerto Rico pushed the U.S. Congress to pass a timid resolution reaffirming "its commitment to respect and support the right of the people of Puerto Rico to determine their own political future through a peaceful, open, and democratic process."[27] The resolution was dead on arrival, of course. But these conversations reveal that, regardless of political or ideological differences, members of Puerto Rico's political establishment all recognized that Puerto Rico was a colonial possession of the United States.[28]

As the UN conversations took place, the MPI continued promoting unity across all pro-independence organizations and efforts. This, however, was easier said than done. When the MPI allowed its members to vote in elections, some influential members abandoned the organization. Then, when the MPI decided to transform itself from a multiclass organization to a socialist one, conflicts and tensions arose once again from its rank-and-file members. And while the Cuban Revolution had not originally been a socialist struggle—it was only declared Marxist-Leninist by Fidel Castro in 1962—socialism proved highly influential in Puerto Rico too. In the PIP, which had maintained an emphasis on electoral politics, a group of young radicals were expelled because they tried to move the party toward socialism.[29]

The Puerto Rican left was also inspired by the anti–Vietnam War movement taking place in the United States and around the world. University students from the FUPI joined forces with the MPI and others in organizing against U.S. militarism in Puerto Rico. One of their most successful campaigns was opposing the military draft. The strategy was to arrive at recruitment offices when summoned but decline to swear allegiance to the United States. A pro-independence student named Sixto Alvelo was the first of many to be arrested in the movement against the compulsory draft.[30]

Another heated campaign led by leftist organizations was against the Reserve Officers' Training Corps (ROTC) program at the University of Puerto Rico. From 1960 until 1971, militant strikes and other actions left dozens of students, professors, and activists suspended or arrested. There were bombs found in the ROTC building on one occasion, and it was set on fire on another. There were also student and police casualties. Ultimately, the movement, with the support of a coalition of radical organizations, succeeded in forcing ROTC off campus.

The revolutionary furor also gave way to a new wave of working-class militancy. The labor movement's combativeness had dwindled since the

FIGURE 10.1. Dollar used to promote the MPI's Eighth Assembly on November 28, 1971, where the Socialist Party was created. The front side has a photograph of Governor Luis A. Ferré and notes in Spanish: "The Socialist Party Is Coming"; "This note has no value. The original was robbed by the one in the photo." Author's personal collection.

1950s when the PPD came to dominate the world of unions. By the 1960s, the resurgence of labor's militancy was due in part to the grassroots organizing of socialist and pro-independence groups. Perhaps the best example was the strike at a General Electric plant that lasted nine months, from October 1969 to July 1970. The strike signaled the emergence of a new working-class radicalism that openly advocated for independence and socialism. Both the MPI and the FUPI were integral in the radicalization of workers.[31]

A new labor federation created in 1971 under the name of Movimiento Obrero Unido (MOU) also coordinated various strikes and was composed of militant unions. More than 45,000 workers participated in the 166 strikes that took place between 1974 and 1975.[32] The

MOU played a crucial role in a strike at the newspaper *El mundo*, which lasted seven months. The newspaper decided to bring in scabs using a fleet of rented helicopters. In solidarity with striking workers, an underground armed guerrilla movement destroyed four of those helicopters, causing damages estimated in the millions of dollars.[33]

In 1971, the MPI announced that it would become the Puerto Rican Socialist Party (PSP). Given its Marxist-Leninist orientation, its leadership originally envisioned a working-class party. It was to become an instrument in their struggle for Puerto Rican independence which, they believed, would only be attainable through socialism. While it attracted less than 1 percent of the vote in the 1976 and 1980 elections, the party's impact extended beyond the ballot box.[34]

Following the MPI's grassroots strategy, the PSP was able to create an impressive national network of municipal sections or *núcleos*. These núcleos organized in schools and universities, job sites, and neighborhoods.[35] The party strongly influenced both the organized labor movement and leftist student organizations. Too often ignored is the fact that its leadership believed in a plurality of tactics in their struggle for independence. Their newspaper *Claridad*, for example, became a bulletin board used by many organizations to claim responsibility for certain military actions or to simply send messages to the government.[36] Ex-MPI member Ángel Agosto also claims that the party created an "armed unit" of 247 members organized in six columns dispersed throughout the archipelago.[37]

By 1975, a PSP internal document noted that the party had 2,635 active members, 14,310 sympathizers, and 1,056 card-carrying militants.[38] While these may have seemed like promising numbers, the MPI started to lose steam shortly afterward. Internal debates and tensions began to tear the party apart. While it started as a working-class organization, it later advocated for multiclass coalitions. This produced tensions that were only heightened by internal critiques of the party's decision to join electoral races. Their crushing defeats exacerbated the discontent. As a former MPI-PSP militant once argued, "esto se jodió cuando se fundó el PSP" (this got fucked when the PSP was founded).[39] By the end of the 1980s the party was debilitated, and many of its members abandoned it.

The PSP was part of a broader radical tradition stemming from the MPI, the Nationalist Party, and the PIP: all parties that understood the centrality of the Puerto Rican diaspora in the struggle for independence. Since its creation, the MPI had sustained and organized missions in the diaspora that sought to radicalize the vibrant Puerto Rican communities in the United States. Known as La Seccional (The Sectional), this diasporic PSP successfully organized núcleos in New York, California, New Jersey, and Pennsylvania, as well as in cities in the Midwest and the Northeast.[40] For some of its members, the party helped them polish their Spanish-language skills, expand their Puerto Rican consciousness, and deepen their relationship to the archipelago.[41] The Seccional produced a short-lived English supplement to the *Claridad* newspaper and focused on pressing local issues affecting Puerto Ricans in the diaspora, as well as collaborating with other civil rights organizations.

By the 1970s and 1980s, the term "Nuyorican," which referred to Puerto Ricans living in New York, was used pejoratively by those who lived in the archipelago. In fact, some English-speaking PSP members felt that they, too, were treated differently by their comrades in Puerto Rico. Officially, however, the PSP stated that Puerto Ricans in the diaspora were part of the Puerto Rican nation and should work toward the independence of Puerto Rico while also advancing revolutionary and socialist struggles in the United States. While their reach and political influence might have been limited, this idea became an important intellectual counterpoint to think about the Puerto Rican nation as not simply contained within the Caribbean archipelago. Echoing the Cuban intellectual José Martí's famous phrase "in the entrails of the beast," a 1972 PSP official document titled *In the Entrails* laid out the party's official stance. The PSP believed that "Puerto Rico was a nation, with its own national territory, language, culture, and history of colonialism and racism."[42] The migration and settlements of Puerto Ricans in the United States "represented a new *extension* of that nation, not the *creation* of a new people, in the form of a national minority."[43] They also believed that only after Puerto Rico's independence could Puerto Ricans be considered a national minority in the United States.[44]

The PSP was not the only organization reimagining the concept of the nation. As part of the broader civil rights movement in the United States, a younger generation of Puerto Ricans born in the diaspora began to combine the struggle for independence with a desire to transform the precarious realities of their families in their barrios. They were tired of the poverty and discrimination that affected their working-class neighborhoods. For this younger generation, poverty, both at home and in Puerto Rico, was the product of imperialism, capitalism, and racism.

Influenced by the Black Panther Party, the Chicano civil rights movement in the West, and the anti–Vietnam War movement, a street gang led by José "Cha Cha" Jiménez became the Young Lords Organization in 1969. It quickly spread to New York, Philadelphia, and Chicago. The New York branch broke away from Chicago and became the Young Lords Party. Many of its members were young adults and teenagers, second-generation Puerto Ricans living in impoverished communities.[45] Imbued in the moment's radical ethos, the Young Lords saw themselves as part of an anti-imperialist internationalist movement that sought to topple capitalism. In the process, they also challenged ideas about race, sexuality, and gender in their local communities.[46]

While the Young Lords Party existed only until 1976, their effective use of mass media and the boldness of some of their actions caught the public's imagination. They burned their neighborhood's trash in the middle of the street when the city failed to pick it up. Members ran community programs around childcare and free meals. They also occupied several churches, parks, and hospitals. In 1970, for example, the Young Lords occupied Lincoln Hospital for several hours after a series of deaths due to negligence on the part of health-care workers and substandard facilities. The event garnered national attention and the Young Lords who took part escaped without arrest.[47]

Because these groups often moved between the archipelago and the United States, they were heavily surveilled. When the Young Lords decided to expand operations to the archipelago, for example, their movements were tracked by undercover agents. Similarly, the FBI's COINTELPRO not only sought to infiltrate and disband groups like the Black Panther

Party but also targeted Puerto Rican groups that were considered extremist. Surveillance was something that, as scholar Marisol LeBrón argues, "united the insurgency across the diaspora."[48]

The Young Lords and the Seccional were not the first organizations to claim rights for Puerto Ricans in the United States. They built their projects on the shoulders of community activists and civic organizations that had been operating in the diaspora for decades. These new organizations signaled a turning point in how colonialism and the urgency of Puerto Rico's independence were linked to everyday life in the diaspora.[49]

Armed Resistance and Repression

An important aspect of the new struggle for independence in Puerto Rico and the diaspora was the appearance of armed guerrilla movements. Inspired by the success of Cuban revolutionaries and Third World liberation struggles, these organizations operated clandestinely in both urban and rural settings. Since they did not have popular support, they believed that strategic actions would weaken U.S. colonialism in Puerto Rico. In part, their plan was to make Puerto Rico inhospitable to U.S. corporations and investors.[50]

One of the first armed organizations to emerge was the Comandos Armados de Liberación (CAL), which operated from 1963 to 1972.[51] They were responsible for 137 bombings between 1968 and 1972, generating more than $100 million in losses and resulting in the deaths of two U.S. Marines.[52] In the diaspora, Chicago activists organized the Fuerzas Armadas de Liberación Nacional (FALN), which carried out 120 bombings between 1974 and 1981. Five people lost their lives in FALN-led actions.[53]

Such events did not take place in a vacuum. These organizations understood their actions as part of a war against U.S. imperialism in Puerto Rico. For example, in 1971 the CAL declared Condado, a tourist destination and one of San Juan's wealthiest neighborhoods, a war zone.[54]

Armed guerrillas responded to state-sponsored terror with equal violence. On March 4, 1970, for example, students clashed with police

FIGURE 10.2. Day of Solidarity with Puerto Rico organized by the PSP in New York City's Madison Square Garden on October 27, 1974. Photograph by Pucho Charrón. Courtesy of the Archivo Histórico del Periódico *Claridad*.

officers outside the UPR in Río Piedras. As the police violently dispersed the students, some began running through adjacent Ponce de León Street. From her balcony, Antonia Martínez Lagares, a twenty-year-old who was studying to become a Spanish teacher, screamed at the police to stop. One officer raised his gun and shot at the balcony, killing Antonia and wounding another student, Celestino Santiago Díaz. The only police officer accused of the assassination, Marcos A. Ramos, was later absolved in court. Much later, in 1991, an investigation led by the Judicial Commission of the Puerto Rican Senate stated that Ramos had been falsely accused to protect the real perpetrator.[55] In response to Antonia's murder, the CAL organized "Antonia Operation," in which they killed two U.S. Marines in retaliation.[56]

Right-wing paramilitary groups operating in Puerto Rico also ramped up the severity of their actions against the independence movement in the 1970s. Juan Mari Brás and the PSP were often targets. In

FIGURE 10.3. Passport photograph of Santiago "Chagui" Mari Pesquera. Courtesy of the Archivo Histórico del Periódico *Claridad*.

December 1975, Mari Brás was elected as the party's candidate for governor in an assembly with more than ten thousand people in the audience. The previous year, in 1974, the PSP Seccional in New York organized an event in Madison Square Garden at which more than twelve thousand people demanded independence for Puerto Rico. The PSP's expansion worried right-wing groups operating in Puerto Rico. When the PSP was preparing for the 1976 elections, Mari Brás received a brutal blow. His twenty-three-year-old son, Santiago "Chagui" Mari Pesquera, was kidnapped in front of his house. Chagui's body was found

the following day. Although one of his neighbors was arrested and subsequently convicted of the murder, a prosecutor stated in court that he
could not have acted alone.[57]

These events were part of a broader trend toward extreme violence
and state repression. There were politically oriented assassinations,
bombings, and indiscriminate arrests throughout the decade. The police
and the FBI also expanded their efforts and successfully infiltrated several leftist organizations.[58]

In 1978, for example, a young revolutionary named Alejandro
González Malavé created two organizations, Comandos Revolucio-
narios Armados and Frente Armado Anti-Imperialista. In the span of
a year, they claimed responsibility for four armed actions: burning
down the Americans for Democratic Action Committee building; attacking guard headquarters at the UPR; shooting up the residency of
Luis Muñoz Marín; and planting a bomb in a post office.[59] González
Malavé's enthusiasm and daring actions enabled him to recruit two
young men, Arnaldo Darío Rosado-Torres and Carlos Soto Arriví, for
his next act: blowing up a radio tower at Cerro Maravilla, a mountainside about fifty miles from San Juan.[60] The date they selected, July 25,
1978, was not arbitrary: it was the anniversary of the U.S. occupation
and the same day that the commonwealth and the Puerto Rican Constitution had been inaugurated in 1952. The three men hijacked a taxi,
forcing the driver, Julio Ortiz Molina, to take them to their destination. They were surrounded by police officers the moment they got
out of the car.

It was a trap.

The group's leader and seasoned revolutionary with years of experience under his belt, González Malavé, immediately surrendered. Darío
Rosario and Soto Arriví were likely astonished when he began scream-
ing at the police officers not to shoot him, he was one of theirs. Alejandro González Malavé was an undercover agent. Darío Rosado-Torres
and Soto Arriví were executed after they had surrendered. Governor
Carlos Romero Barceló from the Partido Nuevo Progresista (PNP)
called the officers "heroes," arguing that "those who carry guns and pis-
tols, who go with bombs. . . . Those who kill must be prepared to die."[61]

Maravilla's Aftermath

The events at Maravilla did not end that day; they dominated the election cycles of 1982 and 1986.[62] Governor Romero Barceló won his second bid for governor in 1982 but his party lost the Senate majority to the Populares. The government's official account of what had happened at Maravilla was that the young men had shot at the police, who had killed them in self-defense. When the taxi driver was interviewed, however, he contradicted that narrative. The PPD-dominated Senate ordered an investigation into what had happened that day. The public hearings began in 1983. They were televised and garnered national attention. It was proven in court that the young men had been executed and the agents involved had committed perjury.[63]

The case created a political storm. In 1986, Romero Barceló lost his third reelection bid. Ten officers were suspended. Alejandro González Malavé was removed from the force, acquitted on all charges, and then assassinated by an armed leftist organization. But the televised court cases revealed more than just that the government had officially lied. A police officer misspoke under pressure while being interviewed and gave away another state secret that everyone had suspected for years: the Puerto Rican police's Department of Intelligence had been surveilling people for decades and had *carpetas* (files) on thousands of Puerto Ricans.[64]

In an unprecedented move, the Puerto Rican courts later concluded that the carpetas had been illegally created and ruled they should be given to those affected. The pages detailed how for three decades the Puerto Rican government had created a sophisticated system of surveillance. But the state had not acted alone. The carpetas confirmed that neighbors, coworkers, and even comrades in the struggle had been collaborating with the police. These documents had also served as a database to target and blacklist those deemed subversives. As sociologist José Anazagasty has noted, those who were *carpeteados* were denied job and study opportunities and suffered discrimination, persecution, illegal arrest, imprisonment, and even death.[65]

The term *carpeteo* became part of Puerto Rican slang for being surveilled, demonstrating the impact that this program had on the collective

FIGURE 10.4. Protest against Governor Romero Barceló. Photograph by
Ricardo Alcaraz Díaz. Courtesy of the Archivo Histórico del Periódico *Claridad*.

imaginary. The carpetas became an archive of state anxieties, fears,
and everyday violence. Unlike other truth and reconciliation processes
in different parts of the world, there was no state-led reckoning that
could provide some meaning to the carpetas while acknowledging the
government's wrongdoing. These events served as the backdrop for an
economic crisis that would profoundly impact Puerto Rico for decades
to come.

CHAPTER 11

THE ROAD TO COLLAPSE

The 1970s and 1980s were decades of economic turmoil in Puerto Rico. The recession that took hold of the U.S. economy after the 1973 oil crisis created a ripple effect in its Caribbean colony. Attracting foreign investment had been a cornerstone of the government's economic agenda under Operation Bootstrap, hailed by *Time* magazine as an economic miracle. The annual gross national product fell from 7 percent in the 1960s to 2.1 percent in the 1980s.[1] By the following decade, 58.9 percent of the Puerto Rican population lived below the poverty level and unemployment reached 20.4 percent.[2] The miracle had lost its divine agency.

Faced with this dire situation, in 1974 Governor Rafael Hernández Colón created a committee to analyze the country's fiscal and economic conditions. Led by James Tobin, a Yale University professor who would later receive the Nobel Prize in Economics, it was charged with drafting a series of recommendations.[3] The committee concluded, among other things, that Puerto Rico needed an economic strategy that was less reliant on U.S. capital.[4]

In 1976, the Hernández Colón administration successfully lobbied the U.S. Congress to implement Section 936 of the U.S. Internal Revenue Code. Previously, any U.S. corporation operating in Puerto Rico paid a 48 percent tax to transfer their earnings back to the United States. Section 936 allowed foreign corporations in Puerto Rico to repatriate their earnings tax free.[5] While moderately successful at first, it consolidated Puerto Rico's dependency on foreign investment, precisely what the Tobin Committee had warned against.

The economic situation affected the multiple Puerto Ricos that co-existed within the archipelago in different ways. Many families migrated from the countryside to urban centers in search of better opportunities, but they faced housing shortages that forced them to settle in *arrabales* (shanty towns). This process had begun decades earlier, in the 1920s and 1930s. It was not uncommon for the police to conduct raids and engage in other acts of violence to evict members of communities living on rescued lands. Their residents, however, demanded rights and often defiantly argued that they would not move.[6]

On February 6, 1980, the tactical unit of the Puerto Rican police surrounded the house of Adolfina Villanueva Osorio and Agustín Carrasquillo, a Black couple from the town of Loiza. They had been fighting in court to claim ownership of the land where their humble house made from wood and zinc stood. The Catholic Church, who claimed to own the land, demanded the couple's immediate eviction.[7]

As the police surrounded Adolfina and Agustín's house, one officer shouted: "We will take you out dead or alive." They proceeded to shoot gas canisters and bullets at the house. Agustín came out and was hit in the legs by four bullets. Adolfina ran inside trying to collect her two children still at home (her other four children were in school). When she came out the door, Adolfina was shot sixteen times. The bullets perforated her lungs and liver; she died on the spot, just thirty-four years old. Police sergeant Victor Estrella was accused of Adolfina's murder but later absolved of any crime.[8]

While Adolfina's case made headlines, the government continued to attack other squatter settlements. On May 18, 1982, the police forcefully and violently removed three hundred families residing in the town of Carolina's Villa Sin Miedo. One police officer died in the operation, many residents were wounded, and houses were set on fire. The government of Carlos Romero Barceló told the press that "the hand of subversive leftists" was operating in Villa Sin Miedo.[9] The criminalization of poverty and the poor only increased over the following decade.[10]

These events and their public reception caused the Puerto Rican government to take a new approach to the housing crisis. As legal scholar Érika Fontánez Torres has noted, the death of Adolfina Villanueva Osorio

and the events at Villa Sin Miedo forced the government to make cos-
metic changes in its public policy with regard to housing through the
reorganization of agencies and bureaucracy. And it also created new legislation seeking to facilitate buying property for poor and marginalized
populations. In practice, however, not much changed. After Hurricane
Hugo in 1989, for example, many poor families lacked housing, leading
the government to create the Programa de Vivienda Permanente para los
Damnificados del Huracán Hugo (Permanent Living Place for the Victims of Hurricane Hugo Program) to assist poor families that had been
impacted by the storm. In 2018, almost three decades after the hurricane,
the Puerto Rican government acknowledged that many people who participated in the program never received their property titles. The program
had been a failure.[11]

For the Puerto Rican middle classes, the crisis affected them in different ways. New patterns of consumption and market-driven ideologies
influenced their spending habits. The proliferation of cars in mid-
twentieth-century Puerto Rico also changed the physical landscape of
urban centers; increasingly, shopping malls became important spaces for
socialization.[12] Credit cards also facilitated consumption and particular
lifestyles at times when the economy was at a standstill. From 1985 to
1992, for example, Puerto Rican credit card debt rose from $455 million
to $848 million.[13]

Debt prevailed among the middle classes at the same time that it
became integral to governing. Margaret Thatcher in the UK and Ronald
Reagan in the United States championed free-market ideologies that
were circulating in the global economy. Termed "neoliberalism" by
scholars, these ideas promised a new way to understand the economy.
But neoliberalism was also a new way to understand citizenship and
social relations through the promotion of individualism, entrepreneur-
ship, and privatization. The Puerto Rican government relied on debt to
maintain the economy. The totality of debt from the commonwealth,
municipalities, and corporations was about $1.6 billion in 1960. By 1990,
however, this number was around $12.7 billion.[14] As the contracting
economy impacted Puerto Rican society, people on different sides of

the political spectrum once again began to carefully think about the meanings of Puerto Ricanness.

Reimagining the Nation, Again

Ideas of "the nation" have loomed large in Puerto Rican intellectual production since the nineteenth century. Works of history and literature attempted to lay the foundations of a national identity distinct from Spanish colonizers. By the 1930s, conversations that had once taken place in private *tertulias* or literary soirees were now being held in public at the University of Puerto Rico (UPR). A new generation of scholars began using the classroom and scholarship to define the essence of Puerto Ricanness, often articulating ideas that were rooted in racism and elitism.[15]

In the 1970s, the university served, once again, as a space where ideas could be put into practice. Influenced by events taking place around the world—the anti–Vietnam War movement, the Cuban Revolution, and global student protests, among other social movements—along with the invigoration of the Puerto Rican working classes, the militancy of the student movement, and the new struggle for independence, a young generation of intellectuals sought to move away from traditional understandings of history.

New readings of Marxism from non-Soviet sources and less dogmatic understandings of socialism led to other ways of doing history. A new generation of scholars, most of whom had studied in France, England, and the United States, returned to Puerto Rico as professors at the UPR during a moment of social and intellectual upheaval. While not all of them knew each other, the urgency of the moment drew them together in what became known as the Centro de Estudios de la Realidad Puertorriqueña (Center for the Study of Puerto Rican Reality; CEREP).[16]

These young intellectuals were part of what became known as La Nueva Historia, but not all of them were trained historians. Those who came together under the CEREP banner in the early 1970s had been trained in different disciplinary traditions like anthropology, theater, sociology, education, and economics. The phrase "history from below" was being discussed in academic seminars from London to Buenos Aires, from Cuba to New York; in Puerto Rico, faculty at CEREP took up the mission to think "from below" and shed light on those histories that had been purposefully overlooked by traditional historians. Their conversations and publications covered a wide range of then-novel topics such as the histories of plantations, women and social action, and workers.[17]

These young intellectuals believed that to understand Puerto Rican reality, one needed to take into consideration marginalized groups first and foremost. While workers, women, and enslaved peoples had been traditionally ignored, they too had rich and vibrant histories from which scholars could draw examples and inspiration. For the members of CEREP, scholarship was political. It was an attempt to understand reality in order to transform it.[18] While members of CEREP organized seminars and workshops, they also met with unions and other groups beyond academia in Puerto Rico.

Community leaders, student activists, and university professors in the New York City diaspora also came together to create an intellectual space to think about the Puerto Rican experience. Their struggles led to the creation of Puerto Rican Studies as a distinct field within U.S. academia. As María E. Pérez y González and Virginia Sánchez Korrol note, "The underrepresented, 'powerless' black and brown students had stormed the citadel, the symbolic ivy-covered towers of the senior colleges and the community colleges, transforming higher education in ways the activists could not then imagine."[19] In 1969, the City of New York's Board of Higher Education secured funding for the creation of Puerto Rican Studies programs, departments, centers, and institutes. By 1972, new academic departments and programs were established at Lehman, Hunter, City, Brooklyn, John Jay, and Queens colleges.[20]

Demands from students, faculty, and community activists in New York City also paved the way for the Centro: Center for Puerto Rican Studies in 1973. This space served as a library, archive, and intellectual hub. Similar to scholars in the archipelago, Centro researchers "helped forge an interpretive paradigm grounded in historical materialist and critical cultural theory."[21] There was also intellectual dialogue and collaboration between scholars in the archipelago and the diaspora. Rafael Ramírez, one of the founders of CEREP, was recruited by Centro and was instrumental in creating their Culture Task Force program.[22] These intellectual efforts led to new interpretations of the Puerto Rican past as scholars attempted to center voices, histories, and experiences that had been ignored. Such scholarship was a political project that they hoped could help transform their realities. That is, the past was not simply something that had happened but something from which they could build new futures.

While the meaning of Puerto Rico was being debated in university classrooms, armed movements for independence continued through the 1980s. One of the most active militant groups was the Macheteros. From 1978 to 1986, they committed eighteen armed actions that called attention to Puerto Rico's colonial reality and sought to expropriate funds for their cause.[23] The Macheteros shocked everyone. To avenge the two independentistas killed in Cerro Maravilla, they attacked a U.S. Navy vehicle in December 1979, killing two marines and wounding dozens. In October 1983, they fired an M-72 rocket at the FBI offices in Hato Rey, in solidarity with "the brotherly people of Grenada," during the U.S. occupation of the Caribbean country.[24]

The Macheteros understood these tactics in terms of propaganda. Their boldest actions were covered by local media and garnered international attention as well. On January 11, 1981, a Machetero commando snuck into San Juan's Muñiz Air National Guard Base and successfully bombed and destroyed a fleet of nine fighter jets. There were no casualties but damages were estimated at $40 million.[25] Two years later, the Macheteros successfully infiltrated and robbed $7 million from a Wells Fargo facility in Hartford, Connecticut.[26] To counter the pro-independence armed struggle, local and federal governments moved from infiltration and state-sponsored terrorism to legal action. Shortly after the Macheteros attacks, many independentistas accused of participating in armed actions were arrested and convicted.[27] Their actions not only challenged local government officials but also reminded the international community about U.S. colonialism in Puerto Rico.

"The nation" was also a powerful way to mobilize people to the ballot box. A bipartisan era began in Puerto Rico after the PNP defeated the PPD in the 1968 elections, ending its sixteen-year streak of victories. Since then, both parties have alternated power. The question of Puerto Rico's colonial status was the driving force in the three dominant political parties: the PNP supported annexation of Puerto Rico, the PPD favored commonwealth status, and the PIP organized for independence. The only commonality among the three was their belief in the existence of the Puerto Rican nation, at least from a cultural standpoint.

During the 1970s and 1980s the PIP continued advocating for independence. The party's founder, Gilberto Concepción de Gracia, had been a UPR and George Washington University–trained lawyer and journalist. When he died in 1968, membership oscillated between radical and socialist interpretations of what a postcolonial Puerto Rico might look like and more moderate social-democratic stances. These different views and aspirations gave way to inevitable tensions and splits. Eventually the more moderate strand took hold and was represented by Concepción de Gracia's successor, Rubén Berrios.

Rubén Berrios was an up-and-coming lawyer in 1970, when he became the PIP's president. Just thirty-one and educated at Georgetown, Yale, and Oxford, his more moderate stance on independence allowed him to unify the party after the more radical sector was expelled. For the PIP, the Puerto Rican nation was already a reality. But because of its colonial status, it lacked judicial and political sovereignty. For them, only independence could provide a viable future for Puerto Rico.[28]

While the PPD did not advocate for independence and instead defended commonwealth status, they agreed on the existence of a cultural nation. In fact, the PPD had been crucial in detaching nationalism from Puerto Rico's political status. When the party came to power in the 1940s, its ideologues promoted a sense of national belonging that did not pose a challenge to the relationship established with the United States after the creation of the commonwealth and the Puerto Rican Constitution in 1952. Anthropologists such as Arlene Dávila and Jorge Duany have demonstrated how the PPD created a cultural apparatus through the Instituto de Cultura and the División de Educación de la Comunidad (DIVEDCO) to promote the idea of the Puerto Rican nation from a cultural, not political, perspective.[29]

It was clear by the 1980s that Operation Bootstrap had not accomplished what it was meant to. The PPD's economic project had failed and was now collapsing. But the cultural nationalism that had accompanied the PPD's rise continued to operate in Puerto Rico with great force. It was so powerful that although the PNP openly and aggressively advocated for annexation to the United States, they did so without abandoning the idea of a cultural Puerto Rican nation.

The PNP had been created two decades earlier, emerging as part of the debates and tensions that took place over the 1967 plebiscite. When the plebiscite was announced, members of the Partido Estadista Republicano were divided as to whether or not they should participate. Some argued that it would only give power to the PPD, while others saw it as an opportunity to advance their pro-statehood agenda. From those tensions, the PNP emerged on August 20, 1968, under the leadership of businessman Luis A. Ferré.

The revolutionary fervor and radical politics of the 1960s not only impacted those who advocated for socialism and independence but also altered conservative parties like the PNP. For example, when Ferré was elected the party's first president, Vicente Hita Jr., a former labor leader and lawyer, approached the podium and asked to speak. He had a gavel in his hands. Hita told the audience that the gavel had belonged to Santiago Iglesias Pantín, one of the most important labor leaders at the beginning of the twentieth century. He gave it to Ferré, who noted, "I accept this gavel with a humble spirit and a sense of great responsibility because this gavel belonged to a great man who was the redeemer of Puerto Rico's humble classes."[30]

To make statehood appealing to different social sectors, Ferré created the idea of the "estadidad jíbara," or Puerto Rican statehood. For Ferré, statehood would grant more rights, protections, and federal funds. This could take place, he argued, without losing Puerto Rican culture. Culture became a dominant theme in conversations about statehood and, ultimately, in their party's platform. When Carlos Romero Barceló took over the PNP in 1974, he published a book titled *La estadidad es para los pobres* (Statehood is for the poor) in hopes of attracting the laboring masses to the party. The book reproduced nineteenth-century ideas that had been consolidated by the PPD in the 1940s, chief among them the notion of Puerto Rico as the mixture of three races: Indigenous, African, and Spanish. Now, however, Barceló added the North American influence as well. The book declared that Puerto Ricans were proud of their heritage. Because of that, Barceló argued, "Our language and our culture are non-negotiable!"[31]

These discourses were undoubtedly influenced by the civil rights movements in the United States as well as local situations in Puerto Rico. But they did not mean that the PNP became a politically radical institution. Puerto Rican scholars Rafael Bernabe and César Ayala have noted, "As a party committed to the preservation of the existing economic and property relations acting in a period of austerity, the PNP could not but turn against militant labor, student, community, and poor people's struggles when they did emerge."[32] Even when Romero Barceló publicly stated that statehood was pro-poor, his government unleashed extreme state violence against students, land rescuers, and pro-independence activists.

Romero Barceló lost his third reelection bid in 1984 to Rafael Hernández Colón from the PPD. Having served as governor in the 1970s, it was Hernández Colón's second time in office. He continued his party's emphasis on the cultural dimensions of the Puerto Rican nation to maintain the ambiguity of the commonwealth's juridical status. This entailed strengthening the Hispanic legacy of the racial and cultural triad of the "Great Puerto Rican Family" myth.

In 1987, Hernández Colón received Spain's King Juan Carlos I and Queen Sofía in the governor's mansion.[33] A running joke at the time noted that he had ordered a golden toilet for the monarchs. To commemorate the fifth centenary of the colonization of the Americas, his administration organized a series of high-profile events. In 1991, the Puerto Rican government welcomed replicas of the *Santa María*, *Pinta*, and *Niña*, the three ships used by Christopher Columbus and the Pinzón brothers during their first trip to the Americas, and sponsored massive cultural and artistic events in "honor" of colonization. The following year, in 1992, Puerto Rico participated in the organization of the "Gran Regata Colón '92," a race across the Atlantic with more than 250 small boats.[34]

In the midst of all of this celebratory fervor, the Hernández Colón government successfully passed a law in 1991 making Spanish the country's official language. As a symbol of gratitude for upholding its Hispanic legacy, Hernández Colón was awarded Spain's prestigious Prince of Asturias Prize.[35] The law was revoked the following year when Pedro Rosselló from the PNP was elected. His administration continued to promote Puerto Rico as a cultural, rather than political, "nation." While neoliberal ideas had been circulating in Puerto Rico since the 1980s, the election of Rosselló ushered in a new era in Puerto Rico's history: one of punitive and neoliberal governance.

The Era of Rosselló I

Pedro Rosselló was elected in 1992 with 49 percent of the vote. In a country embattled by economic distress, rampant criminality, and political corruption, people were drawn to a new face. Rosselló was young, energetic, and charming. My grandmother, fifty-two years old at the time, joked about how she was going to move with her boyfriend to the Fortaleza as soon as he took office. Rosselló was not a traditional politician—he was also respected in the medical community and had a clean political record.[36]

The PNP's record-breaking victory was complemented by their winning the majority in the legislature and 53 out of 78 municipalities.[37] Former mayor and governor Carlos Romero Barceló was elected resident commissioner in Washington, D.C. One of the marketing strategies of Rosselló's first campaign was to downplay the political status of Puerto Rico and focus on the social problems that affected different sectors of society. This caused tensions within the party, and Romero Barceló—then a high-profile party member—publicly criticized Rosselló for not making the annexation of Puerto Rico the focus of his platform.[38]

Given the election results, the PNP was certain that they would emerge victorious in the 1994 status plebiscite. To their surprise, the commonwealth won with 48 percent of the vote.[39] The results proved that not everyone who had voted for Rosselló supported statehood. But the question of Puerto Rico's political status was not the only focus of Rosselló's administration.

In 1993, Rosselló named Pedro Toledo superintendent of the Puerto Rico police. He had been the FBI's second in command in Puerto Rico. In line with the Hernández Colón administration's policy toward crime, Toledo made the Mano Dura Contra el Crimen (Strong Hand Against Crime) a centerpiece of the Rosselló government. Rather than approaching crime holistically and seeking to change the social conditions that produced it, the Rosselló administration militarized the fight against crime.[40]

In February 1993, Rosselló gave a public speech declaring a war on crime. He activated the U.S. National Guard to support the police in controlling drug-related crimes.[41] This entailed the physical occupation of *caseríos* (housing projects). Caseríos had been imagined in the mid-twentieth century as a response to the housing crisis. The government built these structures next to middle-class enclaves to promote social integration. Over time, however, caserío residents—mostly Black and Brown Puerto Ricans—were stigmatized as dangerous and problematic.[42] So much for the racial harmony myth of cultural nationalism. Neighboring middle classes gated their communities while the government mostly ostracized these populations. Such conditions were ripe for the creation of massive drug empires that connected some caseríos while pitting others against each other.[43]

The Rosselló administration showcased their policy toward crime during the first Mano Dura operation. On June 5, 1993, the residents of Villa España were awakened by the sound of helicopters. A full-scale military operation occupied the five-hundred-unit housing project. As scholar Petra Rivera-Rideau has noted, this was "the first of seventy-four raids by the National Guard and Puerto Rican police department over the course of three years."[44] The raids and occupation of caseríos continued until 1999.[45]

The Mano Dura policy sought to control, contain, and eliminate crime using militarized force; in fact, the policy criminalized poverty and treated the caserío residents like criminals. Meanwhile, the Rosselló administration was busy implementing its economic agenda. In line with global economic trends, the administration sought to shrink the Puerto Rican government through privatization. Rosselló's first test of the new model was the announcement of legislation known as the Health Reform, which would privatize the health system by auctioning off health services to private companies, with the government partly subsidizing each patient. To manage the new program, the government created the Administración de Seguro de Salud de Puerto Rico. During Rosselló's second term in office, his administration also privatized seven of the major public hospitals in the archipelago.[46]

Rosselló continued the PNP's strategy of appealing to the masses while also advancing a neoliberal agenda—neoliberalism with a populist face. For example, Rosselló's *tarjetitas*—a reference to the medical insurance card that many Puerto Ricans had for the first time—were presented as options to democratize access to medical plans. In practice, however, the reform created hierarchies between those who could afford private health insurance and those who carried the government's tarjetita. Because of bureaucratic complications, many physicians and doctors claimed that they did not receive payments on time and thus declined to accept patients on the government plan.[47]

Nonetheless, Rosselló easily won a second term in office. In the 1996 elections, his ticket was elected with the biggest margin in the country's electoral history.[48] Two years later, the party organized another plebiscite where statehood was once again defeated.[49] While the Mano Dura policy and the privatization of the health system were seen as moderate successes by Puerto Ricans, Rosselló's administration was plagued with scandals and corruption. More than eighty people from or close to the Rosselló administration were either accused of, convicted on, or imprisoned on corruption charges.[50] In the coming years, *El nuevo día*, the country's leading newspaper, would publish an editorial arguing that the Rosselló administrations had been "the most corrupt period in the history of Puerto Rico.

There has not been a government as corrupt as the Pedro Rselló administration in 100 years."[51]

Rselló's popularity began to wane. It waned even more when he announced plans to privatize the Puerto Rican Telephone Company (PRTC). The previous governor, Rafael Hernández Colón, had also sought to privatize the PRTC, but widespread discontent had stopped the process. On June 18, 1997, telephone workers went on strike with massive support from different sectors of society. Under the banner of "Puerto Rico no se vende (Puerto Rico Is Not For Sale)," protests took place in San Juan and across the archipelago. Some turned violent. Images of protesters bloodied by police circulated in the national media. There was also a general strike where thousands of people took to the streets to demand a stop to the privatization process. Ultimately, the strike ended on July 21, 1997, with a weakened labor movement and the official privatization of the PRTC.[52]

Two years after the anti-privatization protests, another movement captured the nation's attention. This time it originated in the island-municipality of Vieques. Puerto Rico's two island municipalities, Vieques and Culebra, had been used as training grounds by the U.S. Navy for decades. This, however, did not go unchallenged. In the 1970s, a grassroots effort led by fishermen expelled them from Culebra. Fishermen also led the fight against the United States in Vieques during the same period. But it was not until 1999 that massive national mobilizations began to echo and amplify Vieques's demands.

For decades, residents of Vieques had complained about the U.S. Navy's occupation of the island where they would farm or fish; the occupation also endangered their lives. A study prepared for the secretary of the navy noted that the United States bombed Vieques as part of their exercises approximately 180 days per year. In 1998, they dropped 23,000 bombs—17,000 of them with live munitions—or an average of 80 bombs per day.[53] Historian Marie Cruz Soto has shown that Vieques, an impoverished "community of nine thousand people with limited and unreliable means of transportation to nearby islands," "has suffered from higher morbidity and mortality rates than the rest of the archipelago" due to their inability to access health care.[54] Cancer rates, which some trace to the U.S. Navy's contamination, are higher there than in the rest of the Puerto Rican archipelago.[55]

On April 19, 1999, a U.S. Navy jet misfired a bomb and killed civilian guard David Sanes. Public outcry was immediate. Hundreds of protesters broke into and camped on navy-controlled land. National and international celebrities joined the cause and called for the U.S. government to immediately remove the U.S. Navy from Vieques. On February 21, 2000, approximately 150,000 people took to the streets demanding an immediate exit, the largest march recorded in Puerto Rican history until that point. The struggle continued until 2003, when the U.S. Navy officially left the island.[56]

Social movements proliferated at the end of the twentieth century, yet the government continued its Mano Dura approach even after Rosselló stepped down. Punitive governance, as Marisol LeBrón has demonstrated, continued uninterrupted and became an integral part of subsequent political administrations. The FBI also maintained its punitive approach toward the pro-independence movement.[57]

On September 23, 2005, thousands of Puerto Ricans celebrated the Grito de Lares. Filiberto Ojeda Ríos, the leader of the Macheteros, sent a recorded message from the underground. He had been living clandestinely for decades, evading local and federal authorities. As independentistas listened to his voice through the speakers, the FBI, in collaboration with Governor Rafael Acevedo Vilá's administration, raided Filiberto's house in the western town of Hormigueros where he lived with his life partner, Elma Beatriz Rosado Barbosa. The FBI operation had been surveilling the property for days. At 4:28 p.m., agents began shooting at the house. Fearing for his life, Filiberto responded. In the gunfire, a bullet perforated his lung. Although he could have been taken alive, he was left to bleed to death.[58]

The assassination of Filiberto Ojeda Ríos served as a powerful reminder of how the FBI had operated in Puerto Rico for decades. Thousands of people attended his wake at the Puerto Rican Athenaeum and the Bar Association of Puerto Rico. As they transported his remains to his hometown of Naguabo, Puerto Ricans from different political orientations stood on the side of the road to bid the commander one last farewell.[59]

CHAPTER 12

BROKEN PROMISES AND ONGOING RESISTANCE

At the turn of the twenty-first century, Puerto Rico was trapped in an hourglass and the sand was quickly running out. For decades, the archipelago's economy had depended on foreign investments. Attracting U.S. corporations had been the hallmark of the mid-twentieth-century Operation Bootstrap. When that so-called economic miracle came to an end, Section 936 of the Internal Revenue Code made Puerto Rico a tax haven. In 1996, however, the U.S. Congress began to phase out Section 936; it would officially end on April 30, 2006.

After Governor Rosselló left office, two PPD administrations—those of Sila María Calderón (2001–5) and Aníbal Acevedo Vilá (2005–9)—all but continued the neoliberal policies of the 1990s. No plan was put in place for when 936 ended and no decisions were made about how to address the inevitable exodus of corporations that would come with it. For the pro-statehood movement, the passing of Section 936 had been a victory that made Puerto Rico equal to the states of the union. Bill Clinton presented himself as a strongman who was able to close this "tax loophole." For Puerto Rico, however, the lack of a coherent economic plan after the end of 936 was a fiscal disaster. Over 40 percent of the companies that had benefited from this local tax exemption left the island after 2006, resulting in the loss of 67,800 jobs between 2009 and 2015.[1]

April 30, 2006, arrived, and the Puerto Rican Legislative Assembly was deadlocked. Its members could not agree on Puerto Rico's fiscal budget as Section 936 finally expired. The following day, May 1, 2006, the Puerto Rican government officially shut down for two weeks: 95,762 employees were furloughed, and 1,600 public employees were temporarily dismissed.[2] Beyond the immediate impact, the end of 936 marked the beginning of an economic recession that plagued Puerto Rico for the following decades. It also confirmed what everyone knew and feared. The fiscal collapse of Puerto Rico was not some future event to theorize. It was already happening.

As Puerto Ricans looked with dismay at the unraveling crisis, others took to the streets to protest. May Day or International Workers Day had been celebrated in Puerto Rico since 1899, the year after the U.S. occupation. The event continued to be commemorated with public demonstrations, militant actions, and cultural events throughout the twentieth and twenty-first centuries.[3] On May 1, 2006, labor unions and radical organizations marched through the Milla de Oro, Puerto Rico's financial district. Thousands of people protested the dire fiscal and social situation that seemed to be spiraling out of control. In the crowd, a group of workers, students, musicians, and artists launched a new theater project, Papel Machete. One of its members, Jorge Díaz Ortiz, noted that they were a community-based educational arts program that agitated for social struggle. "Through the use of paper mâché as a medium," argued Díaz Ortiz, "we explore a wide range of art forms and styles. . . . We perform in communities, theaters, streets, and protests using puppets, masks, objects, and music to denounce exploitation, build solidarity, and agitate people to bring them to action in the struggles of the frontline communities of the working class."[4]

Papel Machete used street theater to educate people. They also created giant puppets that would stand tall in the massive protests that began to take place in Puerto Rico. The group was part of a broader culture of resistance that proliferated as the fiscal crisis worsened. In the lead-up to the 2008 elections, Papel Machete launched their own political candidate for the governor's race, Ninguno, which they translated as "NoOne." Its slogan was "Todos prometen, Ninguno cumple" (All of them make promises, NoOne fulfills them). Armed with a paper-mâché head, Ninguno's campaign traveled

FIGURE 12.1. Promotional poster for Ninguno. Courtesy of Papel Machete and AgitArte. Photograph by Michel Collado Toro.

through working-class neighborhoods across the archipelago, accompanied by Papel Machete's cultural offerings.[5]

The 2008 elections left the archipelago's bipartisan tradition intact, however. Governor Acevedo Vilá ran for a second term in office. During his campaign, Acevedo Vilá was charged with twenty-four federal counts of corruption.[6] It came as no surprise that his contender from the PNP, Puerto Rico's Resident Commissioner in Washington Luis G. Fortuño, won the ticket by the biggest margin in the country's electoral history—224,894 votes. It was time for Puerto Rico's *medicina amarga* (bitter pill), as Fortuño referred to his economic program.[7]

Fortuño's Bitter Pill

Luis G. Fortuño ran as a father figure. He was presented as the responsible adult who would fix Puerto Rico's problems. When it came to the economy, he borrowed arguments from other Latin American politicians who embraced neoliberal policies: Puerto Rico needed a dose of medicina amarga.[8] Shortly after taking office, he organized the Consejo Asesor de Reconstrucción Económica y Fiscal (Fiscal and Economic Reconstruction Advising Committee; CAREF). It was composed of bankers and businesspeople, an elite group that operated as Puerto Rico's colonial administrators.[9]

As expected, CAREF recommended an austerity package, including massive layoffs, freezing collective bargaining agreements, and eliminating other workers' rights. U.S. economists had often complained about the labor protections that Puerto Rican workers enjoyed. As a result, Governor Fortuño signed a fiscal emergency law, colloquially known as Public Law 7. It was followed by the layoff of 17,000 government employees. The public sector was the largest employer in the archipelago; Public Law 7 devastated its ranks. Following Rosselló's neoliberal ethos, Fortuño sought to shrink the government through privatization and layoffs.[10]

After the 2008 elections, the PNP dominated the executive branch, the legislature, most townships, and even the Supreme Court. Law 7 was signed without challenge. Fortuño also moved the PNP to the right, aligning himself with the most conservative factions within the U.S. Republican Party. During his administration, Puerto Rico accrued almost $11 billion in debt.[11] If Pedro Rosselló's era is known for consolidating punitive governance, Fortuño perfected the art of governance through austerity.

Even before Public Law 7 went into effect, unemployment had reached 16.1 percent. Criminality grew accordingly. Feuds between drug lords intensified and people were caught in the crossfire, both figuratively and literally. Instead of treating drug addiction as a medical problem, the government continued its punitive measures in response to the crisis. Homelessness reached a staggering 35.1 percent in 2009. As had happened in the past, many Puerto Ricans migrated to the United States in search of better living conditions. From 2004 to 2010, more than 176,000 people left the archipelago in search of jobs.[12]

The U.S. media has coined various economic processes in Puerto Rico "miracles," suggesting there must be something truly divine about Puerto Rico. In U.S. conservative circles, Fortuño's policies were considered a "miracle" and "a godsend to the GOP." His bitter pill consisted of austerity measures that exacerbated an already fragile social crisis and went hand in hand with a worsening fiscal situation. As Puerto Rican economist José Alameda noted, Fortuño's medicine "was so sour that it killed the patient. The reduction in public costs and employments, and the incapacity of public-private alliance to create private investment made the medicine sourer."[13] Instead of jump-starting, the economy contracted from −1.2 percent in 2007 to −3.8 in 2010.[14] Those affected by his measures took to the streets to voice their discontent and make their demands.

Three years after the protests against the government response to the end of 936, May Day was again a scene of resistance. The labor movement used the 2009 May Day celebrations to publicly condemn Law 7 as a direct attack on rights they had obtained through decades of struggle. A protest atmosphere could soon be felt throughout Puerto Rico. Political graffiti and posters adorned urban walls, small and sporadic protests took place in different parts of the archipelago, and some activists carried out acts of civil disobedience. Perhaps the most iconic action was when Roberto García Díaz, a laid-off employee, threw an egg at Governor Fortuño during a press conference. García Díaz became known in cultural and political circles as *tipo común* (common guy). It was not unusual for protest banners and posters to display drawings or messages alluding to the incident.[15]

On October 15, one hundred thousand people united under the banner of "All Puerto Rico for Puerto Rico" to demand that the strictest measures of Law 7 be relaxed.[16] Protesters marched from eight different points in San Juan's urban area and converged in front of Plaza las Américas, the Caribbean's largest shopping mall and a powerful symbol of consumerism. It was also the site where Luis Muñoz Marín had given his famous speech after returning from exile in 1972. According to Puerto Rican scholar Arlene Dávila, "The selection of Plaza las Américas as the gathering point showcased a key predicament of neoliberalism: that if there are no jobs, there can't be shopping."[17]

The massive demonstration was to converge in front of Plaza las Américas and adjourn after a series of speeches by various members of different social and activist organizations. But people were angry and desperate. The protest soon involved more than simply condemning Law 7. University students promised to challenge the Fortuño administration if he proceeded with slashing the UPR's already dire budget, and a group of students and members of radical organizations occupied Highway 52, one of San Juan's main expressways.[18]

The protesters first clashed with commuters demanding to pass. The demonstrators explained that they needed to stop traffic to rebuild Puerto Rico. After a few hours, the police and march organizers tried to convince those occupying the highway to leave. But protesters started burning tires and constructing makeshift barricades to protect themselves from the highly militarized police force that grew by the minute. When it seemed that a violent clash was inevitable, Rafael Cancel Miranda, a former political prisoner who had attacked the U.S. Congress in 1954, arrived on the scene. He had been at home when he saw images of the highway occupation on the local news. Cancel Miranda tried to dissuade protesters from continuing their standoff with the police. It was going to be a bloodbath, he argued. If students and protesters had weapons, he would join them in fighting the police. But that was not the case. They were outnumbered and outgunned. As someone with a lifelong record of militancy, Cancel Miranda struck a chord with protesters. They organized an impromptu assembly on the occupied highway and democratically decided to march back to the UPR. The October 15 demonstrations were a prelude to a massive university strike that took place barely six months later.[19]

To assess the national situation and how it impacted the university, the UPR's General Study Assembly of the Río Piedras campus created Comités de Acción based on the university's colleges: Humanities, Social Sciences, Natural Sciences, Education, and the School of Law. These Comités de Acción organized a series of protests and short-lived strikes. In the process, they laid the groundwork for a system-wide strike. When the UPR announced that it planned to eliminate admission-fee exemptions and was looking to impose an $800 increase in tuition to address the government's austerity measures, students called for a General Assembly on April 13, 2010. They decreed a forty-eight-hour work stoppage that became a massive strike, shutting down ten of the eleven UPR campuses.[20]

The UPR strike occurred in two phases. The first consisted of the student occupation of campuses for more than two months, from April to June 2010. They accomplished their objectives: the administration froze the proposed elimination of fee exemptions and the $800 increase. The second phase took place the following semester as the UPR sought to reimplement the increase again, and students responded with another strike in spring 2011. While students had occupied the campuses during the initial phase of the strike, by the second phase, the police and university administration reacted by taking out the gates of the university and inviting the Puerto Rican police to enter the campus, something that had not happened since the strikes of the 1970s and 1980s.

From 2010 to 2011, UPR students were on strike intermittently for almost a full academic year, redefining the way people protested in Puerto Rico. During the occupation of the campuses, students created horizontal forms of organizing. They also planted communal gardens to feed themselves, organized cultural events, and even created a pirate radio station, Radio Huelga, which was broadcast outside the university gates. Instead of following the traditional modes of protest, students relied on direct action, democratic assemblies, and occupations. This process radicalized a generation of activists who felt empowered by creating street art, barricades, and lifelong friendships. These experiences served as a catalyst for many who continued their grassroots activism after graduating. Others honed their political skills and later served in government positions.

Death Spiral

When Fortuño announced his reelection bid, it was clear that most Puerto Ricans were unhappy with his economic policies. Without a clear political program or fiscal plan, the PPD's candidate, Alejandro García Padilla, relied on that discontent to rally votes that could "punish" the PNP and Fortuño for his actions. García Padilla won the 2012 elections. But he did not deviate from the privatization measures that were integral to the Fortuño administration.

In fact, one of García Padilla's first acts was to privatize the Luis Muñoz Marín Airport. While the news was received with a wave of social protests, the privatization process continued and was consolidated in 2013.[21] To cope with the fiscal situation in the archipelago, Governor García Padilla's administration successfully passed Act 66. While it did not entail the elimination of public jobs, it did hamper the bargaining power of unions and employees from the private sector. The law effectively froze wages while eliminating previously negotiated increases. It also reduced public employees' benefits, including vacations, promotions, and bonuses.[22]

In February 2014, the credit-rating agency Standard and Poor's downgraded Puerto Rico's bonds to junk status. Most owners of these bonds remain anonymous despite demands for transparency from journalists, civic society, and the Puerto Rican government. Instead of scaring investors away, a month after Puerto Rico's credit was downgraded, a total of $3.4 billion in new bonds were sold, mainly to hedge funds. Why Puerto Rico's bonds were attractive to hedge funds goes back to the early days of U.S. colonialism. The Jones-Shafroth Act of 1917 not only granted Puerto Ricans their citizenship, it also made Puerto Rican bonds triple-tax exempt, meaning they would not be taxed at the municipal, state, or federal level. The Puerto Rican Constitution of 1952 made repayment of public debt a priority over the finance of public services. Then, in 1984, Congress explicitly excluded Puerto Rico from Chapter 9 of the U.S. Bankruptcy Code, hampering any possibility of refinancing its debt. This meant that as Puerto Rico's bonds were downgraded to junk status and their prices plummeted, vulture funds bought them knowing that Puerto Rico would be forced to pay them back.[23]

The fiscal situation triggered a series of difficult conversations about Puerto Rico and its colonial condition. Major media outlets noted that it was going to be the largest bankruptcy in U.S. history. Like other states, Puerto Rico could not claim bankruptcy exemptions. Unlike states, however, Puerto Rican corporations or municipalities could not file for bankruptcy. This had not always been the case, but Puerto Rico had this right mysteriously revoked in the early 1980s. By 2014, the debt had reached unprecedented levels. The commonwealth owed $72 billion with another $42 billion owed to pensions. The economic situation only exacerbated social problems, creating a humanitarian crisis. The median household income was $19,518, one-third of that of the United States. About 46 percent of the population lived below the federal poverty level, with 57 percent of children living in poverty.[24]

On June 29, 2015, Governor García Padilla delivered a national message to the people of Puerto Rico. For journalist Ed Morales, García Padilla's speech was perhaps the second most important message delivered by a Puerto Rican statesman since Luis Muñoz Marín's 1952 proclamation of the commonwealth. García Padilla said what everyone already knew. The debt was unpayable. Puerto Rico did not have access to a bankruptcy court, and it did not have access to international financing institutions like the International Monetary Fund or the World Bank. Describing the situation as a death spiral, García Padilla declared that the Puerto Rican government could not continue paying the debt.[25]

News of Puerto Rico's situation spread, and Washington addressed it the following year. A bailout was out of the question, more so in an election year. Instead of proposing an audit to explore the reasons for the debt and to also verify its legality—many activists and professionals noted that most of the debt might have been illegally accrued—the Obama administration opted to create a fiscal oversight board.

In a tense atmosphere of negotiations between Republicans and Democrats, high-profile individuals used their platforms to lobby for the PROMESA bill. Playwright Lin-Manuel Miranda, whose family is part of the New York Democratic establishment, rapped on *Last Week Tonight with John Oliver* about the need to help Puerto Rico, even offering Democrats tickets to his award-winning Broadway show *Hamilton*.[26] On June 30, 2016, President Barack Obama signed the PROMESA bill into law. As political theorist Francisco Fortuño Bernier notes, with PROMESA, "a Republican-conceived bill that garnered Hillary Clinton's support and Barack Obama's signature, any veneer of autonomy in Puerto Rico has been stripped from the islands' relation to the United States and financial capital: Puerto Rico has reverted from the self-managed colonialism inaugurated by the commonwealth in 1952 to a reconstructed direct colonialism articulated in a specifically neoliberal way."[27]

The signing of the PROMESA bill took place just weeks after the Supreme Court once again ratified Puerto Rico's colonial status in *Puerto Rico v. Sánchez Valle*. The case was heard after two individuals, Luis M. Sánchez and Gómez Vázquez, were prosecuted on gun charges in both federal and local courts. While they pleaded guilty at the federal level, they argued that they could not be tried in the local courts. The case made it all the way to the Supreme Court, which ended up agreeing with them by a vote of 6–2. By not allowing the Puerto Rican courts to litigate the case separately, the decision shattered any lingering illusion of Puerto Rico's sovereignty.[28]

The PROMESA law created Puerto Rico's Fiscal Oversight and Management Board. Composed of seven unelected members directly named by the president of the United States, the board also has five unelected officers. Colloquially known by Puerto Ricans as La Junta, the board's objective is to guarantee the repayment of the commonwealth's debt and to "provide a method for a covered territory to achieve fiscal responsibility and access to the capital markets," as established in Title I of the bill.[29] To conduct its business, the Junta was given ample power and allowed to operate independently of the Puerto Rican legislative and executive branches. In May 2023, the U.S. Supreme Court ruled that the Junta had "sovereign immunity" and does not need to comply with requests from journalists for documents about the board's operations—even when those requests stemmed from a provision in the Puerto Rican Constitution.[30]

Given its mandate, the Junta did not arrive in Puerto Rico seeking to strike a balance between social and fiscal needs. It proposed a series of austerity measures that impacted every part of Puerto Rican society. Junta-approved fiscal budgets slashed funds for public services. The health department, for example, received a massive cut at a moment when the country was dealing with a failing hospital infrastructure and a health epidemic due to the spread of Zika, chikungunya, and dengue, all tied to the *Aedes aegypti* mosquito. This was happening as doctors and nurses left the island en masse looking for better job opportunities in the United States. As feminist scholar Marisol LeBrón notes, "The debt crisis, of course, didn't create all these problems, but it has deepened them."[31]

The Junta proposed budget cuts as protests intensified. When the Junta organized their First PROMESA Conference in August 2016, dozens of demonstrators and activists from different organizations blocked the Condado Plaza Hilton where the event was to take place. Some activists arrived at five in the morning. For hours, the police tried to disperse the crowd using force and pepper spray. As people saw what was happening on TV, more protestors showed up. The event was so successful that the conference attendees needed to be escorted to the seaside hotel by boat because protesters had blocked all the main entrances.[32]

The Junta began its work just as another election cycle took place. Ricardo Rosselló, son of former governor Pedro Rosselló, won the governorship for the PNP in 2016. He won the ballot box with only 42 percent of the vote, the lowest number in Puerto Rico's electoral history. Ricky Rosselló, as he was colloquially known, received his BA from the Massachusetts Institute of Technology and a PhD in biomedical engineering from the University of Michigan. He was the second youngest governor elected to office. In 2014, Bolivian author Lupe Andrade accused him of plagiarizing one of his concepts for a newspaper column.[33] He spent some time as an assistant professor at the Universidad Ana G. Méndez, which has ties to the PNP, and later at the UPR's medical school. Some people questioned his credentials and cried favoritism.[34]

Following in his predecessors' footsteps, Ricardo Rosselló's first executive order was to declare a fiscal emergency in Puerto Rico, allowing the government to promote and pass unpopular legislation. The labor movement became a target of both the Junta and the Rosselló administration. An article published in the *Economist* in April 2018 noted that "Puerto Ricans enjoy among the most generous protection of any American worker, including mandatory holidays and severance pay." What the article failed to mention, however, was that Puerto Rican workers were paid a third of what U.S. workers earned. The Junta echoed the sentiments against labor when it stated that Puerto Rican benefits were "far beyond those required by any mainland state."[35]

On February 5, 2018, the Junta sent a letter to Rosselló emphasizing the need to offset labor costs because such costs made Puerto Rico noncompetitive. The following month the Rosselló administration announced their plan to repeal Act 80, which provided protections against arbitrary dismissals and benefits to those unjustly fired. While the announcement was seen as a victory for the Junta, the backlash from different social sectors and members of his own party was immediate. Eight days after his declaration, Rosselló changed his attitude toward repealing the labor legislation, saying that the Junta had pressured him to repeal the act.[36]

Education was also gravely impacted by the policies enacted by the Rosselló administration with the Junta's approval. Rosselló appointed Julia Keleher to head Puerto Rico's Department of Education. The Junta had noted that the government needed to save at least $40 million every month. Part of their recommendations included closing almost three hundred schools. The closing of schools was not new; as social justice education scholar Aurora Santiago Ortiz has noted, the Puerto Rican government closed sixty-three schools from 2015 to 2016, citing low enrollment due in part to migration.[37]

Parents, students, and a large swath of the population opposed the school closings. Keleher responded to the critiques in a *New York Times* interview by saying, "We have to close schools. We are going to close schools."[38] In May 2017, Keleher announced the closing of 165 schools. The following year, she added another 263 schools. The social impact was immediately felt in poor and working-class communities that suffered the most.[39] Keleher's policies also opened the door to the privatization of the public school system.

The UPR again became a target. Governor Rosselló proposed cutting the university's already precarious annual budget by $300 million for the 2017–18 academic year. Responding to the announcement, the Junta noted, "The Board is supportive of the Governor's difficult decision to reduce subsidies to the University of Puerto Rico by $300 million in FY19. The magnitude of the Government's structural deficit, however, requires that this reduction in annual subsidy grow to a minimum of $450 million by FY21."[40] This was almost half of the UPR's entire budget.[41] The student body found this unacceptable. They feared that such cuts would effectively kill the university.

On March 21, 2017, the UPR's Río Piedras campus was again shut down by students on strike. Two weeks later, on April 5, ten thousand students from the UPR's thirteen campuses met in San Juan for a General Assembly. Some of their chants showcased their combative yet joyful spirits: "Si en vez de vino, bebieran malta, estos recortes no harían falta" (If instead of wine, they drank malta, these cuts would not be necessary).[42]

Eleven of the thirteen campuses declared a strike with six demands: no penalties for students participating in the strike, reforms to allow representation from all sectors of the university community, zero tuition hikes or elimination of enrollment exemptions, zero budget cuts to the UPR, the restitution of a civic commission to audit the Puerto Rican debt, and a moratorium on debt payments before and during the auditing process.[43]

Strikes were nothing new at the UPR. But unlike previous strikes, students' call to audit the debt was a political demand that transcended the university gates and forced the government to challenge the Junta.[44] After seventy-two days, all campuses lifted the strike. Eleven students faced criminal charges but these were eventually dropped.[45] While the

UPR did not meet striking students' demands, some participants argued that the best outcome was the strike itself as it radicalized a new generation of students, as had happened in 2010. During the strike, students also gave serious thought to the debt and the proposed cuts to the UPR. They developed alternative fiscal plans that were delivered to the Puerto Rican legislature and were ultimately ignored.[46]

As had happened in the past, May Day celebrations became a boiling point. The 2017 celebration was the first May Day since the Junta's creation. On that day, protests began early in the morning. The Afrofeminist group Colectiva Feminista en Construcción began an unexpected *cacerolazo* at 5:00 a.m. in front of the governor's mansion. They were attacked and dispersed by the police. Meanwhile, another group, Jornada Se Acabaron Las Promesas, obstructed the entrance to the Luis Muñoz Marín Airport, while other groups blocked congested city roads, making their anger felt throughout San Juan's urban landscape.[47] All these actions took place before the official labor-sponsored celebrations began.

Those participating in this May Day did not come from the traditional worlds of labor. New organizations composed of students, queer folks, and non-unionized, precarious workers took center stage. As one of their slogans declared, they'd had everything taken away from them, even fear. As the groups marched through Puerto Rico's financial district, protesters began throwing objects at banks, shattering several glass walls. This triggered police intervention and led to the arrest of seventeen. One of them, Nina Droz, served a thirty-seven-month sentence in a federal prison on charges of arson. She was accused of trying to set fire to a building owned by Puerto Rico's Banco Popular. José Carrión III, the Junta's chairman, is related to Richard Carrión, the bank's owner.[48]

The May Day events demonstrated that a collective rage was brewing in Puerto Rico. Protesters understood the symbolic power of the buildings they threw rocks at; to them, these banks were robbing people of their future. The protests concerned the Puerto Rican government greatly. But any tensions between protesters, the government, and the Junta came to a halt four months later when Hurricane María barreled through Puerto Rico.

FIGURE 13.1. "Huracán," by Cristián Guzmán Cardona. Courtesy of Cristián Guzmán Cardona.

CHAPTER 13

THE NIGHT EVERYTHING
WENT SILENT

I called my seventy-eight-year-old grandmother late in the afternoon on September 19, 2017. Her voice sounded calm. She assured me that she was safe. In a matter of hours Puerto Rico would feel the wrath of a category 5 hurricane, barely weeks after Hurricane Irma had barreled through the Caribbean. While Irma did not directly impact Puerto Rico, it demonstrated that the archipelago was not ready for a massive storm. Irma alone caused $700 million in damages and four deaths and left one million people without electricity.[1]

Most houses in Puerto Rico are built with cement, precisely because of our long history with storms and hurricanes. My grandmother's house, however, was made of wood. It was not the same house I grew up in—that one was also made of wood and had burned down in an electrical fire. While it might have been beautiful, the building material marked my grandmother's working-class status.

"I love you. Don't worry about me, everything will be okay." Those were her last words before hanging up the phone. That night the winds howled, haunting everyone's sleep, but Puerto Rico itself seemed to go silent. Hurricane María made landfall the next morning. "That noise," she later recalled. "I will never forget the hurricane's noise; it sounded like the devil was howling."

I would not hear anything from her for days. I was one of thousands of people from *allá 'fuera* desperately waiting for any news. Phone communication was impossible. There was no internet. On social media, someone recommended a phone app that resembled a radio scanner. People organized dozens of channels trying to search for loved ones. It seemed as if there was a channel for each of the seventy-eight municipalities in Puerto Rico. I quickly joined the Aguadilla channel only to find that everyone on it was in the United States. Like me, they were desperate for news.

Several days after the hurricane, I received a call from one of my abuela's neighbors and a dear family friend. "Your abuela is fine. I don't have much time. I found cell phone reception and I have a list of people that I need to call to let them know their family members are well. But she's fine. Her house is fine." I cried with relief. I cried with guilt. Guilt for having electricity and potable water. I cried because I had lived through other hurricanes in the archipelago and had spent months without essential services. I cried because I knew that there were no recent precedents for what had just happened in Puerto Rico. I still cry; I cry as I write these words.

As a result of Hurricanes Irma and María, the island of Barbuda was left uninhabitable. Dominica resembled a war zone. And while the government failed to admit it, experts estimated Puerto Rico's death toll to be in the thousands. Some people had to bury their loved ones in their backyards because their houses were effectively cut off after bridges collapsed and landslides covered what once were roads. Hurricane María left the people of Puerto Rico without electricity and potable water for months on end; it hit an island already suffering a stagnating economy and deep social crises.

The storm did not stop the following day. Its aftermath continued with great might and fury, taking the lives of thousands of people. Its effects continued because of Puerto Rico's failing infrastructure and, as we know now, colonial neglect.

The Storm

I could write a detailed narrative about the suffering that people went through that night. There are thousands of stories of people struggling for their lives, thousands of stories of people who failed in that struggle. I will refrain from doing so, however. The wounds from those stories are still raw, as if the hurricane never left the archipelago. And including those stories for the sake of advancing this book's narrative could end up perpetuating violence, trauma, and pain, as historian and literary scholar Saidiya Hartman has powerfully demonstrated in her work.[2]

Puerto Ricans have been dealing with hurricanes for centuries. Indigenous communities adapted to them. They harvested tubers like yuca and yams. They identified caverns to hide in during storms, which they tended to predict according to weather patterns. One of their deities was also named Jurakán—some scholars have argued that the word "hurricane" comes from this term.[3] Colonial governments, from both Spain and later the United States, also came to terms with hurricanes. The first challenge that the U.S. occupation faced in Puerto Rico was not resistance or insurrection but the fury of San Ciriaco, a category 4 hurricane in 1899 that left 3,370 people dead and caused millions in damages.[4]

Puerto Rico was hit by six major hurricanes during the twentieth century alone.[5] Álvarez Guedes, a Cuban comedian, has commented on how hurricanes have become ingrained in Puerto Rican culture. In one of his jokes, he notes that he was visiting San Juan before a major hurricane. Everyone was joyful in the streets and the stores had sold out of alcohol. That time the island got lucky, and the hurricane changed its course. The next day, however, Guedes noted that there was a depressive aura around San Juan. The mayor came on TV and said, "Do not lose the faith, we might have better luck the next time around."[6]

There's a hidden truth behind Guedes's story. Hurricanes have been imagined as a time when people come together and obligations are suspended. As Puerto Rican scholar Aurora Santiago Ortiz has argued, "As a child, I romanticized hurricanes, remembering nights playing dominoes, listening to the radio, telling ghost stories."[7] When people learned that a hurricane was on the way, they began their ritual of flocking to supermarkets and gas stations, nailing wooden panels to their windows, and praying to their deity of choice. But as many survivors noted, nothing prepared them for María.

On the night of September 19, 2017, Puerto Ricans braced them-selves for a category 5 hurricane with sustained winds of 175 miles per hour. After wreaking havoc on the island of Barbuda, its winds slowed to 155 mph. María had become a category 4 hurricane by the time it made landfall in the town of Yabucoa the following day at 6:15 a.m. For hours, the people of Puerto Rico submitted to its merciless wrath. Over forty inches of rain were reported in parts of the island, and the winds seemed to destroy everything in their path. Zinc roofs that protected poor and working-class families flew away and danced in the air.

For some, disasters like Hurricane María can be regarded as great equalizers. Natural events do not care about class, race, or gender. While this might be true, disasters are not natural. They are natural events that cause human-made disasters. Poor and working-class communities, which in Puerto Rico are also often predominantly Black and Brown, live in high-risk spaces with much greater chances of experiencing flooding, landslides, and other calamities. Their humble houses are often made of materials that cannot withstand such winds. While shel-ters are often provided by municipal governments, many return to their homes only to see what little they had accrued throughout their life destroyed in the blink of an eye. Again, there are many Puerto Ricos. And, depending on which Puerto Rico they inhabited, people experi-enced Hurricane María differently.[8]

Thousands of buildings were damaged by María, bridges collapsed, and hundreds of people went missing in the floods that swept through the archipelago. In the town of Yabucoa, located in the main island's eastern region, 99 percent of the municipal buildings collapsed.[9] A re-port from the RAND Corporation painted a dire picture: 100 percent of the power grid, 95 percent of cellular sites, and 43 percent of waste-water treatment plants were inoperable. There were more than 40,000 landslides and more than 97 percent of Puerto Rico's roads were impass-able. This created a health crisis as more than 95 percent of the popula-tion lacked drinking water for weeks and 28 percent of state-run health centers that receive federal funds were damaged.[10] It took the central government several days before they could communicate with all of Puerto Rico's seventy-eight municipalities.

María wasn't the only reason behind such devastation. Puerto Rico's infrastructure had been vulnerable for decades. Power outages had become part of everyday life. Puerto Ricans drank contaminated water on an almost daily basis. A report from the Natural Resources Defense Council noted that in 2015, "99.5 percent of Puerto Rico's population was served by community water systems in violation of the Safe Drinking Water Act [SDWA], and 66.4 percent of the people of the island[s] were served by water sources that violated SDWA's health standards." The situation was so dire that from 2005 to 2015, Puerto Rico had "a total of 33,842 violations to the Safe Drinking Water Act, including violations of health-based standards, monitoring violations, and reporting violations."[11]

In the southern town of Guayama, Applied Energy Services (AES), a multinational corporation based out of Arlington, Virginia, produced about 800 tons of coal ash daily. It began operations in 2002 and for almost two decades dumped ash into a toxic waste site more than twelve stories tall. A study by the UPR noted that chronic illnesses like cancer and respiratory problems had doubled between 2016 and 2018 in Guayama. Ignoring residents, activists, and even the Puerto Rican government, AES did not cover the ashes before Hurricane María. They relocated them next to an aquifer that supplied potable water to a large part of the archipelago's main island.[12] As local activists in Guayama had made clear, the state's neglect and AES's greed did not take into consideration the health of nearby residents.

The fiscal crisis and austerity measures imposed by several administrations had also heavily impacted public services, including health-care provision. When the storm hit, these conditions exacerbated its impact. The government originally noted that the hurricane had only resulted in sixteen deaths. But given Puerto Rico's conditions before the storm, everyone knew those numbers were false. María's death toll did not stop when the storm left the archipelago. Infrastructural collapse, colonial neglect from the U.S. government, and mishandling by local officials caused the deaths of thousands of people.

After the Storm

"This room is full of love. You can feel the love," uttered President Donald J. Trump as he entered a church full of desperate Puerto Ricans. Most of them had been displaced by María's wrath. Some had been transported from different shelters in the San Juan area. It was a staged event for a few photographs; Trump sported a rain jacket. Some Puerto Ricans had not had electricity for almost a year. Trump spent less than five hours in the archipelago.[13]

This event became a powerful symbol that ignited rage across the archipelago and the Puerto Rican diaspora. Trump's visit took place shortly after a press conference that included the president, First Lady Melania Trump, Governor Ricardo Rosselló, and Puerto Rico's first lady, Beatriz Rosselló. As Trump spoke to the cameras, the Puerto Rican governor took selfies in the background. "This governor did not play politics," noted Trump. "He didn't play it at all. He was saying it like it was, and he was giving us the highest grades. And I want to—on behalf of our country, I want to thank you."[14]

Trump noted, "Now, I hate to tell you, Puerto Rico, but you've thrown our budget a little out of whack because we've spent a lot of money on Puerto Rico, and that's fine. We've saved a lot of lives." He went on to argue that Katrina had been a real catastrophe with "tremendous hundreds and hundreds and hundreds of people that died." "What happened here," he noted, "was just totally overpowering. . . . What is your death count as of this moment—17?" The governor replied, "Sixteen certified." The president touted, "Sixteen people versus in the thousands. You can be very proud of all of your people, all of our people working together." The reality, however, was very different. The official figure was wrong. Thousands of people died because of María and its aftermath.

Shortly after the hurricane, people began reporting deaths that had not been included in the official count. It seemed like everyone knew someone who had lost a loved one in the storm. By November 2017, the government had declared fifty-five deaths. The Centro de Periodismo Investigativo published a report on November 16 noting they had discovered at least forty-four previously unreported deaths.[15] That number is now in the hundreds. Ten months after the hurricane, there were more than three hundred unidentified bodies stored in air-conditioned containers at Puerto Rico's Forensic Science Institute.[16]

The mounting pressure for accountability pushed the Puerto Rican government in February 2018 to request an external report from the University of Puerto Rico and George Washington University about María-related deaths.[17] Another study led by the Universidad Carlos Albizu in San Juan and an institution in Cambridge, Massachusetts, took place simultaneously. Their results were published on July 12, 2018, in the *New England Journal of Medicine*. They concluded that "the number of excess deaths related to Hurricane María in Puerto Rico is more than 70 times the official estimate." They surveyed 3,299 randomly chosen households across Puerto Rico and estimated a mortality rate of 14.3 deaths per 1,000 persons from September 20 to December 31, 2017. They concluded, "Our estimate of 4,645 excess deaths . . . is likely to be conservative since subsequent adjustments for survivor bias and household-size increase this estimate to more than 5,000."[18] The number 4,645 became a recurrent theme in the protests that took place the following months.

For the Trump administration, the low number of originally reported deaths was a good story. U.S. media outlets also picked up the story but highlighted how federal incompetency was creating a humanitarian crisis. Journalists flocked to Puerto Rico looking for stories. In the process, Puerto Ricans were portrayed as hopeless and in need of saving. In the immediate aftermath, people desperately sought to leave the island and arrived at the Luis Muñoz Marín Airport in droves trying to find flights at an inoperative airport. The way this event was covered in the media, anthropologist Hilda Lloréns has argued, reproduced several stereotypes about what she calls "the disastrous tropics." "Imagery from the disastrous tropics," notes Llorens, "quintessentially depicts individuals, groups, and crowds who look variously stunned, bewildered, dejected, destitute, traumatized, unfit, ill, disabled, dying, or dead."[19]

The idea that Puerto Ricans needed to be saved from the "disastrous tropics" and themselves was accompanied by a justification. Puerto

Ricans are U.S. citizens. The federal government had an obligation to help, not because of their humanity but because of their citizenship status. This created what filmmaker, writer, and scholar Frances Negrón-Muntaner has called "rhetorical citizenship." U.S. journalists, corporations, and citizens began arguing about the need to help "the 3.5 million American citizens of Puerto Rico." Even Moe, the bartender from *The Simpsons*, raised funds to help Puerto Rico.[20] This rhetorical citizenship obscures three things, according to Negrón Muntaner. It does not recognize the U.S. occupation of Puerto Rico as an act of colonialism. It also ignores the intimate ties between colonialism and racism for "citizenship has never offered full protection for racialized, colonial, and otherwise minoritized legal citizens in the United States." Lastly, it fails to accept "colonial responsibility or shared humanity."[21]

While Puerto Ricans were portrayed as U.S. citizens, the federal government did not respond to María's destruction the same way it did to hurricanes in Florida and Texas. A study conducted by *BMJ Global Health* concluded that there had been "a marked disparity in the time it took victims of Hurricane Maria [*sic*] in Puerto Rico to receive assistance as opposed to the US mainland."[22] When the mayor of San Juan claimed on U.S. national television that Puerto Ricans were dying, Donald Trump began an online feud. Addressing Mayor Yulín "and others," Trump tweeted: "They want everything done for themselves when it should be a community effort."[23] What he failed to recognize, or willfully ignored, was the fact that without the rapid response of communities working in solidarity with one another, the death toll would have been much higher.

Community as Survival

After María, many Puerto Ricans felt that they were living in a stateless country. For those inland, government relief, local or federal, took weeks to arrive. In the town of San Sebastián, retired workers from the Puerto Rico Electric Power Authority (PREPA) reconnected the service for their communities. Impromptu neighborhood brigades began clearing roadways. And communities without power gathered all they had left in their fridges to prepare collective meals. When food did arrive from FEMA, it was without any nutritional value. A study by George Washington University noted that the food sent to Puerto Rico after María did not meet federal dietary standards.[24]

In the wake of the storm, volunteer-run centers of mutual aid known as CAMs (Centros de Apoyo Mutuo) began to appear throughout the archipelago. In their study of these CAMs, sociologists Jacqueline Villarrubia-Mendoza and Roberto Vélez-Vélez found that the experience with Hurricane Irma had already initiated conversations about what could happen in a major catastrophe. The first CAM opened its doors in the eastern town of Caguas nine days after María. While it emerged in the post-storm context, its members had been part of grassroots projects around food justice since the 2010 UPR strike.[25]

Shortly after they appeared in Caguas, fourteen additional CAMs began operating in different parts of the archipelago, including the island-municipality of Vieques. Villarrubia-Mendoza and Vélez-Vélez note that the majority opened in the inland municipalities that had been most affected and were also most neglected by the state. Each CAM had goals based on the community's needs. While autonomous, there were also efforts to bring the CAMs together in national dialogues to share strategies and actions. Their programs were organized around themes like agriculture, nutrition, culture, economy, education, geriatrics, health, sustainability, reconstruction, and housing.[26]

In Las Carolinas, a neighborhood in the municipality of Caguas, anthropologist Sarah Molinari noted that "residents went without water service for three months, without electricity for seven months, and without storm municipal debris pickup for eighty days."[27] To make things more complicated, "sixty to seventy percent of the community's twenty-five hundred residents are over fifty-five years old, and one in three households lives under the poverty level." Las Carolinas was a woman-led CAM occupying a school that had been closed in pre-María austerity measures. While FEMA officials complained about a supposed culture of "wanting everything to get done for them," the Las Carolinas CAM offered one hundred lunches three times a week to elderly and bedridden residents while also providing company and support.[28] In the words of Molinari, the Las Carolinas CAM created "a space of healing, care work, and learning that has shifted in response to the community's needs from the emergency to longer-term recovery and local transformation."[29]

Other spaces were also transformed by community needs. Before the storm, El Local was a dive bar in Santurce where multiple underground scenes met to dance, sing karaoke, or listen to local punk bands. The space began as an anarchist public library and events space but turned into a node in San Juan's underground nightlife.[30] In the wake of the storm, El Local reopened its doors with another purpose. Bands took the stage but, lacking power, they played acoustic sets during the day to take advantage of the sunlight. They also opened La Cocina Huracanada, a space to share meals, resources, basic support, information, and knowledge.[31] Armed with a commercial gas stove and a host of volunteers, La Cocina Huracanada prepared meals for anyone who needed them.[32]

Professional organizations also mobilized their resources to help communities in need. Social psychologist Blanca Ortiz-Torres noted that a month after the emergency, she was part of an initiative organized by the Puerto Rican College of Physicians and Surgeons. They organized ten groups "composed by physicians of several specialties (e.g., pediatricians, family MDs, endocrinologists), nurses, and at least one behavioral health professional, which could include psychologists, counsellors, or social workers." After meeting with residents of the Valle Hill community—a poor neighborhood in the northeastern region heavily impacted by the hurricane—Ortiz-Torres initiated an eight-month collaboration. Their intervention was intended to empower community members to organize autonomously and gain access to essential services.[33]

These efforts demonstrate that in the absence of relief from the state, communities relied on themselves to survive. Some media outlets began circulating tropes of resilience. The hashtag #PuertoRicoSeLevanta was also used. But focusing on resilience ignores the fact that people who had suffered multiple traumas were doing what they needed to survive. Celebrating resilience shifted blame away from the state and toward the individual. For many, María painfully revealed that the U.S. government continued to view Puerto Ricans as second-class citizens at best, lazy and in need of saving at worst.

The storm's impact laid bare Puerto Rico's frail infrastructure caused by decades of social, political, and fiscal crises. It also demonstrated the colonial reality of the archipelago. María was not a singular event. It was part of broader processes that preceded it and continue long after its winds have passed.

CHAPTER 14

THE STORM AFTER MARÍA

Many people died in the aftermath of Hurricane María because they lacked basic necessities like water. A few days after the storm, the mayor of Rincón sent a desperate message to the central government via satellite phone asking for water as residents were "being driven to despair" in a municipality that looked "as if a nuclear bomb" had been dropped on it.[1] Lack of access to potable water led to a rise in cases of leptospirosis, a bacterial disease transmitted through infected animals' urine.[2] Without electricity, water-pumping stations could not operate and the archipelago suffered massive flooding, leaving Puerto Ricans to drink from contaminated waterways.[3] Five days after the hurricane made landfall, a picture from the eastern town of Humacao went viral. In an act of desperation, its residents had painted on a street "S.O.S. We Need Water/Food" for passing helicopters.[4]

In August 2017, a month before the hurricane, FEMA admitted to having lost a truck full of water.[5] It was not the first time, and it wouldn't be the last. On September 11, 2018, almost a year after María made landfall in Puerto Rico, an amateur photographer flew a drone over an abandoned military airport in the eastern town of Ceiba. The pictures he took sparked public outrage. There were 20,000 pallets laden with unopened water bottles. In total, about 1,440,000 bottles had been left to spoil in the sun. FEMA blamed the local Puerto Rican government, who then blamed the U.S. federal government. The following year, in July 2019, another shipment of thousands of water bottles was found unused in an empty lot in the town of Dorado.[6]

Whether these were cases of corruption or mishandling of supplies, many Puerto Ricans were incensed. As reports confirmed that deaths numbered in the thousands and not dozens as the government had initially claimed, the huge quantities of water bottles triggered conversations about how many lives could have been saved if not for local and federal neglect. The number provided by the Universidad Carlos Albizu report—4,645—began gracing protest banners and posters, and it was spray-painted throughout San Juan.

Immediately after the hurricane, the Puerto Rican global diaspora came together to seek ways to help those in the archipelago. The diaspora's response once again highlighted the idea of the nation as unbound from a fixed location. Puerto Ricans around the world organized to send funds, food, and medical supplies.[7] Millions of dollars were raised to help rebuild Puerto Rico. The question then became how to best deliver money and supplies. The Puerto Rican first lady, Beatriz Rosselló, created a nonprofit organization called Unidos Por Puerto Rico. The organization received more than $41.1 million from private individuals and corporations. Many did not trust the Rosselló administration and decided to use other organizations like the María Fund, which served as an umbrella for grassroots groups.[8]

Intuitive distrust in the government proved to be well placed. On August 10, 2018, Radio Isla 1320, a local radio station, posted a video on their Facebook page showing twelve containers full of supplies originally received through Unidos Por Puerto Rico on the premises of Puerto Rico's Electoral Commission. The video revealed desperately needed first-aid supplies covered in animal feces. The National Guard who oversaw their distribution said some had arrived already expired.[9] The FBI later launched an investigation into Unidos Por Puerto Rico.[10]

A few weeks before the media found the containers, Ricardo Rosselló fired Puerto Rico's secretary of the treasury, Raúl Maldonado Gautier. Before being fired, the secretary had publicly compared the Rosselló administration to an "institutionalized mafia."[11] Angered by his father's dismissal, Raúl Maldonado Nieves wrote a series of incendiary Facebook posts that led him to be interviewed on public radio.[12] What he said was shocking. According to Maldonado Nieves, his father had been fired for investigating Beatriz Rosselló's involvement with the Electoral Commission containers. He went even further, arguing that Ricardo Rosselló, in collaboration with the tax consulting firm BDO-Puerto Rico, had altered a report regarding the management of supplies to benefit his wife.[13] Instead of distributing supplies, argued Maldonado Nieves, Rosselló wanted "to make news out of them."[14]

Beatriz Rosselló responded that the allegations made against her and her husband were false. But instead of dealing with the political fallout, the governor and his family left the country for a European vacation. While Rosselló traveled, several members of his administration were arrested. Federal agencies began an investigation of ASES (Administración de Seguros de Salud de Puerto Rico), the administration of health plans, which eventually led to the resignation and later arrest of Ángela Ávila Marrero. Perhaps more explosive was the news that Secretary of Education Julia Keleher—who had closed hundreds of schools—had also been arrested.[15] Two others close to the administration, Fernando Scherrer Caillet from the tax firm BDO and Mayra Ponce from the Department of Education, were arrested as well. Six members of Ricardo Rosselló's inner circle were federally charged with corruption, conspiracy, and fraud by a grand jury.[16]

Then came the leaks.

Verano 2019

On July 9, 2019, as Ricardo Rosselló and his family enjoyed their European vacation, PPD legislator Carlos Bianchi Angleró published a few pages of a text chat between the governor and his inner circle. In the leaked conversation, the governor and his friends, whom he called "los brothers," mocked Secretary of Justice Wanda Vázquez and the Senate's president, Thomas Rivera Schatz.

The officials had been using the Telegram phone application, which encrypts messages and self-destroys the content from its server.[17] Rosselló's "brothers" were an inner circle of eleven cabinet members and friends in the private sector, all young professionals and entrepreneurs. As its first pages demonstrated, the chat not only mocked political adversaries but also shaped policy. It gave members of the private sector access to confidential and privileged government information.[18] The backlash was immediate. As the first pages were leaked, people began calling for the resignation of everyone involved. The president of the Senate, also a member of the governor's party, declared, "All of them need to go."[19]

The following day, local news broke the story of the arrest of Secretary of Education Julia Keleher and other members of the Rosselló administration. By the end of the day, a small group had gathered in front of the governor's mansion to protest. That same day, the Twitter hashtag #RickyRenuncia went live. In the coming weeks, protests intensified and proliferated; meanwhile #RickyRenuncia became, according to Twitter, "the most relevant and transcendental" hashtag in the history of the platform thus far, garnering 1.3 million interactions.[20]

There were many reasons to be angry. People were living through ongoing political and fiscal crises. Government inefficiency had created a death sentence for thousands after Hurricane María. Now, they were reading seemingly live transcripts detailing the corrupt ways that government officials schemed with the private sector to shape public policy for the benefit of a handful of people.

As political tensions grew, another section of the controversial chat was leaked: twenty-six pages of Ricardo Rosselló's responses to the Junta's policies. "My authorized expressions," noted the governor, "*Dear Oversight Board . . . Go Fuck Yourself. . . .*" The new pages not only demonstrated how the governor handled politics but also showcased shockingly casual sexism. Chat members referred to Natalie Jaresko, chair of the Junta, as a *gatita* (pussycat). In reference to Melissa Mark-Viverito, former speaker of the New York City Council, Rosselló wrote, "Our people need to come out and defend Tom [Pérez, former chair of the Democratic National Committee] and jump on that whore." He also used similar words to refer to Alexandra Lúgaro, who ran for governor in 2016 and 2020.[21]

The maelstrom forced the governor to cut his vacation short. Back in Puerto Rico, he was greeted by an infuriated populace banging pots in protest. Rosselló begged for forgiveness, arguing that the chat was just a way to let off steam after long workdays. His lukewarm response was followed by another leak on July 12. The newly released pages documented a continued pattern of sexist comments against women; they also showed chat members scheming to shape public narratives about the administration.

The night of July 12, an anonymous source contacted Omaya Sosa Pascual, a journalist who had cofounded the Centro de Periodismo Investigativo (CPI). The source offered her the complete transcript of the infamous chat. Sosa Pascual assembled a team of journalists who spent all night reading and verifying the document. The following morning, the CPI published the 889-page chat. A political storm without precedent in the country's electoral history had started.[22]

The chat's publication confirmed what everyone already knew. But it also sadly demonstrated the ways in which Rosselló and his inner circle poked fun at the misery Puerto Ricans were living through. They joked about dead bodies and María's destruction of a humble house next to the governor's cottage. The chat was also rife with sexist, homophobic, fatphobic, classist, and degrading comments toward politicians, public figures, activists, and everyday citizens. Finally, the chat clearly documented the ways in which people from the private sector had gained access to confidential government information that benefited their businesses.[23]

What began as a small protest in front of the governor's mansion grew into a massive movement with no clear leaders. Every single day there were calls for protests and marches. It seemed like all it took to begin a protest was a flyer on social media. With each passing day, the events drew larger crowds. On July 17, 2019, for example, almost half a million people flooded the streets of San Juan demanding the resignation of Ricardo Rosselló. It was, without a doubt, one of the largest protests in the country's history, comparable to the movement against the U.S. Navy in Vieques in the early 2000s and the strike against the privatization of the telephone company in 1998. Celebrities like rapper Residente, rap artist Bad Bunny, and pop star Ricky Martin, among others, joined the movement.[24]

The huge protest that took place on July 17 was not a one-time event. Five days later another massive march of more than half a million people took over San Juan's main expressway. When Chief of Police Henry Escalera asked that event organizers meet with the police, he was ridiculed on social media—there were no organizers.[25] These events were not isolated. They are part of a vibrant culture of protest that emerged since at least 2006 in response to austerity measures, university budget cuts, and punitive logics.

Unlike the protests of the past, plurality was the marker that defined the protest movement that emerged against Rosselló and his administration. There seemed to be new forms of protest every day. The movement was not solely confined to Puerto Rico's metropolitan area but expanded throughout the archipelago. People protested on horseback, on bicycles, in kayaks, and through yoga and acts of civil disobedience. In the morning, there were activities for children and families. Evening *cacerolazos* (pot-banging sessions) could be heard throughout the city. Many of these events were centered around the joy of coming together to enact change. But people were also angry. Rage had ignited action.[26]

In Fortaleza Street, later symbolically renamed Resistance Street, clashes between police and protesters took place almost every night. While daily activities were for everyone, "nights were for combat," as a member of the Movimiento Socialista de Trabajadores noted.[27] At around 11:30 p.m. the police called the protests done for the day. When people refused to leave, they would disperse them using force. On July 17, a police officer declared through a megaphone that the constitution had been suspended.[28] The heavily militarized police force then proceeded to use rubber bullets, pepper spray, and tear gas against the assembled crowd. People resisted with rocks, water bottles, and anything they could find. Media coverage focused on the protesters' actions, but the American Civil Liberties Union noted that police had infiltrated the crowd.[29]

In the past, protests were dismissed as solely attended by "los pelús," a reference to socialists and students, typically thought of as long-haired and unruly. What happened in Puerto Rico that summer severely challenged preconceived notions of the protest movement. People from different backgrounds and lived experiences came together under #RickyRenuncia.

Although the governor's resignation was their clear goal, other demands were articulated by different groups. One example of this was Rey Charlie, a young garbage collector and motorcycle enthusiast who took social media by storm. During the July 17 protests, Rey Charlie led a 3,000-strong motorcade through San Juan's metropolitan area. His working-class followers made sure to stop at different housing projects, inviting others to join them. As social justice scholar Aurora Santiago Ortiz and I have noted, "When he addressed both the procession members and a Puerto Rican news network via live feed, Charlie transmitted the message of not only calling for the resignation of Rosselló but also mused discursively about marginalization and oppression, acknowledging the political potential of the 'poor and humble.'" Ultimately, this "overturned and directly challenged many assumptions of both the left and right about the marginalized classes' disinterest in political processes beyond the ballot box."[30]

While protests happened every day over a two-week period, other protest repertoires also occurred in different parts of the archipelago, including queer balls and *perreo combativo* (combative perreo dances). And social media became yet another space where people came together both across the islands and in the diaspora to actively demand Rosselló's resignation. When the police were ready to disperse crowds in front of Fortaleza Street, those watching live feeds from any part of the world could alert their friends and loved ones on the ground. Protesters also set up crowdfunding accounts to buy protective gear like water, gas masks, and first-aid kits.[31]

For many, it was the first time they had attended a political rally; others had participated in Puerto Rico's long history of protest. They were reminders that this protest movement was not spontaneous. There were veterans from Afro-descendant groups like Colectivo Ilé, students who had participated in the 2010 and 2017 UPR strikes, and participants from the long-standing and vibrant environmental justice movements all taking to the streets.

One of the most vocal groups was the Colectiva Feminista en Construcción, a Black feminist organization that began organizing in 2013. While La Cole was publicly ignored by the Rosselló administration, those who participated in the chat had mocked Shariana Ferrer-Núñez, the organization's spokesperson—they were paying attention to the organization's actions. The variety of tactics La Cole used to capture media attention in previous years laid the groundwork for some of the actions and discourses amplified in the Verano '19 protests. Through actions like camping in front of the governor's mansion and organizing impromptu protests in the Puerto Rican Senate or Plaza las Américas, people had noticed La Cole's actions. One of their most important campaigns was their demand for the Puerto Rican government to declare a state of emergency due to the high number of femicides in the archipelago before that summer, and these demands only increased during the Verano '19 protests.[32]

In a desperate attempt to control the narrative, Rosselló agreed to be interviewed by Fox News journalist Sheppard Smith on July 22. During seventeen excruciating minutes, Rosselló struggled to answer Smith's questions. Repeating his rehearsed prompts, he also maintained he would not resign. When Smith asked Rosselló to name people who had come forward in his support, the governor ignored the question. The reporter asked again and Rosselló vaguely answered, "I've talked to people from different groups. A lot of people from my administration." Smith asked him to name a single person. "The mayor of San Sebastián," a municipality located in northwest Puerto Rico, Rosselló answered. The interview was a public relations disaster. A few hours later, Javier Jiménez, the mayor of San Sebastián, denied the governor's claim.[33]

As the protests continued, members of the PNP distanced themselves from Rosselló. Meanwhile, his closest allies were resigning. His father, Pedro Rosselló, traveled to Puerto Rico to see if he could close ranks within the party but was unsuccessful. To make matters worse, the protest movement had been picked up by international news outlets. On July 23, the day after hundreds of thousands marched through the streets of San Juan, the protests were front-page headlines in the *New York Times, Washington Post, Wall Street Journal*, and *Miami Herald*.[34]

Then, on July 24, rumors began circulating that Rosselló would resign. Journalists were alerted that the governor was going to address them in his mansion at five in the afternoon. The minutes turned into hours, and journalists were moved from the patio to a room inside. These improvised decisions signaled the chaos happening behind closed doors. By seven that evening, a crowd had gathered in front of the Fortaleza—the usual evening protests would start soon. This time, however, there was a celebratory aura. A perreo combativo had been convened in front of the mansion but because of the massive turnout, it moved a few blocks away to the steps of San Juan's cathedral.[35]

Seven minutes to midnight—on the eve of the anniversary of the 1898 U.S. occupation, the 1952 creation of the commonwealth, and the assassination of two young independentistas at the Cerro Maravilla in 1978—a prerecorded message from the governor was aired. Silence fell on the streets, households, and the global Puerto Rican diaspora. The speech lasted fourteen minutes. When Rosselló announced his resignation, effective August 2, millions of Puerto Ricans celebrated an unprecedented historical moment in the archipelago.[36]

After the celebrations came the crucial question: what now? Pedro Pierluisi, who had lost the 2016 primaries and served as the Junta's attorney, had been named Puerto Rico's secretary of state by Rosselló and was thus next in the chain of succession. The Puerto Rican Senate, however, had blocked his confirmation. When Rosselló resigned, there was no clear successor. In the political vacuum, Pierluisi claimed the governorship and was sworn in by a judge at his sister's house on August 2. Three days later, the Senate met and did not confirm his appointment as secretary of state. Pierluisi could not claim the governor's seat. The Supreme Court stepped in and agreed that his appointment had been unconstitutional. Next in the chain of succession was Wanda Vázquez Garced, the secretary of justice. She became the new governor of Puerto Rico.[37]

For many of those who had participated in the summer protests, Governor Vázquez Garced was more of the same. After all, she had been part of the Rosselló administration accused of failing to properly investigate irregularities with, for example, Beatriz Rosselló's missing containers. Impromptu popular assemblies began to appear throughout the archipelago. Known as "The People's Assemblies," these were autonomously organized. Each had a different set of priorities, but they shared collective concerns about the auditing of the Puerto Rican debt, the privatization of essential services, and the social impacts of the ongoing fiscal crisis.[38] The People's Assemblies promised a continuation of the movement, but fatigue had set in and the Assemblies quickly dispersed. The everyday experiences of living in economic scarcity likely also played a factor. Some members, however, went on to join other community grassroots groups that became part of the Assemblies' afterlives.[39]

The continuation of the Rosselló administration even after his resignation should not be considered a failure. In fact, the Verano '19 protests challenge the fixed binary of success or failure. As philosopher Pedro Lebrón notes, "The beauty of the summer of 2019 was the collective subject that emerged across ideological differences for that moment (e.g., pro-statehood, pro-commonwealth, pro-independence, atheists, Christians, anti-colonial, feminist, queer, etc.). While it is certain that the summer of 2019 changed us in some way, its effects on an intersubjective level are unknown."[40] Participating in the summer events allowed many Puerto Ricans to envision a future otherwise, a future they could build collectively.

Ongoing Disaster

"What is going on?" I was suddenly awake. The room was violently shaking and the walls shrieking. I stood up but fell to the ground. My wife crawled to our child's bedroom. It was January 7, 2020. For a few seconds that went on for eternity, we felt the might of a 6.4-magnitude earthquake.

After the initial quake, we rushed outside to meet with neighbors. Everyone shared experiences and then went silent. The power was out, and we stood next to each other without a sense of what would happen next. But at least we were all together.

When we finally went back to our apartment to get some much-needed rest, the shaking came back. It was the first of many aftershocks for us, but for many others it was not the first. Beginning on December 28, 2019, Puerto Rico's southern district experienced a swarm of more than 9,000 earthquakes, eleven of them greater than 5.0 magnitude.[41] A report by the United States Geological Survey noted that aftershocks "will persist for years to decades."[42]

We experienced the earthquake while living in the northern town of Manatí. The quake's epicenter, however, had been in the southern town of Guánica. As the day progressed, news of damage in southern municipalities circulated. Images of collapsed houses appeared on social media and local news outlets. The photographs shed light on the geographical inequities in Puerto Rico. While the southern district had been the center of industrialization projects in the 1960s, it had receded economically in later decades and was now home to abandoned oil refineries.[43] The residents in the most impacted municipalities, and in the communities that had been most affected, were mostly non-white and Black Puerto Ricans.[44]

When anthropologist Hilda Llorens interviewed a medical doctor who had worked in the region for forty years, he noted that sharp increases in illnesses were due to "contaminants from the AES [Applied Energy Services] coal power plant, the Aguirre Power Complex, and the GMO [genetically modified organisms] agrochemical industries." But, most importantly, he noted, "The worst illness afflicting the region is poverty. . . . Because this is a poor region, people are powerless. They have little political clout and voice with which to defend themselves against the onslaught of contaminating industries sited here."[45]

Once again, solidarity efforts became a lifeline for many. Immediately after the earthquake, people organized fundraising campaigns to help those in the greatest need. The government discouraged traveling to the southern municipalities in the immediate hours after the earthquake because some bridges and roads needed to be assessed for infrastructural damages. Once travel was possible, thousands of people made their way to the town of Guánica with donations.

As had happened with Hurricane María, the earthquake laid bare Puerto Rico's frail infrastructure. A collapsed school in Guánica triggered conversations about children's safety. A day after the January 7 earthquake, Puerto Rico's College of Engineers noted that only 500 of the 857 public schools in Puerto Rico that had not been closed by the

Rosselló administration were reinforced to sustain an earthquake.[46] The town of Guánica endured aftershocks that continued to worsen its already fragile infrastructure. The situation became so dire that people slept outside their houses for weeks. Some were lucky enough to find shelter in truck containers; others slept in cars or tents.[47]

The earthquake's aftermath was one of multiple disasters caused by the country's fiscal crisis. It exacerbated social problems that many people had already been living with for years. And as the aftermath of María had shown, people could not depend on the local or federal government for any sort of relief. Many mayors in the affected municipalities complained about the lack of help from Puerto Rico's central government.[48]

As people struggled to survive, a Facebook live feed once again triggered collective rage. On January 19, an investigative blogger known as Leon Fiscalizador began a livestream at a warehouse in the southern municipality of Ponce. In what felt like déjà vu for many of us watching, the live video showed a warehouse full of supplies that had not been distributed: thousands of products ranging from water to diapers, from stoves to sleeping cots. The blogger had received an anonymous tip from someone within the PNP administration claiming to be loyal to the party but fed up with such abuses. The video went viral, garnering more than seven hundred thousand views. Groups began arriving at the warehouse and stormed it, redistributing the supplies until the police arrived and cleared them away.[49]

Governor Wanda Vázquez Garced denied knowledge of the warehouse but was forced to publicly retract her statement. The government also confirmed that there were other warehouses full of supplies. As feminist scholar Marisol LeBrón has noted, "Many felt that she was handling the earthquake recovery efforts in a similar manner to how her predecessor, the disgraced former governor Ricardo Rosselló, handled Hurricanes Irma and María." Governor Vázquez Garced denied responsibility and blamed the previous administration, but as LeBrón notes, "The irony, of course, is that Vázquez was part of the previous administration . . . and many of her advisors and cabinet members were also part of the Rosselló government and, thus, implicated in the very corruption and ineptitude from which she was now trying to distance herself."[50]

The warehouse incident triggered a series of protests that evoked the Verano '19 protests. Night after night, protesters banged pots, marched, and demanded the resignation of Vázquez Garced. They even created a life-size guillotine as a symbol of what needed to be done with Puerto Rico's political class. Such corruption was systemic, a malaise that permeated Puerto Rico's elites, or what scholar-activists Joaquín Villanueva, Martín Cobián, and Félix Rodríguez have called "the criollo bloc." This bloc is a managerial class and political elite who administers the colony and whose "wealth has been generationally inherited by virtue of their privileged racial position and their historical class alliances."[51] Although many people expected a sequel to the Verano '19 events, political exhaustion was apparent as the low turnout and the ephemeral nature of these protests demonstrated.[52]

As different social sectors demanded the resignation of Governor Vázquez Garced, the country's frail health infrastructure was about to face another challenge: the coronavirus pandemic. In March 2020, the Puerto Rican government activated the U.S. National Guard and imposed a two-week lockdown. It was followed by strict curfews. As the pandemic continued, many Puerto Ricans complained that tourists used the archipelago as their playground. They also criticized the ways the government catered to wealthy foreigners and crypto-impresarios through tax exemptions. Meanwhile, hundreds of thousands of Puerto Ricans—far more than those who participated in the Great Migration of the mid-twentieth century—left the archipelago, possibly for good.

CHAPTER 15

BROKEN MEMORIES AND FUTURE-ORIENTED HISTORIES

In the Verano '19 protests, activists used banners and social media to argue that the Puerto Rican government hated its people. The Rosselló group chat on Telegram seemed to confirm just that. On January 18, 2019, the "brothers," as the chat members referred to themselves, commented about an announcement that President Trump was going to make the following day about the humanitarian crisis unfolding at the U.S. southern border. They joked that Trump would declare that he was selling Puerto Rico to Russia. One of the "brothers" was Edwin Miranda, a publicist who tried to conceal his propaganda work for the Rosselló administration once the chat was leaked. But the Centro de Periodismo Investigativo showcased multiple instances in which he used his agency to promote the former governor's image in social media and news outlets.[1] Miranda jested, "I saw the future . . . is [*sic*] so wonderful . . . there are no puertorricans."[2]

His words became almost prophetic. Puerto Rico's population fell to 3.3 million in the 2020 census, meaning the archipelago had lost 11.8 percent of its peoples in a decade. Hundreds of thousands left in the wake of the fiscal crises, natural disasters, and colonial neglect. In the mid-twentieth century's Great Migration, the state facilitated the relocation of people, intending to pave the way for modernization. The postwar economy created a labor market that allowed Puerto Ricans to find a "plethora of limited opportunities."[3] Many migrated without knowing that they were numbers in a broader structural plan laid out by the Puerto Rican government. Migration became part of the state's official policy.

Unlike previous large-scale migrations, however, Puerto Rico is not headed toward industrialization or modernization in the first decades of the twenty-first century. Quite the opposite. The archipelago is moving toward collapse as there is no clear government plan or agenda to address the fiscal crises aside from a strategy to attract wealthy U.S. foreigners, the latest iteration of Puerto Rico's fiscal dependency on foreign investment.

As Puerto Ricans continue to arrive in the United States in the thousands, they find a precarious labor market. The global pandemic, skyrocketing oil prices, and military conflicts have created a dire international economic situation. Puerto Ricans also face structural racism. White supremacy, or the idea of white people's superiority, has been a foundational ideology in the United States. A wave of protests has highlighted the racial inequities in the country after a series of police-led assassinations of African American people, including Tamir Rice, George Floyd, and Sandra Bland, to mention just a few. The presidency of Donald Trump emboldened white supremacist groups, which have become more vocal and active ever since.[4]

In 2014, a few months after I moved to the United States for graduate school, I was told to go back to my country by an older gentleman when he overheard me speaking Spanish to my daughter at a store. It was a subtle reminder that for some people Puerto Ricans are not welcome in the United States. But since Puerto Ricans have U.S. citizenship, albeit second-class, we carry privileges that other Latinx communities do not have. Race and class also play an important role in how Puerto Ricans are racialized in the United States. My position as an educated light-skinned Puerto Rican affords me privileges that I cannot overlook. There are still many Puerto Ricos and hundreds of thousands of migration stories.

The demographic changes the Puerto Rican nation is facing are not only triggered by migration. A report published by City University of

New York's Centro: Center for Puerto Rican Studies noted that by 2017, senior citizens (those older than sixty-five) were "the only demographic group [of Puerto Ricans] with positive growth rates." This is in part due to lower fertility rates, increased life spans, and the migration of people of child-bearing age.[5] The older population's growth is taking place at a moment when the Puerto Rican government has slashed the retirement pensions of teachers, university professors, and government employees to tackle the fiscal crisis.[6]

When I was growing up, any conversation about the potential independence of Puerto Rico was met with the same comment: "Do you want to become another Cuba or Dominican Republic?" Beneath the xenophobic and racist undertones of these comments, there was a concern about poverty and lack of infrastructure that made life difficult in those countries. I was told about food and gas shortages, about unreliable electric grids. Independence never arrived in Puerto Rico, yet in 2022 Puerto Ricans faced electrical outages daily. Soaring poverty—particularly affecting children—makes life in Puerto Rico difficult. The lack of employment has also pushed many people from all social classes to migrate.

The future without Puerto Ricans that Edwin Miranda dreamed about was not an abstract joke but a political project that sought to make Puerto Rico a disappearing archipelago. As many Puerto Ricans struggle to survive or make ends meet, a new class of wealthy U.S. foreigners has arrived in the archipelago to take advantage of the government's tax incentives. Some of these new foreigners dream of creating utopic projects based on crypto currencies. For many in Puerto Rico, as the messages spray-painted with graffiti through the streets of San Juan attest, this is just another form of colonialism.

New Forms of Colonialism

"They call what they are building Puertopia," read the first line of a *New York Times* article published on February 2, 2018. For many Puerto Ricans, this article was the first they had heard of entrepreneurs who had made their fortunes through Blockchain and Bitcoin migrating to the archipelago. "They want to build a crypto utopia," read the article, "a new city where the money is virtual and the contracts are all public, to show the rest of the world what a crypto future could look like. Blockchain, a digital ledger that forms the basis of virtual currencies, has the potential to reinvent society—and the Puertopians want to prove it."[7]

By the time the article was published, a handful of crypto investors had already settled in San Juan, making a former children's museum their base of operations. They would later buy the building, a symbolic gesture that showcased their desire to stay. These crypto investors also had conversations about buying the former Roosevelt Roads military base in the country's eastern district to begin their Puertopia, later renamed Sol. These colonial fantasies were also infused with New Age spiritual discourses. Brock Pierce, the former child-actor turned movement guru, argued, "A billionaire is someone who has positively impacted the lives of a billion people."[8] While being interviewed by a *New York Times* reporter, Pierce stood in front of a tree and prayed for Puertopia.[9]

After Hurricane María, Puertopians saw the archipelago as a "blank slate."[10] Instead of challenging these colonial desires, the Puerto Rican government encouraged the arrival of crypto investors. In March 2018, it sponsored a conference, "Blockchain Unbound," and eight hundred people attended.[11]

Many were lured by tax breaks. In 2012, Governor Fortuño's administration passed two pieces of legislation to attract foreign capital, effectively making the country a tax haven. Acts 20 (Export Services Act) and 22 (Individual Investors Act) offered tax incentives to new residents or business arriving in the archipelago.[12] While these acts did not include crypto businesses, it was extended to them through Act 60 of 2019. As legal scholar José Atiles notes, "At present, any individual who spends three months in Puerto Rico can receive exemptions from federal and local taxes, capital gains tax, and taxes on passive income until the year 2035."[13]

For decades, the town of Rincón in the western side of Puerto Rico has been a surfing destination, attracting many white U.S. residents. In recent years, Puerto Rican residents have complained that tax breaks have accelerated the migration process, displacing Puerto Ricans due to the high housing prices. Samuel Sánchez Tirado, a Rincón resident, noted that those arriving "don't ask for a price" when they want to buy a property. "They just hand you a check and ask you to fill out how much you think the house is worth."[14]

A report in *El nuevo día*, Puerto Rico's largest newspaper in circulation, noted that the archipelago had 22,426 rooms being used for short-term rentals in 2022. In Old San Juan, 25 percent of livable units—one out of every four residences—was a short-term rental.[15] According to government data, the rental industry grew by 99 percent in 2020.[16] Puerto Ricans have also complained that tourists began venturing outside of the metropolitan area, triggering gentrification processes that increase rent and the cost of living in other municipalities.

Tourism has been an important part of Puerto Rico's economy since the mid-twentieth century. In 2019, before the pandemic began, for example, tourism contributed 5.1 percent of Puerto Rico's total GDP.[17] The government has used film and media to present Puerto Rico as a tropical paradise that U.S. residents can visit without a passport. It was no coincidence that the Puerto Rican government's slogan to attract these new crypto entrepreneurs was "Paradise Performs."[18] But tourism is not always benign or beneficial. Caribbean peoples have long critiqued the ways that tourism has perpetuated colonial hierarchies between nations and exacerbated economic dependency.

In 2020, as Puerto Rico was in the midst of the Covid-19 pandemic, Governor Wanda Vázquez Garced requested that the Federal Aviation Agency close the Luis Muñoz Marín International Airport due to the high number of Covid cases. Her request was denied.[19] Instead, travel continued despite the government's strict Covid restrictions and protocols. In 2021, the Puerto Rican government announced that tourism was generating record-breaking profits during the pandemic, particularly through rental taxes.[20]

The number of tourists flocking to San Juan during the pandemic created tensions with locals. News reports of trashed rentals, large brawls in public spaces, and fights with service-industry workers became commonplace. Puerto Ricans responded by using social media to

FIGURE 15.1. Mural along San Juan's Baldorioty de Castro expressway.
Photograph by the author.

share memes, videos, and critiques. This created a sense that Puerto
Rico was a playground for tourists, eerily reminding everyone of Edwin
Miranda's dream of "Puerto Rico without Puerto Ricans."

Contrary to the mostly white, U.S. foreigners whom the tax exemptions attracted, many tourists during the first stages of the pandemic
were African Americans. In reaction to the tourist boom, some Puerto
Ricans articulated a racist discourse toward them as anthropologist
Yarimar Bonilla noted in the Puerto Rican press: "Instead of focusing
on the type of tourism that we are receiving, we should reflect on how

tourism represents a violent act in itself—not only based on colonial legacies and the destruction of nature, but also in racist and sexist imaginaries that are reproduced by those who are also victims of it."[21] Bonilla was not the only person warning against the violence of tourism.

Beyond social media, Puerto Ricans use street walls as bulletin boards. In the Baldorioty de Castro Avenue, one of the busiest highways in the archipelago, the activist art collective La Puerta painted a mural that said in bold letters: GRINGO GO HOME. END COLONIALISM. This was complemented by similar phrases from anonymous people throughout urban hubs. Phrases like "Gringo, You're Not Welcomed" and "Act 20/22 = Ethnic Genocide" were painted in bathroom stalls and on city walls or pasted on street poles. These are forms of everyday protest and resistance by those who seek to resist Edwin Miranda's dream.

The Politics of Debt and Everyday Life

Since 1968, Puerto Rico's electoral history has been dominated by two traditional parties: the Partido Popular Democrático (PPD) and the Partido Nuevo Progresista (PNP). Each one defended a particular political status for the archipelago. The PPD created the commonwealth during the 1950s while the PNP advocated for statehood, or the incorporation of Puerto Rico into the United States. The Partido Independentista Puertorriqueño (PIP) had been the runner-up shortly after its creation in 1946 but then became a minority party. And although the two parties alternating power had different views on the political status of the archipelago, as time went by both parties became more and more alike.

At the turn of the twenty-first century, the people of Puerto Rico began losing faith in their political apparatus. Voter turnout dwindled. More than 82 percent of eligible voters had cast their ballot in 2000, yet only 55 percent did in 2018.[22] The second decade of the twenty-first century also saw the emergence of new political parties like the Puertorriqueños por Puerto Rico (Puerto Ricans for Puerto Rico) in 2003, Movimiento Unión Soberanista (Sovereignist Union Movement) in 2010, and the Partido del Pueblo Trabajador (Party of the Working

Peoples) in 2010. While their numbers continued to be small and all of them eventually dissolved after a few electoral runs, their existence demonstrated growing discontent with traditional politics. These parties accrued, along with the PIP, a marginal percentage of the overall ballots cast. In the 2012 elections, for example, minority parties only garnered 5 percent of the total ballots cast in Puerto Rico.[23]

In 2019, various social groups, including the former Partido del Pueblo Trabajador, joined forces to create a new political party, Movimiento Victoria Ciudadana (Citizens' Victory Movement; MVC). The party began as a coalition and internally elected Alexandra Lúgaro for the governor's ticket. Lúgaro is an entrepreneur who led a successful campaign for the governorship as an independent candidate in the 2016 elections, where she received more than 11 percent of the vote, an impressive number for a woman running without a party apparatus behind her. But MVC was not Alexandra Lúgaro's party. Rather, it is a coalition composed of seasoned activists, community organizers, and politicians from traditional political parties.

After the summer 2019 events led to the ousting of Governor Ricardo Rosselló, both the MVC and the PIP went through a moment of political effervescence. This was in part due to grassroots political campaigns focusing on a younger generation who did not feel represented by traditional political parties. These parties, then, articulated stances around gender, race, and sexuality that resonated with activists and young people tired of the bipartisan system they grew up in.

The 2020 elections were the first since Rosselló left office, and they demonstrated that the bipartisan model had entered a moment of crisis. Pedro Pierluisi of the PNP party—a lawyer for La Junta who sought to take over the government when Rosselló resigned but whose appointment was ruled unconstitutional by Puerto Rico's Supreme Court—won the governor seat with less than 33 percent of the vote. Other parties saw their numbers grow drastically. The PIP, which had struggled to survive for decades, accrued 14 percent of the vote, something they had not been able to do since the 1950s. MVC also received 14 percent of the vote and was able to elect two senators and two legislators.

Leftist parties were not the only ones that took advantage of the political moment. In previous years, conservative and religious fundamentalists had complained about their lack of representation in traditional political parties. In 2020 they created a party called Proyecto Dignidad (Dignity Project). While the idea of "dignidad" had been a rallying cry for social movements across Latin America, this group used the name in Puerto Rico to defend conservative ideas and values. They also succeeded in electing one senator and one legislator in the 2020 elections.

Low voter turnout was not limited to elections. In 2020, the Puerto Rican government organized its sixth referendum or plebiscite on the status question. The first plebiscite had taken place in 1967; four others had followed in 1993, 1998, 2012, and 2017. While political parties have always negotiated language to negatively impact their opponents, some version of "commonwealth" had always won these plebiscites except in 2017 when statehood won but with only 27 percent of eligible voters casting ballots. In 2020, statehood clearly won in the plebiscites but less than 50 percent of eligible voters participated. For many Puerto Ricans, these nonbinding referendums are a waste of government resources.

The low number of votes also reflects distrust and discontent, particularly for a younger generation that feels like representative democracy failed them. Instead, they are enacting politics and other forms of participatory democracy beyond the ballot box. Radical street library projects are forcing people to rethink the ways they relate to space and private property. The Colectiva Feminista en Construcción has shown that demands are not made behind closed doors but that in the face of a wave of femicides, the streets need to be public forums. Agricultural collectives are shaping the conversation toward the meanings of food sovereignty in a colony that imports almost 90 percent of the food it consumes. And activists have also created food pantries across the island to combat hunger from a radical standpoint.

For many of the people who participate in these projects, decolonization is an urgent matter. Since they cannot continue to wait for elected officials to help them, they rely on themselves to do so. The phrase "sólo el pueblo salva el pueblo" (only the people will save the people) acquires power in this context. But activists also warn that we cannot romanticize the struggles people face by celebrating resilience. Many of these projects, while radical in their political orientation, stem from necessity. As some activists have argued, to survive in the colony is a radical act. And when that is the case, casting a vote every four years does not carry the promise of changing a situation that seems to be spiraling out of control.

There is a direct correlation between voter turnout and the fiscal crisis that Puerto Rico has battled since 2006. Traditional parties are portrayed as not having done much to deal with the crisis. And, for some, they are directly responsible for it.

In 2017, Chief Justice John G. Roberts of the U.S. Supreme Court assigned U.S. District Judge Laura Taylor Swain to oversee Puerto Rico's bankruptcy case, one of the largest in the history of the United States.[24] After almost three years of deliberations and discussions, Judge Swain agreed to restructure the debt. The deal erased $33 billion of the total debt while cutting $22 billion in bonds to $7 billion.[25] Some of the Junta's members celebrated this as an outstanding victory for Puerto Rico. Natalie Jaresko and David Skeel noted in a *Wall Street Journal* editorial that the United States had not addressed the question of Puerto Rico's status because of its enormous debt. That was, according to them, now resolved. Under their logic, their actions paved the way to solve the perennial problem of status.[26]

However, the refinancing process failed to address a major concern raised by multiple activist and civic groups. Most of the debt had been accrued illegally, but the agreed-upon deal curtailed any possibility of an audit. Further, scholars Marisol LeBrón and Sarah Molinari have noted that La Junta has used austerity measures to slash funds and shrink the government since its creation. The debt's repayment plan, which will be shouldered by the people of Puerto Rico for forty years, did not include any strategy to rebuild or address the many institutions affected by austerity measures. Without a clear national plan, it seems as if the Puerto Rican government's plan depended, once again, on foreign investment once the debt was restructured.

In 2021, the Puerto Rican government effectively privatized the power grid. Luma Energy took over the distribution of electricity in the archipelago. With the privatization came multiple increases in electric bills at a moment when the infrastructure is so weak and unreliable that Puerto Ricans face power outages daily. Rent prices continue to surge as short-term rental companies cater to foreigners with purchasing power. The fiscal crisis that began in 2006 continues without an end in sight. Meanwhile, Jenniffer González, Puerto Rico's resident commissioner in Washington—a position that has no voting power in Congress—works toward the creation of yet another plebiscite to address the status question.

Privatization and corruption continue to plague the Puerto Rican government. From 2020 to 2022, twenty-four government officials or people close to them were arrested on corruption or fraud charges, including former governor Wanda Vázquez Garced.[27] Corruption can mean many things; it does not have a simple definition. According to José Atiles, Gustavo A. García López, and Joaquín Villanueva, international organizations like the United Nations, the World Bank, and the International Monetary Fund broadly define corruption as "the abuse of power for private gain." These scholars argue, however, that it is vastly more complex than that. In the case of Puerto Rico, corruption has served to legitimize U.S. colonialism in Puerto Rico, and "US capitalism," they note, "has routinely pushed for instrumental anti-corruption measures and exceptional practices to ensure wealth extraction and profit-making while functionally pathologizing local leaders as untrustworthy, deviant, and otherwise 'corrupt.'"[28]

But corruption did not begin in 1898 with the U.S. occupation. Spanish merchants smuggled enslaved African peoples while much of the rural population of Puerto Rico depended on contraband. The foundation of Miguel Enríquez's fortune, to the point of becoming the wealthiest Puerto Rican in the early eighteenth century, stemmed from corrupt arrangements he made with Governor Gabriel Gutiérrez de la Riba. Later, in the nineteenth century, the white planter elite accused the laboring masses of being corrupt. In their opinion, the masses needed to be regenerated. This was also a foundational piece of the Great Puerto Rican Family myth.[29]

Before and after the U.S. occupation of 1898, politicians, elites, and government functionaries participated in schemes for personal gain. In a recently published study that used municipal audit reports to create a longitudinal data set, a group of scholars found that partisan politics after 1952—the year that the Puerto Rican Commonwealth was inaugurated—corruption cases "were at the front and center of Puerto Rico's trajectory."[30] Their report also demonstrated that "institutional decay is directly correlated with the normalization of corruption practices over time."[31]

As this book has demonstrated, corruption did not cease during the first two decades of the twenty-first century. The country's colonial condition has created a managerial class that has benefited from Puerto Rico's current relation to the United States. While their corrupt practices have changed throughout time, they have maintained positions of power in Puerto Rico's public and political life. A breaking point came in the summer of 2019 when Puerto Ricans took to the streets to demand the resignation of Governor Ricardo Rosselló. While the masses were considered corrupt by elites in the nineteenth century, now it was the people accusing those in power of being corrupt and demanding change.[32] But these protests were not solely about challenging corruption. As people occupied streets, spray-painted walls, and *perrearon* (twerked) in front of San Juan's cathedral, new forms and understandings of Puerto Ricanness were being negotiated. While not much changed after the 2019 summer protests, those who participated in such events were changed by it.

Corruption continues without an end in sight. In the western coastal town of Aguadilla, people protested an illegal development of a hotel on protected public lands. Acting with a sense of impunity, on January 29, 2023, private security officers shot live ammunition at the crowd, wounding one of the protesters. The event became a metaphor for the way that developers take over public lands, particularly Puerto Rico's beaches, without considering the well-being of Puerto Ricans.[33] One of the lawyers representing the developers is Antonio García Padilla, former governor of Puerto Rico.[34] Meanwhile, a few weeks later, journalist

Sandra Rodríguez Cotto broke the news that a study noted that Governor Pierluisi's son, Anthony Pierluisi, owns 88 percent of all short-term rental properties in the San Juan area. And while this is not illegal in itself, the real estate does receive paid promotion from government agencies like the Tourism Company and Discover Puerto Rico.[35]

All these events take place while the social crisis continues and, with it, criminality, drug-related murders, and petty crimes are on the rise. Instead of presenting a comprehensive social project that is attentive to education, the economy, and holistic, medical approaches to drug use, the government only employs "Mano Dura" policing practices. As this book has demonstrated, those policing practices have been used in the archipelago since the 1990s, and they have failed time and time again.[36]

The current situation—with a defunded educational system, massive displacement and migration, and endless corruption—seems as if it was made by design. But, while former governor Ricardo Rosselló's friends dream of a Puerto Rico without Puerto Ricans, many anonymous people are working to build a Puerto Rico full of Puerto Ricans. That is, people are working to create liberatory futures for Puerto Ricans no matter if they are in Santurce, Cayey, and Cabo Rojo, or New York City, Orlando, or Milwaukee.

El Apagón

Many young people identified as the "Yo no me dejo" generation during the 2019 summer protests. This term was coined by the rap and reggaeton artist Bad Bunny in a song with fellow artists Residente and iLe, released during the protests. Benito Antonio Martínez Ocasio, known as Bad Bunny, was a supermarket grocery bagger before becoming a global superstar. In 2022, he announced three new concerts in Puerto Rico with tickets only sold in person; parts of the San Juan metropolitan area were shut down due to the massive numbers of people camping out in front of the stadium. His music has come to define a generation not only in Puerto Rico but globally.

Unlike the chauvinist and macho ethos that dominated the reggaeton music genre, Bad Bunny represented a queer aesthetic, with his brightly colored outfits, painted nails, and gender-bending performances. In *Un verano sin ti*, his fourth solo studio album, Bad Bunny once again topped the charts and broke streaming records. One track, "El apagón" (The power outage), became an immediate anthem in the archipelago.

An upbeat tempo is accompanied by a crowd shouting "Puerto Rico está bien cabrón" (Puerto Rico is fucking awesome or Puerto Rico is really hard [depending on how you interpret it]). As the title notes, besides the festive tone, the song is also a reminder of the dire reality lived by many in the archipelago. Toward the end of the song, Gabriela Berlingeri sings:

Yo no me quiero ir de aquí.
No me quiero ir de aquí.
Que se vayan ellos.
Que se vayan ellos.
Que se vayan ellos.
Que se vayan ellos.

Lo que me pertenece a mí
se lo quedan ellos.
Que se vayan ellos.

Esta es mi playa.
Este es mi sol.
Esta es mi tierra.
Esta soy yo.

//

I do not want to leave from here.
Do not want to leave from here.
Let them go.
Let them go.
Let them go.
Let them go.

What belongs to me
they keep it.
Let them go.

This is my beach.
This is my sun.
This is my land
This is me.[37]

The song documents a collective rage and discontent. Puerto Rico caters to wealthy U.S. foreigners while Puerto Ricans are forced to leave. Many of those who have left note that they did not want to, just like Gabriela Berlingeri sings in the song. They left because they had no option.

My grandfather left the archipelago in the 1950s, hoping to never come back. I write these final words on an airplane as I leave the archipelago once again. I too am part of what some have called "the flying bus," or the "vaivén," a constant back and forth between the diaspora and the archipelago. I left in 2013 hoping to return for good, but I do not know if that will be possible. Yet, as Bad Bunny's song notes, many Puerto Ricans hope that they—the corrupt officials, capitalists, and ignorant foreigners—leave so we can return to our beaches, our sun, our land. Meanwhile, other Puerto Ricos are currently being imagined *aquí o allá* (here or there), wherever those places might be.

ACKNOWLEDGMENTS

Often, books do not have a single point of origin. That is certainly the case with this one. In fall 2020, I was invited by Laurel Davis-Delano to deliver a lecture at Springfield College. The task was to present a broad historical overview of Puerto Rico, Puerto Ricans, and Puerto Rican-ness in one hour. It was an exercise in narrative building that laid the foundation for this book. The idea to begin writing it, however, stemmed out of a conversation with my editor Priya Nelson after my colleague Matt Delmont facilitated our initial interaction. To all of them I am thankful.

Writing a book is always a collective effort. It is the product of count-less conversations with friends, colleagues, and family members. I am forever indebted to and thankful for all of my history teachers and profes-sors who fostered in me a sense of pride in being from Puerto Rico, the Caribbean, and Latin America. It's also a thank-you note to my students for everything they have taught me in the classroom over the years. I am particularly thankful to my students at Dartmouth College and the Uni-versity of Wisconsin–Madison for carefully engaging with some of the ideas that ended up in the pages of this book.

The writing of this book was informed by being in community with Pedro Lebrón, Mónica Jiménez, Joaquín Villanueva, Karrieann Soto Vega, Marie Cruz Soto, Sarah Molinari, Daniel Nervaez, José Atiles, and Aurora Santiago Ortiz, all of them members of the PfknR Collective. It was also informed by conversations with Francisco Moscoso, Rocío Zambrana, Ronald Mendoza de Jesus, César Salcedo Chirinos, Michael Staudenmaier, Melody Fonseca, Marcelo A. Luzzi, and so many other wonderful people.

My dear student Fionnuala Murphy provided crucial research support during the book's early stages. Another friend and colleague, Nelson Pagán Butler, helped me conduct research in Puerto Rico when the pandemic made travel difficult. During the writing process, I had the invaluable editorial support of Hannah Brooks-Motl.

The book was written between San Juan, Puerto Rico, and Hanover, New Hampshire. It was finished in an airplane on my last flight to New England before I moved to join the University of Wisconsin–Madison. It was in Verona, Wisconsin, where I revised the final manuscript. I mention these sites because they serve as a radiograph of the ways that Puerto Ricans are always on the move. Just like Puerto Ricanness, this book is also diasporic.

During my time at Dartmouth College, I was able to connect with people who transcended the bonds of friendship and became part of my extended family: Ernesto Mercado Montero, Jorge Ramírez-López, Vanessa Castañeda, Melanie Z. Plasencia, MT-Vallarta, Joe Blanco, Charlie Guyer, Shaonta' Allen, Christian Hadome, Bryan Winston, and Audrey Winston. The El Norte Frío crew, as we called ourselves, became a lifeline as I began writing this book. Marisol LeBrón, Margaret Power, Joaquín Villanueva, and Mark Bray read the first drafts of the manuscript and provided invaluable feedback. Students at Manchester University, Indiana, in Michael Staudenmaier's classes also read different parts of this book and engaged with its content. I am also very lucky to be part of a vibrant intellectual community at the University of Wisconsin–Madison. My conversations with Pablo Gómez, Patrick Iber, Marcella "Sally" Hayes, Allison Powers-Useche, Marla Ramírez, Giuliana Chamedes, Daniel Williford, Viren Murthy, and so many other wonderful colleagues have made me feel at home. To all of them I'm grateful.

I could not have written this book without the support of my friend and mentor Blanca G. Silvestrini. Her work, along with that of so many Puerto Rican historians, has been influential in my understanding of the archipelago. My family has always been my number-one support: Iris Meléndez, Robin Guzzo, and Ada Roldán Soto. This is the product of all of their hard work. My family-in-law have always been there to support me as well: Blanca Ortiz, Julio Santana, and Guadalupe Santiago.

Libertad continues to be my source of inspiration. Your joy and sense of humor have been crucial for me to undertake this project. This book also carries an enormous debt to you for all the time it stole from play. I do hope that someday reading it will make you proud and will help you understand the pain and beauty of our people. My main interlocutor has been my partner in life, friend, and colleague, Aurora Santiago Ortiz. You are the engine that pushes me to continue producing work that will hopefully contribute to those freedom futures we so desire. May our love continue to serve as a compass to navigate the rest of our lives together. And may that life continue to be full of laughter, solidarity, and love.

May Puerto Rico be free soon, and forever.

NOTES

Prologue: "I Am Never Coming Back Here"

The epigraph for the Prologue is taken from Arcadio Díaz-Quiñones, *Conversación con José Luis González* (Río Piedras: Ediciones Huracán, 1976). Translated by the author. Reproduced with permission of Arcadio Díaz-Quiñones.

1. For Carlos Alberto Nieves Rivera's age, see "United States Census, 1940," database with images, *FamilySearch* (https://www.familysearch.org/ark:/61903/1:1:KFJ7-WV9), Carlos Alberto Nieves Rivera in household of Herminia Rivera Vda Nieves, Corrales, Aguadilla, Puerto Rico; citing enumeration district (ED), sheet, line, family, Sixteenth Census of the United States, 1940, NARA digital publication T627, Records of the Bureau of the Census, 1790–2007, RG 29, Washington, DC, National Archives and Records Administration, 2012, roll. For Pan Am's first flight, see https://digitalcollections.library.miami.edu/digital/collection/asm0341/id/219732/; for the airborne migration, see Jorge Duany, *Puerto Rico: What Everyone Needs to Know* (Oxford: Oxford University Press, 2017), 138; Edna Acosta-Belén and Carlos E. Santiago, *Puerto Ricans in the United States: A Contemporary Portrait*, 2nd ed. (Boulder, CO: Lynne Rienner Publishers, 2018), 4.

2. Arcadio Díaz Quiñones, *La memoria rota: Ensayos sobre cultura y política* (Río Piedras: Ediciones Huracán, 1993).

3. For some theoretical meditations on the concept of *destierro* or uprootedness, see Yomaira Figueroa Vásquez, *Decolonizing Diasporas: Radical Mappings of Afro-Atlantic Literature* (Evanston: Northwestern University Press, 2020).

4. Francisco Rivera-Batiz and Carlos E. Santiago, *Island Paradox: Puerto Rico in the 1990s* (New York: Russell Sage Foundation, 1996). See also Edgardo Meléndez, *Sponsored Migration: The State and Puerto Rican Postwar Migration to the United States* (Columbus: Ohio State University Press, 2017), 202.

5. Jorge Duany, *The Puerto Rican Nation on the Move: Identities on the Island and in the United States* (Chapel Hill: University of North Carolina Press, 2002).

6. Lesley Gill, *The School of the Americas: Military Training and Political Violence in the Americas* (Durham: Duke University Press, 2004).

7. Frances Negrón-Muntaner, "Our Fellow Americans: Why Calling Puerto Ricans 'Americans' Will Not Save Them," in *Aftershocks of Disaster: Puerto Rico Before and After the Storm*, ed. Yarimar Bonilla and Marisol LeBrón (Chicago: Haymarket Books, 2019), 113–23.

8. José Trías Monge, *Puerto Rico: The Trials of the Oldest Colony in the World* (New Haven: Yale University Press, 2007).

9. See Ángel López Cantos, *Los puertorriqueños: Mentalidad y actitudes, siglo XVIII* (San Juan: Ediciones Puerto, 2001).

10. See Ángel G. Quintero Rivera, "Apuntes para una sociología del análisis social en Puerto Rico: El mundo letrado y las clases sociales en los inicios de la reflexión sociológica," in *Patricios*

y plebeyos: Burgueses, hacendados, artesanos y obreros: Las relaciones de clase en el Puerto Rico de cambio de siglo (Río Piedras: Ediciones Huracán, 1988), 189–279.

11. See Arlene M. Dávila, *Sponsored Identities: Cultural Politics in Puerto Rico* (Philadelphia: Temple University Press, 1997).

12. For recent interpretations, see Michael Goebel, curator, "Rethinking Nationalism," *American Historical Review* 127, no. 1 (March 2022): 311–71.

13. Lisa Lowe, *The Intimacies of Four Continents* (Durham: Duke University Press, 2015).

14. Aurora Santiago Ortiz is developing this concept in a book project titled "Circuits of Self-Determination: Mapping Solidarities and Radical Political Pedagogies in Puerto Rico."

1. Borikén's First Peoples: From Migration to Insurrection

1. Francisco Moscoso, *Sociedad y economía de los Taínos* (Río Piedras: Editorial Edil, 2003); for the Caribbean geographies of waterways in a later period, see Ernesto Bassi, *An Aqueous Territory: Sailor Geographies and New Granada's Transimperial Greater Caribbean World* (Durham: Duke University Press, 2017).

2. Perhaps the most famous account of the conquest's violence was written by Bartolomé de las Casas, a Dominican friar and priest. See Bartolomé de las Casas, *A Short Account of the Destruction of the Indies* (New York: Penguin Books Limited, 2004).

3. Jalil Sued Badillo, *El Dorado borincano: La economía de la conquista, 1510–1550* (San Juan: Ediciones Puerto, 2001), 61.

4. Ibid.

5. Ada Ferrer, *Cuba: An American History* (New York: Scribner, 2021), 17.

6. Cited in Pedro Lebrón Ortiz, "Against the Mythological Machine, Towards Decolonial Revolt," *Theory & Event* 24, no. 3 (July 2021): 799.

7. Walter Mignolo, *The Idea of Latin America* (Malden, MA: Blackwell, 2005), 53, 81; Eric R. Wolf, *Europe and the People without History*, 2nd ed. (Oakland: University of California Press, 2010).

8. According to Jalil Sued Badillo, only caciques were the interpreters of collective and individual histories. See Jalil Sued Badillo, *Caribe taíno: Ensayos históricos sobre el siglo XVI* (San Juan: Editorial Luscinia C.E., 2020), 33.

9. See Mario R. Cancel, *El laberinto de los indóciles: Estudios sobre historiografía puertorriqueña del siglo 19* (Cabo Rojo: Editora Educación Emergente, 2021); Francisco Scarano, "La historia heredada: Cauces y corrientes de la historiografía puertorriqueña, 1880–1970," *Exégesis* 6, no. 17 (1993): 40–52.

10. María de los Ángeles Castro Arroyo, "De Salvador Brau a la 'novísima historia': Un replanteamiento y una crítica," *Boletín del Centro de Investigaciones Históricas*, no. 4 (1988): 9–25.

11. Laurent Dubois and Richard Lee Turits, "The Indigenous Caribbean," in *Freedom Roots: Histories from the Caribbean* (Chapel Hill: University of North Carolina Press, 2019), 14.

12. Luis A. Chanlatte Bail, *Proceso y desarrollo de los primeros pobladores de Puerto Rico y Las Antillas* (San Juan: n.p., 1986); Labor Gómez and Manuel Ballesteros Gabrois, *Culturas indígenas de Puerto Rico* (Río Piedras: Editorial Cultural, 1978); Museo de Historia, Antropología y Arte, Universidad de Puerto Rico, Recinto de Río Piedras, *Culturas indígenas de Puerto Rico* (Río Piedras: Impresos de la Universidad de Puerto Rico, 1996).

13. L. Antonio Curet, "Las crónicas en la arqueología de Puerto Rico y el Caribe," *Caribbean Studies* 34, no. 1 (January–June 2006): 163–99.

14. Irving Rouse, *The Tainos: Rise and Decline of the People Who Greeted Columbus* (New Haven: Yale University Press, 1992).

15. L. Antonio Curet, "The Earliest Settlers," in *The Caribbean: A History of the Region and Its People*, ed. Stephan Palmié and Francisco Scarano (Chicago: University of Chicago Press, 2011), 54.

16. Luis M. Díaz Soler, *Puerto Rico: Desde sus orígenes hasta el cese de la dominación española* (Río Piedras: Editorial de la Universidad de Puerto Rico, 1994), 61–62; for cemís, see Moscoso, *Sociedad y economía de los taínos*, 50.

17. Blanca G. Silvestrini and María Dolores Luque de Sánchez, *Historia de Puerto Rico: Trayectoria de un pueblo* (San Juan: Ediciones Cultural Panamericana, 1992), 62.

18. Jalil Sued Badillo, *La mujer indígena y su sociedad*, rev. ed. (Río Piedras: Editorial Cultural, 2010); Jalil Sued Badillo, "Las taínas en resistencia," in *Caribe taíno*, 257–72.

19. Sebastián Robiou Lamarche, *Tainos and Caribs: The Aboriginal Cultures of the Antilles*, trans. Grace M. Robiou Ramírez de Arellano (San Juan: Editorial Punto y Coma, 2019), 23. Columbus noted the potential mutiny in his diary entry for Wednesday, October 10, 1492; see Cristóbal Colón, *Los cuatro viajes: Testamento*, ed. Consuelo Varela (Madrid: Alianza Editorial S.A., 2007), 57.

20. Jalil Sued Badillo, *Los Caribes: Realidad o fábula* (San Juan: Editorial Cultural, 1978).

21. Jalil Sued Badillo, *Agüeybaná el Bravo* (San Juan: Ediciones Puerto, 2008).

22. Fray Ramón Pané, *An Account of the Antiquities of the Indians*, ed. Juan Arrom, trans. Susan C. Griswold (Durham: Duke University Press, 1999), 30–35.

23. Ibid., xiv.

24. See Edward Wilson-Lee, *The Catalogue of Shipwreck Books: Christopher Columbus and the Quest to Build the World's Greatest Library* (New York: Scribner, 2019).

25. Pané, *An Account of the Antiquities of the Indians*, 53. For more on cemís, see José R. Oliver, *Caciques and Cemí Idols: The Web Spun by Taíno Rulers between Hispaniola and Puerto Rico* (Tuscaloosa: University of Alabama Press, 2009).

26. Pané, *An Account of the Antiquities of the Indians*, 53.

27. Robiou Lamarche, *Tainos and Caribs*, 40.

28. Ibid.

29. Ibid.

30. Ibid.

31. Colón, *Los cuatro viajes*, 60.

32. Ibid., 33, 61.

33. Osvaldo García Goyco, "El yacimiento Jácana (PO-29), su probable participación en la rebellion taína de 1511," in *5to centenario de la rebelión taína, 1511–2011* (San Juan: Instituto de Cultura Puertorriqueña, 2011), 106; Francisco Moscoso, "El sermón de fray Antonio Montesinos, antecedentes de las Leyes de Burgos de 1512–1513: Contextualización histórica," in *5to centenario de la rebelión taína, 1511–2011*, 51.

34. For some of Puerto Rico's first settlers, see Luis Rafael Burset Flores, *Diccionario biográfico de residentes en la cuenca del Caribe* (Santo Domingo: Archivo General de la Nación, 2020), 2:279–380.

35. Ida Altman, *Life and Society in the Early Spanish Caribbean: The Greater Antilles, 1493–1550* (Baton Rouge: Louisiana State University Press, 2021), 1.

36. Olga Jiménez de Wagenheim, *Puerto Rico: An Interpretive History from Pre-Columbian Times to 1900* (Princeton: Markus Wiener, 2006), 39.

37. Juan Ángel Silén, *Historia de la nación puertorriqueña* (Río Piedras: Editorial Edil, 1980), 27.

38. Altman, *Life and Society in the Early Spanish Caribbean*, 194.

39. Sued Badillo, *Agüeybaná el bravo*, 28.

40. Sued Badillo, *El Dorado borincano*, 41.

41. Ibid., 61.

42. See Moscoso, "El sermón de fray Antonio Montesinos," 48–54.

43. Francisco Moscoso, *Fundación de San Juan en 1522* (San Juan: Ediciones Laberinto, 2020), 18–23.

44. Adolfo de Hostos, *Tesauro de datos históricos: Índice compendioso de la literatura histórica de Puerto Rico, incluyendo algunos datos inéditos, periodísticos y cartográficos* (Río Piedras: Editorial de la Universidad de Puerto Rico, 1995), 5:423.

45. García Goyco, "El yacimiento Jácana (PO-29)," 108.

46. For an example of how this myth was reproduced, see Salvador Brau, *Historia de Puerto Rico* (Río Piedras: Editorial Edil, 2000).

47. Sued Badillo, *Agüeybaná el Bravo*, 68.

48. Ibid., 32.

49. Ibid., 71.

50. García Goyco, "El yacimiento Jácana (PO-29)," 111.

51. The first census took place in 1530. Using mining documents, Jalil Sued Badillo estimates that no less than 621 people lived in Puerto Rico by 1510. See Sued Badillo, *El Dorado borincano*, 47.

52. Brau, *Historia de Puerto Rico*, 25–26.

53. Sued Badillo, *Agüeybaná el Bravo*, 184–89.

54. Francisco Moscoso, *Agricultura y sociedad en Puerto Rico, siglos 16 al 18* (San Juan: Instituto de Cultura Puertorriqueña, 2001), 9.

2. Consolidating the Colonial Project

1. For Alonso Manso, see Juan Alberto Delgado Negrón, *La visión y misión evangelizadora del obispo Alonso Manso en las Américas* (Lajas: Centro de Estudios e Investigaciones del Sur Oeste, 2020).

2. Robiou Lamarche, *Tainos and Caribs*, 180.

3. Sued Badillo, *Caribe taíno*, 263; for the role of women in Taíno society, see Sued Badillo, *La mujer indígena y su sociedad.*

4. Jalil Sued Badillo and Ángel López Cantos, *Puerto Rico negro* (Río Piedras: Editorial Cultural, 2007), 20.

5. Ibid., 19.

6. Historian David Wheat has persuasively argued that we cannot solely understand Spanish colonial history during the conquest's early stages through the binary of sugar production or resistance by enslaved peoples. Instead, he notes, scholars need to pay attention to the ways that

African peoples, free or enslaved, became surrogate settlers for the Spanish Crown, particularly in rural areas. While more work is needed for the particularities of Puerto Rico, this might have also been the case there. For more on "surrogate settlers," see David Wheat, *Atlantic Africa and the Spanish Caribbean, 1570–1640* (Williamsburg and Chapel Hill: Omohundro Institute of Early American History and Culture and University of North Carolina Press, 2016).

7. The Crown received two million gold pesos of 450 maravedís each. That would be equivalent to $294,787,584.84 in 2022. See Jalil Sued Badillo, *El Dorado borincano: La economía de la conquista, 1510–1550* (San Juan: Ediciones Puerto, 2001), 426.

8. Luis M. Díaz Soler, *Historia de la esclavitud negra en Puerto Rico* (Río Piedras: Editorial de la Universidad de Puerto Rico, 1981), 29–33; for a history of enslavement in the Spanish Caribbean, see Erin Woodruff Stone, *Captives of Conquest: Slavery in the Early Modern Spanish Caribbean* (Philadelphia: University of Pennsylvania Press, 2021).

9. Sued Badillo and López Cantos, *Puerto Rico negro*, 111; for the sugar economy, see Elsa Gelpí Báez, *Siglo en blanco: Estudio de la economía azucarera en Puerto Rico, siglo XVI* (Río Piedras: Editorial de la Universidad de Puerto Rico, 2000).

10. Sued Badillo and López Cantos, *Puerto Rico negro*, 156–58.

11. See Stuart B. Schwartz, *Sea of Storms: A History of Hurricanes in the Greater Caribbean from Columbus to Katrina* (Princeton: Princeton University Press, 2015); see also Luis Caldera Ortiz, *Historia de los ciclones y huracanes tropicales en Puerto Rico* (Lajas: Editorial Akelarre, 2014).

12. Sued Badillo and López Cantos, *Puerto Rico negro*, 175–76; Caldera Ortiz, *Historia de los ciclones*, 15–16.

13. Sued Badillo and López Cantos, *Puerto Rico negro*, 183.

14. For Garcés's story, see Miguel Rodríguez López, *El indio borincano y el rey emperador: Un encuentro para la historia, 1528* (San Juan: Editorial EDP, 2021). It seems that Garcés's trip was organized and funded by Diego Muriel, another influential vecino and enemy of Villasante.

15. See Moscoso, *Fundación de San Juan en 1522*.

16. For the population estimates, see Sued Badillo, *El Dorado borincano*, 49.

17. For the origins of San Germán, see José Aridio Taveras de León, *San Germán: Comunidad, parroquia y misión, 1511–1556* (Author's edition, 2021).

18. Jorell Meléndez-Badillo, "El cabildo secular en Puerto Rico: Siglos XVI–XVIII," *Kalathos: Revista Transdisciplinaria Metro-Inter* 5, no. 1 (2011), http://kalathos.metro.inter.edu/kalathos _mag/publications/archivo2_vol5_no1.pdf.

19. Francisco Moscoso, *El hato: Latifundio ganadero y mercantilismo en Puerto Rico, siglos 16 al 18* (San Juan: Publicaciones Gaviota, 2020); see also Moscoso, *Agricultura y sociedad en Puerto Rico*.

20. Sued Badillo and López Cantos, *Puerto Rico negro*, 110.

21. Cited in Arturo Morales Carrión, *Historia del pueblo de Puerto Rico: Desde sus orígenes hasta el siglo XVIII* (San Juan: Editorial Cordillera, 1983), 140.

22. Ibid., 138; see also Gelpí Báez, *Siglo en blanco*.

23. Morales Carrión, *Historia del pueblo de Puerto Rico*, 140.

24. Arturo Morales Carrión, *Puerto Rico y la lucha por la hegemonía en el Caribe* (Río Piedras: Editorial de la Universidad de Puerto Rico, 2003).

25. Morales Carrión, *Historia del pueblo de Puerto Rico*, 141–46.

26. Isabel Gutiérrez del Arroyo, *Conjunicón de elementos del medioevo y la modernidad en la conquista y colonización de Puerto Rico* (San Juan: Instituto de Cultura Puertorriqueña, 1974), 26.

27. Díaz Soler, *Puerto Rico*, 170.

28. The last fleet took place in 1776. For more on these institutions, see Bibiano Torres Ramírez, *La Armada de Barlovento* (Sevilla: Escuela de Estudios Hispano-Americanos de Sevilla, 1981); Esteban Mira Caballos, *El sistema naval del imperio español: Armadas, flotas y galeones en el siglo XVI* (Madrid: La Esfera de los Libros, 2005); and Esteban Mira Caballos, *Las armadas imperiales: La guerra en el mar en tiempos de Carlos V y Felipe II* (Madrid: Punto de Vista Editores, 2015).

29. Sued Badillo and López Cantos, *Puerto Rico negro*, 52.

30. For a detailed account of the economy during the second half of the sixteenth century, see Gelpí Baiz, *Siglo en blanco*.

31. "Carta del gobernador Juan de Céspedes al rey sobre varios asuntos: Informa de los daños causados por los indios caribes, sobre el número de esclavos en la obra de la catedral y el despoblamiento de la isla," in *Documentos históricos de Puerto Rico*, ed. Ricardo Alegría (San Juan: Centro de Estudios Avanzados de Puerto Rico y el Caribe, 2009), 5:5–8. The concern about depopulation continued into the following century; see Ángel López Cantos, *Historia de Puerto Rico, 1650–1700* (Sevilla: Escuela de Estudios Hispano-Americanos de Sevilla and Consejo Superior de Investigaciones Científicas, 1975), 13; Morales Carrión, *Historia del pueblo de Puerto Rico*, 144.

32. Sued Badillo and López Cantos, *Puerto Rico negro*, 128.

33. Francisco Moscoso, "La población de Puerto Rico, siglos XVI–XVIII," in *Historia de Puerto Rico*, ed. Luis E. González Vales and María Dolores Luque (Madrid: Consejo Superior de Investigaciones Científicas and Doce Calles, 2010), 31.

34. For debates around indigenous survival in Puerto Rico, see Sherina Feliciano-Santos, *A Contested Caribbean Indigeneity: Language, Social Practice, and Identity within Puerto Rican Taíno Activism* (New Brunswick, NJ: Rutgers University Press, 2021).

35. "Carta del gobernador Diego Menéndez de Valdés al rey confirmando el recibo de dos cédulas que advierten de un posible ataque de Francis Drake: Sobre la presencia de corsarios ingleses y franceses en las cosas y las precauciones tomadas en caso de ataque," in *Documentos históricos de Puerto Rico*, 5:251–55.

36. Morales Carrión, *Puerto Rico y la lucha por la hegemonía en el Caribe*, 42.

37. Fernando Picó, *History of Puerto Rico: A Panorama of Its People* (Princeton: Markus Wiener, 2017), 82.

38. Morales Carrión, *Puerto Rico y la lucha por la hegemonía en el Caribe*, 49.

39. Ibid., 54.

40. "Relación de la entrada y cerco del enemigo Boudoyno Henrico, general de la armada del principe de Orange en la ciudad de Puerto Rico de las Indias; Por el licenciado Diego de Larrasa," in *Biblioteca histórica de Puerto Rico, que contiene varios documentos de los siglos XV, XVI, XVII y XVIII*, ed. Alejandro Tapia y Rivera (San Juan: Editorial Mundo Nuevo, 2010), 424.

41. Brau, *Historia de Puerto Rico*, 103.

42. For a detailed description of the Dutch attack of 1625, see "Relación de la entrada y cerco del enemigo Boudoyno Henrico," 416–32.

43. "Carta del obispo de Puerto Rico.—D. Fray Damián López de Haro á Juan Díaz de la Calle, con una relación muy curiosa de su viaje y otras cosas," in *Biblioteca histórica de Puerto Rico*, 442. Enríquez also noted the same thing in his memoirs; see Ángel López Cantos, *Mi tío, Miguel Enríquez* (San Juan: Ediciones Puerto, 2006), 51.

44. López Cantos, *Historia de Puerto Rico*, 311–40.

45. Cited in Bibiano Torres Ramírez, *La isla de Puerto Rico* (San Juan: Instituto de Cultura Puertorriqueña, 1968), 84.

46. Moscoso, *Agricultura y sociedad en Puerto Rico*, 99.

47. Picó, *History of Puerto Rico*, 95–98.

48. For Miguel Enríquez's life, see Ángel López Cantos, *Miguel Enríquez* (San Juan: Ediciones Puerto, 1998).

49. See Arcadio Díaz Quiñones, *El arte de bregar: Ensayos* (San Juan: Ediciones Callejón, 2003).

50. López Cantos, *Mi tío, Miguel Enríquez*, 19–21.

51. Ibid., 95.

52. López Cantos, *Miguel Enríquez*, 59.

53. Ibid., 367–68.

54. López Cantos, *Mi tío, Miguel Enríquez*, 19–21.

55. "Descripción de la isla y ciudad de Puerto-Rico, y de su vecindad y poblaciones, presidio, gobernadores y Obispos; frutos y minerales: Enviada por el licenciado Don Diego de Torres Vargas, Canónigo de la Santa Iglesia de esta Isla en el aviso que llegó á España en Abril 23 de 1647, al Sr. Cronista Maestro Gil González Dávila," in *Biblioteca histórica de Puerto Rico*, 478.

56. López Cantos, *Los puertorriqueños*, 2.

57. Interestingly, in 1788 Friar Íñigo Abbad y Lasierra used the term "criollo" as a broad category that included anyone born in the archipelago in what some scholars consider Puerto Rico's first history book. For more about the racialization of the term "criollo," see Mario R. Cancel-Sepúlveda, "Jíbaros, criollos, puertorriqueños: Identidad y raza," *Periódico Claridad*, January 25, 2023, https://claridadpuertorico.com/jibaros-criollos-puertorriquenos-identidad-y -raza/.

3. Revolutionary Winds: From Reform to Revolution

1. For the period's naval history, see Morales Carrión, *Puerto Rico y la lucha por la hegemonía en el Caribe*.

2. "The Caribbean Space," in *The Caribbean: Origin of the Modern World*, ed. Consuelo Naranjo Orovio, María Dolores González-Ripoll Navarro, and María Ruiz del Árbol Moro (Madrid: Centro Superior de Investigaciones Científicas, 2022), 18–19.

3. For race relations in nineteenth-century Puerto Rico, see María del Carmen Baerga, *Negociaciones de sangre: Dinámicas racializantes en el Puerto Rico decimonónico* (Madrid: Iberoamericana Vevuert, 2015).

4. Laurent Dubois, *Haiti: The Aftershocks of History* (New York: Metropolitan Books, 2012), 19.

5. Michel-Rolph Trouillot, *Silencing the Past: Power and the Production of History* (Boston: Beacon Press, 1995).

6. Perhaps the most important book written about the revolution is C. L. R. James, *The Black Jacobins: Toussaint L'Ouverture and the Santo Domingo Revolution* (New York: Vintage Books, 1989).

7. Laurent Dubois, "Why Haiti Should Be at the Center of the Age of Revolution," *Aeon*, November 7, 2016, https://aeon.co/essays/why-haiti-should-be-at-the-centre-of-the-age-of-revolution.

8. A book with drawings became a crucial piece of evidence in the aftermath of the 1812 Aponte Rebellion in Cuba. See Matt D. Childs, *The 1812 Aponte Rebellion in Cuba and the Struggle against Atlantic Slavery* (Chapel Hill: University of North Carolina Press, 2009).

9. Lauren Dubois, *A Colony of Citizens: Revolution and Slave Emancipation in the French Caribbean, 1787–1804* (Chapel Hill: University of North Carolina Press, 2012), 7.

10. Germán Delgado Pasapera, "Orígenes del independentismo puertorriqueño," in *En busca de una estrella: Antología del pensamiento independentista puertorriqueño: De Betances a Filiberto*, ed. Juan Mari Brás (Mayagüez: Editora Causa Común, 2007), 22.

11. Díaz Soler, *Puerto Rico*, 365.

12. Jiménez de Wagenheim, *Puerto Rico*, 107.

13. Ibid., 108.

14. Ibid., 109.

15. Francisco Moscoso, *La revolución puertorriqueña de 1868: El Grito de Lares* (San Juan: Instituto de Cultura Puertorriqueña, 2003), 15.

16. Ibid., 16.

17. Delgado Pasapera, "Orígenes del independentismo," 29.

18. Moscoso, *La revolución puertorriqueña de 1868*, 18; Francisco Moscoso, personal communication with the author, July 13, 2022.

19. Delgado Pasapera, "Orígenes del independentismo," 30.

20. Guillermo Baralt, *Esclavos rebeldes: Conspiraciones y sublevaciones de esclavos en Puerto Rico, 1795–1873* (Río Piedras: Ediciones Huracán, 1981), 16.

21. Delgado Pasapera, "Orígenes del independentismo," 22.

22. Baralt, *Esclavos rebeldes*, 17–18.

23. Ibid., 18.

24. Jiménez de Wagenheim, *Puerto Rico*, 120–23.

25. Fernando Picó, *Historia general de Puerto Rico* (Río Piedras: Ediciones Huracán, 1988), 129.

26. Baralt, *Esclavos rebeldes*, 27–29.

27. Jiménez de Wagenheim, *Puerto Rico*, 117.

28. Ibid., 118.

29. For the period's demographic transformations, see Jorge Duany, "Población y migración desde 1815 hasta la actualidad," in *Historia de Puerto Rico*, ed. Luis E. González Vale and María Dolores Luque (Madrid: Consejo Superior de Investigaciones Científicas, 2010), 62–69.

30. Christopher Schmidt-Nowara, "A Second Slavery? The 19th-Century Sugar Revolutions in Cuba and Puerto Rico," in *The Caribbean: A History of the Region and Its Peoples*, ed. Stephan Palmié and Francisco Scarano (Chicago: University of Chicago Press, 2011), 333–46.

31. Moscoso, *La revolución puertorriqueña de 1868*, 23.

32. See Vincent Brown, *Tacky's Revolt: The Story of an Atlantic Slave War* (Cambridge, MA: Harvard University Press, 2020); for maroons in Puerto Rico, see Benjamin Nistal-Moret, *Esclavos, prófugos y cimarrones: Puerto Rico, 1770–1870* (Río Piedras: Editorial de la Universidad de Puerto Rico, 2004). Some scholars are now using the category of "maroon" to think about contemporary liberatory practices; see Pedro Lebrón Ortiz, *Filosofía del cimarronaje* (Cabo Rojo: Editora Educación Emergente, 2021).

33. Moscoso, *La revolución puertorriqueña de 1868*, 26.

34. Lidio Cruz Monclova, *Historia de Puerto Rico: Siglo XIX* (Río Piedras: Universidad de Puerto Rico, 1970), 1:179–81; for more on María de las Mercedes Barbudo, see Raquel Rosario Rivera, *María de las Mercedes Barbudo: Primera mujer independentista de Puerto Rico, 1773–1849* (Author's edition, 1997).

35. Gilberto R. Cabrera, *Puerto Rico y su historia íntima, 1500–1996* (San Juan: Academia Puertorriqueña de la Historia, 1997), 2:92.

36. Baralt, *Esclavos rebeldes*, 48–49.

37. For de la Torre's regime, see Carlos Altagracia Espada, *La utopía del territorio perfectamente gobernado: Miedo y poder en la época de Miguel de la Torre. Puerto Rico, 1822–1837* (Author's edition, 2013).

38. Jiménez de Wagenheim, *Puerto Rico*, 127–28.

39. Baralt, *Esclavos rebeldes*, 57.

40. Cabrera, *Puerto Rico y su historia íntima*, 2:105; Cruz Monclova, *Historia de Puerto Rico*, 1:175–90.

41. Loida Figueroa, *Breve historia de Puerto Rico*, vol. 1 (Río Piedras: Editorial Edil, 1979), 177–80.

42. By 1832, there were fifty-two recognized towns and municipalities in Puerto Rico.

43. Cabrera, *Puerto Rico y su historia íntima*, 2:98–101.

44. Schmidt-Nowara, "A Second Slavery?"; Díaz Soler, *Historia de la esclavitud negra en Puerto Rico*; Badillo and López Cantos, *Puerto Rico negro*.

45. Picó, *Historia general de Puerto Rico*, 173.

46. Ibid.

47. Altagracia Espada, *La utopía del territorio perfectamente gobernado*.

48. Baralt, *Esclavos rebeldes*, 85–144.

49. Cabrera, *Puerto Rico y su historia íntima*, 2:129–42, 173–84, 185–96.

50. Ibid., 2:177–80.

51. Baralt, *Esclavos rebeldes*, 129–30; Cabrera, *Puerto Rico y su historia íntima*, 2:178.

52. Cabrera, *Puerto Rico y su historia íntima*, 2:187.

53. Luz M. Alicea Ortega, *La formación de la clase obrera en Puerto Rico: Aproximación teórico-metodológica, 1815–1910* (Puerto Rico: First Book Publishing of P.R., 2002)

54. Cabrera, *Puerto Rico y su historia íntima*, 2:194.

55. Quintero Rivera, *Patricios y plebeyos*, 195–98; Silvia Álvarez Curbelo, *Un país del porvenir: El afán de modernidad en Puerto Rico, siglo XIX* (San Juan: Ediciones Callejón, 2005), 67.

56. López Cantos, *Los puertorriqueños*, 2.

4. Imagining the Great Puerto Rican Family

1. James L. Dietz, *Historia económica de Puerto Rico* (Río Piedras: Ediciones Huracán, 1989), 72. See also Joaquín Villanueva, "The Criollo Bloc: Corruption Narratives and the Reproduction of Colonial Elites in Puerto Rico, 1860–1917," *Centro Journal* 34, no. 2 (Summer 2022): 27–50.

2. Fernando Picó, *Amargo café: Los pequeños y medianos caficultores de Utuado en la segunda mitad del siglo XIX* (Río Piedras: Ediciones Huracán, 1981).

3. Dietz, *Historia económica de Puerto Rico*, 68–70.

4. See Félix Ojeda Reyes, *El desterrado de París: Biografía del doctor Ramón Emeterio Betances* (San Juan: Ediciones Puerto, 2001).

5. Moscoso, *La revolución puertorriqueña de 1868*, 40–41; Jesse Hoffnung-Garskof, *Racial Migrations: New York City and the Revolutionary Politics of the Spanish Caribbean* (Princeton: Princeton University Press, 2019).

6. See Antonio Rivera, *Acercándonos al Grito de Lares* (San Juan: Instituto de Cultura Puertorriqueña, 1972); Lidio Cruz Monclova, *El Grito de Lares* (San Juan: Instituto de Cultura Puertorriqueña, 1968); Olga Jiménez de Wagenheim, *El Grito de Lares: Sus causas y sus hombres* (Río Piedras: Ediciones Huracán, 2004).

7. "Ramón Emeterio Betances," in *En busca de una estrella: Antología del pensamiento independentista puertorriqueño: De Betances a Filiberto*, ed. Juan Mari Brás (Mayagüez: Editora Causa Común, 2007), 46–47.

8. Ibid., 45.

9. Mario R. Cancel, *Segundo Ruiz Belvis: El prócer y el ser humano* (Bayamón: Editorial Universidad de América, 1994).

10. Moscoso, *La revolución puertorriqueña de 1868*, 58–63.

11. Jiménez de Wagenheim, *Puerto Rico*, 173.

12. See María F. Barceló Miller, "Las mujeres en el Grito de Lares" (paper presented at the University of Puerto Rico's Museum in the Opening of an Exposition on El Grito de Lares, April 27, 2011), https://www.academia.edu/11747718/Las_mujeres_en_el_Grito_de_Lares.

13. Jiménez de Wagenheim, *Puerto Rico*, 174.

14. Moscoso, *La revolución puertorriqueña de 1868*, 62.

15. Ibid., 63.

16. Ojeda Reyes, *El desterrado de París*, 128.

17. Moscoso, *La revolución puertorriqueña de 1868*, 68–72; Jiménez de Wagenheim, *El Grito de Lares*, 221.

18. Ada Ferrer, *Insurgent Cuba: Race, Nation, and Revolution, 1868–1898* (Chapel Hill: University of North Carolina Press, 1999).

19. Cabrera, *Puerto Rico y su historia íntima*, 2:173–74.

20. Picó, *History of Puerto Rico*, 214–16.

21. Fernando Bayrón Toro, *Historia de las elecciones y los partidos políticos de Puerto Rico, 1809–2012* (San Juan: Publicaciones Gaviota, 2016), 101–24.

22. See Jürgen Habermas, *The Structural Transformation of the Public Sphere: An Inquiry into a Category of Bourgeois Society* (Cambridge: Polity Press, 2015).

23. Álvarez Curbelo, *Un país del porvenir.*

24. Jorell Meléndez-Badillo, *The Lettered Barriada: Workers, Archival Power, and the Politics of Knowledge in Puerto Rico* (Durham: Duke University Press, 2021), 7.

25. "Sociedad protectora de la inteligencia del obrero," *El obrero,* November 10, 1899, 2.

26. See Quintero Rivera, *Patricios y plebeyos,* 190–95.

27. Ileana Rodríguez Silva, "Abolition, Race, and the Politics of Gratitude in Late Nineteenth-Century Puerto Rico," *Hispanic American Historical Review* 93, no. 4 (2013): 621–57.

28. Adolfo de Hostos, *Tesauro de datos históricos,* vol. 5 (Río Piedras: Editorial de la Universidad de Puerto Rico, 1990), 461–63; Adolfo de Hostos, *Diccionario histórico bibliográfico comentado de Puerto Rico* (San Juan: Academia Puertorriqueña de la Historia, 1976), 135.

29. Isabel Gutiérrez del Arroyo, "Sociedad recolectora de documentos históricos: Su colección documental," *Revista del Instituto de Cultura Puertorriqueña,* no. 48 (July–September 1970): 36.

30. "Fundación del Ateneo Puertorriqueño: Acta de la primera junta general de socios," April 30, 1876, reproduced in Cayetano Coll y Toste, *Biblioteca histórica de Puerto Rico* 1, no. 1–2 (1914–15): 141–43.

31. Alejandro Tapia y Rivera edited *La azucena,* a magazine dedicated to women. See Alejandro Tapia y Rivera, *La azucena* (San Juan: Ediciones Puerto, 2001).

32. For Barbosa, see Daisy Flores Fernández, *Barbosa en el tiempo* (Author's edition, 2022).

33. For a detailed account of Puerto Rico's world of politics in the nineteenth century, see Cruz Monclova, *Historia de Puerto Rico.*

34. Jiménez de Wagenheim, *Puerto Rico,* 185.

35. Cabrera, *Puerto Rico y su historia íntima,* 2:498.

36. Jiménez de Wagenheim, *Puerto Rico,* 182–88.

37. See Hoffnung-Garskof, *Racial Migrations.*

38. See Patria Figueroa de Cifredo, *Pachín Marín: Heroe y poeta* (San Juan: Instituto de Cultura Puertorriqueña, 1967); José Limón de Arce, *Biografía de Francisco Gonzalo Marín* (Ponce: Casa Paoli del Centro de Investigaciones folklóricas de Puerto Rico, 2007).

39. Cabrera, *Puerto Rico y su historia íntima,* 2:582–88.

40. Germán Delgado Pasapera, *Puerto Rico: Sus luchas emancipadoras* (Río Piedras: Editorial Cultural, 1984), 536–37.

41. Ramón R. O'Neill Santos, "Betances y el anarquismo," *Archipiélago,* no. 92 (April–June 2016): 18.

42. Ibid.

43. Mark Bray, *The Anarchist Inquisition: Assassins, Activists, and Martyrs in Spain and France* (Ithaca: Cornell University Press, 2022), 128.

44. Frank Fernández, *La sangre de Santa Agueda: Angiolillo, Betances y Cánovas del Castillo* (Miami: Ediciones Universal, 1994).

45. See Bray, *The Anarchist Inquisition.*

46. Richard Bach Jensen, *The Battle against Anarchist Terrorism: An International History, 1878–1934* (Cambridge: Cambridge University Press, 2015).

47. Ojeda Reyes, *El desterrado de París,* 350–52.

48. O'Neill Santos, "Betances y el anarquismo," 19.

49. Ojeda Reyes, *El desterrado de París*, 354–57.

50. Ibid.

51. Ibid.

52. Figueroa, *Historia de Puerto Rico*, 2:139–40.

53. Bray, *The Anarchist Inquisition*, 143.

5. Chronicle of a War Foretold

1. Figueroa, *Historia de Puerto Rico*, 2:491–92.

2. U.S. War Department, Porto Rico Census Office, *Report on the Census of Porto Rico, 1899* (Washington, DC: GPO, 1900).

3. For the Ateneo, see Fernando Picó, *History of Puerto Rico: A Panorama of Its People* (Princeton: Markus Wiener, 2017), 221; see also Jesús Manuel Hernández, *Nilita Vientós Gastón y la legitimación de las disidencias políticas bajo su presidencia en el Ateneo Puertorriqueño, 1946–1961* (San Juan: Disonante, 2018).

4. Cited in Edgardo Meléndez, *Patria: Puerto Rican Revolutionary Exiles in Late Nineteenth Century New York* (New York: Centro Press, 2020), 20.

5. Hoffnung-Garskoff, *Racial Migrations*.

6. See, as an example, José Limón de Arce, *Biografía de Francisco Gonzalo Marín* (Ponce: Casa Paoli del Centro de Investigaciones Folklóricas de Puerto Rico, 2007).

7. Armando J. Martí Carvajal, "Rectificaciones históricas: Sobre las banderas de Cuba y Puerto Rico," *Akelarre: historia y ficción*, November 30, 2016, https://editorialakelarre.blogspot.com/2016/11/sobre-las-banderas-de-cuba-y-puerto-rico.html.

8. For the different ideologies within the group of Puerto Rican revolutionary exiles, see Meléndez, *Patria*.

9. Felix V. Matos Rodríguez and Pedro Juan Hernández, *Pioneros: Puerto Ricans in New York City, 1896–1948* (Charleston: Arcadia Publishing, 2001).

10. Díaz Soler, *Puerto Rico*, 690.

11. Germán Delgado Pasapera, *Puerto Rico: Sus luchas emancipadoras* (Río Piedras: Editorial Cultural, 1984), 536–37.

12. Rubén Dávila Santiago, *El derribo de las murallas: Los orígenes intelectuales del socialismo en Puerto Rico* (Río Piedras: Editorial Cultural, 1988), 23.

13. Ibid.

14. Meléndez-Badillo, *The Lettered Barriada*.

15. Ángel G. Quintero Rivera, "Apuntes para una sociología del análisis social en Puerto Rico: El mundo letrado y las clases sociales en los inicios de la reflexion sociológica," in *Patricios y plebeyos*, 189–279.

16. Delgado Pasapera, *Puerto Rico*, 538.

17. Jorell Meléndez-Badillo, *Voces libertarias: Los orígenes del anarquismo en Puerto Rico*, 3rd ed. (Lajas: Editorial Akelarre, 2015), 172–73.

18. José Manuel García Leduc, *Apuntes para una historia breve de Puerto Rico: Desde la prehistoria hasta 1898* (San Juan: Isla Negra Editores, 2002), 231–33.

19. Cabrera, *Puerto Rico y su historia íntima*, 2:604.

20. Francisco Scarano, *Puerto Rico: Cinco siglos de historia* (Mexico City: McGraw-Hill Interamericana Editores, 2008), 629; Silvestrini and Luque de Sánchez, *Historia de Puerto Rico*, 380.

21. Figueroa, *Historia de Puerto Rico*, 2:206.

22. Ibid., 2:447–54.

23. Cabrera, *Puerto Rico y su historia íntima*, 2:604–5.

24. Figueroa, *Historia de Puerto Rico*, 2:206.

25. Ibid., 2:604–5.

26. Scarano, *Puerto Rico*, 629.

27. For sugar during this period, see César J. Ayala, *American Sugar Kingdom: The Plantation Economy of the Spanish Caribbean, 1898–1934* (Chapel Hill: University of North Carolina Press, 1999); Humberto García Muñiz, *Sugar and Power in the Caribbean: The South Porto Rico Sugar Company in Puerto Rico and the Dominican Republic, 1900–1921* (Río Piedras: Editorial de la Universidad de Puerto Rico, 2010); Sidney Mintz, "The Cultural History of a Puerto Rican Sugar Cane Plantation: 1876–1949," *Hispanic American Historical Review* 33, no. 2 (May 1953): 224–51.

28. Almont Lindsey, *The Pullman Strike: The Story of a Unique Experiment and a Great Labor Upheaval* (Chicago: University of Chicago Press, 1964); Priscilla Murolo, "Wars of Civilization: The US Army Contemplates Wounded Knee, the Pullman Strike, and the Philippine Insurrection," *International Labor and Working-Class History* 80, no. 1 (2011): 77–102.

29. See, for example, William Libbey, *Princeton in the Spanish American War, 1898* (Princeton: Princeton Press, 1899); *Harvard Volunteers, 1898* (Cambridge, MA: The Harvard Crimson, 1898); and *The Dartmouth*, April 29, 1898.

30. Amy Kaplan, "Black and Blue on San Juan Hill," in *Cultures of United States Imperialism*, ed. Amy Kaplan and Donald E. Pease (Durham: Duke University Press, 1993), 219–36.

31. Ibid.; Greg Grandin, "The Pact of 1898," in *The End of Myth: From the Frontier to the Border Wall in the Mind of America* (New York: Metropolitan Books, 2019), 132–47.

32. Figueroa, *Historia de Puerto Rico*, 2:201–3.

33. Cited in Luis González Vale, "The Puerto Rican Campaign Revisited: 'A Splendid Little War'" (working paper for the Caribbean Institute and Study Center for Latin America of the Inter American University of Puerto Rico, San Germán, "The American Presence in Puerto Rico Series," November 1998), 9.

34. Edgardo Pratts, *De Coamo a la trinchera de Asomante: Incluye testimonios, anécdotas y el cuento de un combatiente de la batalla de Asomante* (Aibonito: Fundación Educativa Idelfonso Pratts, 2006). The battle has also been the focus of historiographical debates in Puerto Rico. Some of them are summarized in Francisco Serrano, *Seva vive*, DVD (San Juan: Cine con eñe, 2010).

35. See Rubén Nazario Velasco, *La historia de los derrotados: Americanización y romanticismo en Puerto Rico, 1898–1917* (San Juan: Ediciones Laberinto, 2019).

36. Jorge L. Lizardi Pollock, "Palimpsestos y heterotopias: El espacio y sus prácticas en el Viejo San Juan," *Revista mexicana del Caribe* 4, no. 8 (1999): 90–127; Puerto Rico Historic Buildings Drawings Society, "Antigua Prisión La Princesa," July 24, 2014, https://www.prhbds.org/san-juan/2014/7/23/antigua-prisin-la-princesa.

37. Meléndez-Badillo, *The Lettered Barriada*, 12–13.

38. César Andreu Iglesias, "Bosquejo para la historia del movimiento obrero en Puerto Rico," in *Historia del movimiento obrero en Puerto Rico: Brevísima antología documental*, ed. Jesús Delgado (San Juan: Federación de Maestros de Puerto Rico, 1994), 4.

39. See Gervasio L. García and Ángel G. Quintero Rivera, *Desafío y solidaridad: Breve historia del movimiento obrero puertorriqueño* (Río Piedras: Ediciones Huracán, 1997); Ángel Quintero Rivera, *Lucha obrera: Antología de grandes documentos de la historia obrera puertorriqueña* (Río Piedras: CEREP, 1972); Ángel Quintero Rivera and Lydia Milagros González, *La otra cara de la historia* (Río Piedras: CEREP, 1984); Juan Ángel Silén, *Apuntes para la historia del movimiento obrero* (San Juan: Ediciones Gaviota, 2001).

40. Santiago Iglesias Pantín, *Luchas emancipadoras*, vol. 1 (San Juan: Imprenta Cantero Fernández, 1929); Jorell Meléndez-Badillo, "Mateo and Juana: Racial Silencing, Epistemic Violence, and Counterarchives in Puerto Rican Labor History," *International Labor and Working-Class History* 96 (Fall 2019): 103–4.

41. Iglesias Pantín, *Luchas emancipadoras*.

42. Gervasio L. García, *Historia crítica, historia sin coartadas* (Río Piedras: Huracán, 1985), 67–68.

43. Gervasio L. García, "Las primeras actividades de los honrados hijos del trabajo: 1873–1898," *Revista del Centro de Investigaciones Históricas*, no. 5 (1990): 217–27; see also Meléndez-Badillo, *The Lettered Barriada*.

44. Ileana Rodríguez Silva, "Racial Silencing and the Organizing of Puerto Rican Labor," in *Silencing Race: Disentangling Blackness, Colonialism, and National Identities in Puerto Rico* (New York: Palgrave Macmillan, 2012), 159–86; Meléndez-Badillo, *The Lettered Barriada*, 126.

45. Mariano Negrón Portillo, *Las turbas republicanas, 1900–1904* (Río Piedras: Ediciones Huracán, 1990). Because there are no archival sources from the FRT, it is impossible to determine whether their ideas differed greatly from those of the FLT or the island's intellectual elite. For more on their silencing, see Rodríguez Silva, "Racial Silencing"; Meléndez-Badillo, *The Lettered Barriada*.

46. Picó, *History of Puerto Rico*, 239.

47. Arcadio Díaz Quiñones, *Once tésis sobre un crimen* (San Juan: Lusciana C.E., 2019).

48. Luis Cáldera Ortiz, *Historia de los ciclones y huracanes tropicales en Puerto Rico* (Lajas: Editorial Akelarre, 2014), 112.

49. Schwartz, *Sea of Storms*, 195–98.

50. See José Elías Levis Bernard, *Estercolero*, ed. Carmen Centeno Añeses (Río Piedras: Editorial de la Universidad de Puerto Rico, 2008).

51. Cited in Estelle Irizarry, *La voz que rompió el silencio: La novelística singular de J. Elías Levis en Puerto Rico post-1898* (San Juan: Ediciones Puerto, 2007), 58.

52. Schwartz, *Sea of Storms*, 198.

53. This would be the equivalent of $7,139,180 in 2022. See ibid., 200.

54. Ibid.

55. Lanny Thompson, *Imperial Archipelago: Representations and Rule in the Insular Territories under U.S. Dominion after 1898* (Honolulu: University of Hawai'i Press, 2010).

56. Gervasio L. García, "I Am the Other: Puerto Rico in the Eyes of North Americans, 1898," *Journal of American History* 87, no. 1 (June 2000): 39–64.

57. Lanny Thompson, "The Imperial Republic: A Comparison of the Insular Territories under U.S. Dominion after 1898," *Pacific Historical Review* 71, no. 4 (November 2002): 573–74.

58. Ojeda Reyes, *El desterrado de París*, 450–68.

59. Roberto Gytuérrez Laboy, *Pensar y entender a Hostos* (San Juan: Ediciones Situm, 2009).

60. "Carta de Betances a Estrada Palma," in *En busca de una estrella*, 65–67.

6. Foundations of U.S. Colonialism in Puerto Rico

1. Thompson, *Imperial Archipelago*.

2. Aida Negrón de Montilla, *La americanización en Puerto Rico y el sistema de instrucción pública, 1900–1930* (Río Piedras: Editorial de la Universidad de Puerto Rico, 1998), 25.

3. Solsiree del Moral, *Negotiating Empire: The Cultural Politics of Schools in Puerto Rico, 1898–1952* (Madison: University of Wisconsin Press, 2013), 16.

4. Cited in Gervasio L. García, "I Am the Other: Puerto Rico in the Eyes of North Americans, 1898," *Journal of American History* 87, no. 1 (June 2000): 49.

5. Negrón de Montilla, *La americanización en Puerto Rico*, 10.

6. For more on the UPR, see Silvia Álvarez Curbelo and Carmen I. Raffuci, eds., *Frente a la torre: Ensayos del Centenario de la Universidad de Puerto Rico, 1903–2003* (Río Piedras: Editorial de la Universidad de Puerto Rico, 2005); Axel Hernández, *Políticas imperiales sobre la educación de Puerto Rico, 1800–1920* (Lajas: Editorial Akelarre, 2015), 173–83.

7. Del Moral, *Negotiating Empire*, 17.

8. Ibid., 87–90.

9. Blanca G. Silvestrini, "El impacto de la política de salud pública de los Estados Unidos en Puerto Rico, 1898–1913," in *Politics, Society, and Culture in the Caribbean*, ed. Blanca G. Silvestrini (San Juan: Universidad de Puerto Rico, 1983), 78–80.

10. Raúl Mayo Santana, Silvia E. Rabionet, and Ángel A. Román Franco, *Historia de la medicina tropical en Puerto Rico en el siglo XX* (San Juan: Ediciones Laberinto, 2022).

11. Silvestrini, "El impacto de la política de salud pública de los Estados Unidos en Puerto Rico," 82–83; Nicole Trujillo-Pagán, *Modern Colonization by Medical Intervention: U.S. Medicine in Puerto Rico* (Leiden: Brill, 2013).

12. "Reforms in Puerto Rico: Commissioner Carroll Returns and Tells of Conditions There," *New York Times*, March 9, 1899, 9; for religion, see Silvestrini and Luque de Sánchez, *Historia de Puerto Rico:* 386–87; Samuel Silva Gotay, "La iglesia protestante como agentre de americanización en Puerto Rico, 1898–1917," in *Politics, Society, and Culture in the Caribbean*, 37–66; Pedro A. González-Vélez, *El impacto socio-político de la evangelización de Vieques por la Iglesia Metodista, 1902–1954* (Lajas: Editorial Akelarre, 2016).

13. Eileen Findlay, *Imposing Decency: The Politics of Sexuality and Race in Puerto Rico, 1870–1920* (Durham: Duke University Press, 1999), 120.

14. For the history of sex work, see Nieve de los Ángeles Vázquez Lazo, *Meretrices: La prostitución en Puerto Rico de 1876 a 1917* (Hato Rey: Publicaciones Puertorriqueñas, 2008); Mario R. Cancel, "Flores de la noche: Las mujeres públicas y el orden a fines del siglo 19," in *Historias*

marginales: Otros rostros de Jano (Mayagüez: CePa, 2007); Eileen J. Findlay, "Decent Men and Unruly Women: Prostitution in Ponce, 1890–1900," in *Imposing Decency*, 77–109.

15. L. J. Texidor, "El nuevo código penal," *La correspondencia de Puerto Rico*, January 31, 1902, 2.

16. Javier Laureano, *San Juan Gay: Conquista de un espacio urbano, 1948–1991* (San Juan: Instituto de Cultura Puertorriqueña, 2016).

17. Jorell Meléndez-Badillo, "Imagining Resistance: Organizing the Puerto Rican Southern Agricultural Strike of 1905," *Caribbean Studies Journal* 43, no. 2 (July–December 2015): 35.

18. Ibid., 33–81. For more about workers' living conditions from 1898 to 1920, see Erick J. Pérez Velazco, "La condición obrera en Puerto Rico," *Plural* 3, no. 1–2 (January–December 1984): 157–70.

19. Jorell Meléndez-Badillo, "A Party of Ex-Convicts: Bolívar Ochart, Carceral Logics, and the Socialist Party in Early Twentieth-Century Puerto Rico," *Hispanic American Historical Review* 101, no. 1 (February 2021): 76–77.

20. Meléndez-Badillo, "Imagining Resistance," 55; Federación Libre de Ponce, *16 de abril: Crímenes policiacos* (Ponce: Imprenta M. López, 1905).

21. The phrase is from a letter; see Karl Marx to Dr. Kugelmann, "Concerning the Paris Commune," London, April 12, 1871, https://www.marxists.org/archive/marx/works/1871/letters/71_04_12.htm.

22. The phrase is from the title of García and Quintero Rivera, *Desafío y solidaridad*.

23. Women became important figures within the early twentieth-century Spiritist movement. See Clara Román-Odio, *Mujeres espiritistas en Puerto Rico, 1880–1920* (Humacao: Self-published, 2021); Nancy Herzig Shannon, *El Iris de Paz: El espiritismo y la mujer en Puerto Rico, 1900–1905* (Río Piedras: Ediciones Huracán, 2001).

24. Silvestrini and Luque de Sánchez, *Historia de Puerto Rico*, 419; César Ayala and Rafael Bernabe, *Puerto Rico in the American Century: A History since 1898* (Chapel Hill: University of North Carolina Press, 2007), 68.

25. See María de Fátima Barcelo Miller, *La lucha por el sufragio femenino en Puerto Rico, 1896–1935* (Río Piedras: Ediciones Huracán, 2006).

26. Meléndez-Badillo, *The Lettered Barriada*, 15.

27. Ibid.

28. Ibid., 121.

29. Ibid.

30. Meléndez-Badillo, *The Lettered Barriada*, 108–33; Silvestrini and Luque de Sánchez, *Historia de Puerto Rico*, 420–21.

31. Norma Valle Ferrer, *Luisa Capetillo: Historia de una mujer proscrita* (Río Piedras: Editorial Cultural, 1990), 39–58.

32. For some of Capetillo's writings, see Julio Ramos, ed., *Amor y anarquía: Escritos de Luisa Capetillo* (Cabo Rojo: Editora Educación Emergente, 2021).

33. Meléndez-Badillo, *The Lettered Barriada*, 90; Jorell Meléndez-Badillo, "Luisa Capetillo and the Caribbean's Counter-Republic of Letters," *Small Axe: A Caribbean Journal of Criticism* 69 (November 2022): 112–20.

34. See Aracelis Tinarejo, *El Lector: A History of the Cigar Factory Reader* (Austin: University of Texas Press, 2010).

35. Jorell Meléndez-Badillo, "Luisa Capetillo en La Habana: Sus escritos en la prensa anarquista cubana, 1910–1914," in *Amor y anarquía*, 214–21; "Notas diversas," *¡Tierra!: Periódico anarquista*, March 12, 1910, reproduced in *Páginas libres: Breve antología del pensamiento anarquista en Puerto Rico, 1900–1919*, ed. Jorell Meléndez-Badillo (Cabo Rojo: Editora Educación Emergente, 2021), 80.

36. "Ecos y notas," *El tipógrafo*, April 16, 1911, 3.

37. "Luisa Capetillo," *Justicia*, April 17, 1922, 3.

38. Meléndez-Badillo, "Luisa Capetillo and the Caribbean's Counter-Republic of Letters."

39. See Vanessa Valdés, *Diasporic Blackness: The Life and Times of Arturo Alfonso Schomburg* (Albany: State University of New York Press, 2017); Eleanor Des Verney Sinnette, *Arthur Alfonso Schomburg: Black Bibliophile and Collector, A Biography* (New York: New York Public Library, 1989), 41–42; Jesse Hoffnung-Garskof, "The Migration of Arturo Schomburg: On Being Antillano, Negro, and Puerto Rican in New York, 1891–1938," *Journal of American Ethnic History* 21, no. 1 (Fall 2001): 3–49.

40. See Jesús Colón, *A Puerto Rican in New York and Other Sketches* (New York: International Publishers, 1982); Jesús Colón, *The Way It Was and Other Writings*, ed. Edna Acosta-Belén and Virginia Sánchez Korrol (Houston: Arte Público Press, 1993); Bernardo Vega, *Memorias de Bernardo Vega: Contribución a la historia de la comunidad puertorriqueña en Nueva York*, ed. César Andreu Iglesias (Río Piedras: Ediciones Huracán, 2009).

41. Edward Maldonado cited in Carmen Teresa Whalen and Víctor Vázquez-Hernández, eds., *The Puerto Rican Diaspora: Historical Perspectives* (Philadelphia: Temple University Press, 2005), 13.

42. See Virginia Sánchez Korrol, *From Colonia to Community: The History of Puerto Ricans in New York City* (Berkeley: University of California Press, 1994); Michael Staudenmaier, "'Mostly of Spanish Extraction': Second-Class Citizenship and Racial Formation in Puerto Rican Chicago, 1946–1965," *Journal of American History* 104, no. 3 (December 2017): 681–706.

43. Ayala and Bernabe, *Puerto Rico in the American Century*, 24–26.

44. Mónica Jiménez, "Puerto Rico under the Colonial Gaze: Oppression, Resistance, and the Myth of the Nationalist Enemy," *Latino Studies* 18 (2020): 16.

45. See García, "I Am the Other."

46. See Paul B. Niell, "Architecture, Domestic Space, and the Imperial Gaze in the Puerto Rico Chapters of *Our Islands and Their People* (1899)," in *Imperial Islands: Art, Architecture, and Visual Experience in the US Insular Empire after 1898*, ed. Joseph R. Hartman (Honolulu: University of Hawai'i Press, 2022), 103–21; Hilda Llorens, "Imaging Puerto Rican Natives, 1890–1920," in *Imaging the Great Puerto Rican Family: Framing Nation, Race, and Gender during the American Century* (Lanham, MD: Lexington Books, 2014), 1–30.

47. José de Olivares, *Our Islands and Their People as Seen with Camera and Pencil*, 2 vols. (New York: N. D. Publishing, 1899).

48. Llorens, "Imaging Puerto Rican Natives."

49. García, "I Am the Other." For more on this, see Nazario Velasco, *Los derrotados*, and Kelvin Santiago-Valle, *Subject People and Colonial Discourses: Economic Transformations and Social Disorder in Puerto Rico, 1898–1947* (Albany: State University of New York Press, 1994).

50. See Robert McGreevey, *Borderline Citizens: The United States, Puerto Rico, and the Politics of Colonial Migration* (Ithaca: Cornell University Press, 2018); Sam Erman, *Almost Citizens: Puerto Rico, the U.S. Constitution, and Empire* (Cambridge: Cambridge University Press, 2019).

51. McGreevey, *Borderline Citizens*, 33–40.

52. Ibid., 96.

53. McGreevey, "The Rise of National Status," in *Borderline Citizens*, 41–66; see also Staudenmaier, "'Mostly of Spanish Extraction.'"

54. McGreevey, *Borderline Citizens*, 155.

55. Meléndez-Badillo, "A Party of Ex-Convicts," 89.

56. Juan José Baldrich, *La huelga como instrumento de lucha, 1915–1942* (Río Piedras: Universidad de Puerto Rico, Departamento de Sociología y Antropología, Recinto de Río Piedras, 2012).

57. This is carefully detailed in Rafael Alonso Torres, *Hurto Menor: El célebre caso del allanamiento de morada contra la Federación Libre y el proceso de hurto menor contra el Secretario General de la institución* (San Juan: Privately printed, 1919).

58. Balzac v. Porto Rico, 258 U.S. 298 (1922), Justia U.S. Supreme Court, https://supreme .justia.com/cases/federal/us/258/298/.

59. Meléndez-Badillo, "A Party of Ex-Convicts," 89–90; Francisco Ortiz Santini, *Balsac vs. El Pueblo de Puerto Rico: Su historia, sus protagonistas* (San Juan: Self-published, 2018).

7. A Turbulent Decade

1. Picó, *History of Puerto Rico*, 231.

2. Miguel Á. Náter, "Ciencia, progreso y escepticismo en *Momentos*, de José A. Lanauze Rolón," *Revista de Estudios Hispánicos* 1, no. 1 (2014): 157–58.

3. José A. Lanauze Rolón, *Momentos: Poesías y cuentos fantásticos* (Ponce: Tipografía El Aguila, 1916).

4. Jorell Meléndez-Badillo, *Voces libertarias: Los orígenes del anarquismo en Puerto Rico* (Lajas: Editorial Akelarre, 2015), 178–79.

5. José A. Lanauze Rolón, *El mal de los muchos hijos: Polémica sobre el neo-maltusianismo* (n.p.: Privately published, 1926).

6. José A. Lanauze Rolón, *Por los caminos de la violencia: La idea comunista* (Ponce: Casa Editorial América, 1932).

7. See Blanca G. Silvestrini, *Los trabajadores puertorriqueños y el Partido Socialista: 1932–1940* (Río Piedras: Editorial de la Universidad de Puerto Rico, 1979); José R. Rivera Caballero, *De lobos y corderos: Afirmación Socialista y la disidencia interna del Partido Socialista de Puerto Rico, 1915–1934* (n.p.: Self-published, 2016).

8. For the concept of the "Black radical tradition," see Cedric Robinson, *Black Marxism: The Making of the Black Radical Tradition* (Chapel Hill: University of North Carolina Press, 1983).

9. See Michel-Rolph Trouillot, *Silencing the Past: Power and the Production of History* (Boston: Beacon Press, 1995).

10. Erick J. Pérez Velazco, "La condición obrera en Puerto Rico, 1898–1920," *Plural* 3, no. 1–2 (January–December 1984): 157–70.

11. Silvestrini and Dolores Luque, *Historia de Puerto Rico*, 500.

12. Schwartz, *Sea of Storms*, 253–55.

13. That would be equivalent to $1,070,877,108.43 in 2022.

14. Dietz, *Historia económica de Puerto Rico*, 156–57.

15. For needleworkers, see María del Carmen Baerga, "Exclusion and Resistance: Household, Gender, and Work in the Needlework Industry in Puerto Rico, 1914–1940" (PhD diss., State University of New York at Binghamton, 1996); Rose Pessota, "I Go to Puerto Rico" and "Island Paradise and Mass Tragedy," in *Bread upon the Waters* (Ithaca: ILR Press, 1987), 103–24.

16. Cabrera, *Puerto Rico y su historia íntima*, 2:832.

17. Ibid., 2:835.

18. Ibid., 2:835–36; Juan Carreras, *Escuelas para el hombre olvidado* (San Juan: Imprenta Venezuela, 1932); Bianca M. Medina Báez, *Teresa Angleró Sepúlveda: Primera organizadora de las trabajadoras de la industria de la aguja en Puerto Rico* (San Juan: Publicaciones Gaviota, 2019), 195–206.

19. Jorell Meléndez-Badillo, "Becoming Politicians: The Socialist Party and the Politics of Legitimation," in *The Lettered Barriada*, 108–33.

20. Meléndez-Badillo, *The Lettered Barriada*, 139–42.

21. Ayala and Bernabe, *Puerto Rico in the American Century*, 102.

22. Ibid.

23. See Silvestrini and Luque de Sánchez, *Historia de Puerto Rico*, 488; Fernando Picó, *Historia general de Puerto Rico* (Río Piedras: Ediciones Huracán, 1988), 252–54.

24. Dietz, *Historia económica de Puerto Rico*, 181; Taller de Formación Política, *No estamos pidiendo el cielo: Huelga portuaria de 1938* (Río Piedras: Ediciones Huracán, 1988); Silvestrini, *Los trabajadores puertorriqueños y el Partido Socialista*.

25. Cited in Meléndez-Badillo, *The Lettered Barriada*, 123–24.

26. Meléndez-Badillo, *The Lettered Barriada*, 134–55.

27. Ibid.

28. See Taller de Formación Política, *¡Huelga en la caña! 1933–1934* (Río Piedras: Ediciones Huracán, 1982).

29. Dietz, *Historia económica de Puerto Rico*, 184.

30. Ibid.

31. Mónica Jiménez, "Puerto Rico under the Colonial Gaze: Oppression, Resistance, and the Myth of the Nationalist Enemy," *Latino Studies* 18 (2020); Taller de Formación Política, *La cuestión nacional: El Partido Nacionalista y el movimiento obrero puertorriqueño. Aspectos de las luchas económicas y políticas de la década de 1930–40* (Río Piedras: Ediciones Huracán, 1982).

32. Truman R. Clark, *Puerto Rico and the United States, 1917–1933* (Pittsburgh: University of Pittsburgh Press, 1975), 153; "Medicine: Porto Ricochet," *Time*, February 15, 1933, https://content.time.com/time/subscriber/article/0,33009,743163,00.html.

33. Daniel Immerwahr, *How to Hide an Empire: A History of the Greater United States* (New York: Picador, 2019), 137–53.

34. For a history of the Nationalist Party, see Luis Ángel Ferrao, *Pedro Albizu Campos y el nacionalismo puertorriqueño* (Río Piedras: Editorial Cultural, 1990); José Manuel Dávila

Marichal, *Pedro Albizu Campos y el ejército libertador del Partido Nacionalista de Puerto Rico, 1930–1939* (San Juan: Ediciones Laberinto, 2022); Margaret Power, *Solidarity across the Americas: The Puerto Rican Nationalist Party and Anti-Imperialism* (Chapel Hill: University of North Carolina Press, 2023).

35. See Carmen Dolores Hernández, *Ricardo Alegría: Una vida* (San Juan: Editorial Plaza Mayor, 2002).

36. See Cristina Meneses Albizu Campos and Silvia Lora Gamarra, *Una vida de amor y sacrificio: Laura Meneses de Albizu Campos: Una vida dedicada a la lucha* (N.p.: n.p., 1997).

37. Margaret Power, "The Puerto Rican Nationalist Party, Transnational Latin American Solidarity, and the United States during the Cold War," in *Human Rights and Transnational Solidarity in Cold War Latin America*, ed. Jessica Stites Mor (Madison: University of Wisconsin Press, 2013), 21–46.

38. Bayrón Toro, *Historia de las elecciones y los partidos políticos de Puerto Rico*, 239–47.

39. Ayala and Bernabe, *Puerto Rico in the American Century*, 109.

40. See Ché Paralitici, *Sentencia impuesta: 100 años de encarcelamientos por la independencia de Puerto Rico* (San Juan: Ediciones Puerto, 2004).

41. Ché Paralitici, *Historia de la lucha por la independencia de Puerto Rico: Una lucha por la soberanía y la igualdad social bajo el dominio estadounidense* (Río Piedras: Publicaciones Gaviota, 2018), 90.

42. Ibid., 89.

43. Junta Pedro Albizu Campos, *Nervio y pulso del mundo: Nuevos ensayos sobre Pedro Albizu Campos y el nacionalismo revolucionario* (San Juan: Talla de Sombra Editores, 2014).

44. Picó, *History of Puerto Rico*, 257.

45. See Manuel E. Moraza Ortiz, *La masacre de Ponce* (Mayagüez: Publicaciones Puertorriqueñas, 2012).

46. Frank Otto Gatell, "Independence Rejected: Puerto Rico and the Tydings Bill of 1936," *Hispanic American Historical Review* 38, no. 1 (1958): 25–44.

47. See Néstor R. Duprey Salgado, *A la vuelta de la esquina: El Proyecto Tydings de independencia para Puerto Rico y el diseño de una política colonial estadounidense* (Humacao: Author's edition, 2016).

48. See Sandra Pujals, *Un caribe soviético: El comunismo internacional en Puerto Rico y el Caribe, 1919–1943* (Madrid: Ediciones Complutense, 2022).

49. Ayala and Bernabe, *Puerto Rico in the American Century*, 139. There are several MA and PhD theses that are exploring these topics; see Emmanuel Figueroa Rosado, "Borinquen rojo: Procesos sociales y politicos del comunismo en Puerto Rico durante la Tercera Internacional, 1919–1945" (PhD thesis, Universidad Interamericana de Puerto Rico-Recinto Metropolitano, 2023); Carlos Román Espada, "César Andreu Iglesias: Ante un inmortal de la historia" (PhD thesis, Centro de Estudios Avanzados de Puerto Rico y el Caribe, 2023); Félix V. Arroyo Ríos, "El gobierno de Luis Muñoz Marín: La persecución política hacia el Comité Central del Partido Comunista Puertorriqueño de 1953 a 1960" (PhD thesis, Centro de Estudios Avanzados de Puerto Rico y el Caribe, 2019); and Luis A. Díaz Feliciano, "El Partido Comunista Puertorriqueño y la táctica del Frente Popular, 1934–1945" (MA thesis, Centro de Estudios Avanzados de Puerto Rico y el Caribe, 2015).

50. Rivera Caballero, *De lobos y corderos.*

51. Meléndez-Badillo, *The Lettered Barriada*, 182.

52. Ibid., 141.

53. José Vasconcelos, *Indología: Una interpretación de la cultura ibero-americana* (Barcelona: Agencia Mundial de Librería, 1939), xxiv.

54. Luis Ángel Ferrao, "Nacionalismo, hispanismo y elite intelectual en el Puerto Rico de la década de 1930," in *Del nacionalismo al populismo: Cultura y política en Puerto Rico*, ed. Silvia Álvarez Curbelo and María Elena Rodríguez Castro (Río Piedras: Ediciones Huracán, 1993), 37–60.

55. "Antonio S. Pedreira," in *Biografías puertorriqueñas: Perfil histórico de un pueblo*, ed. Cesáreo Rosa-Nieves and Esther M. Melón (Sharon, CT: Troutman Press, 1979), 327–30.

56. Antonio S. Pedreira, *Insularismo* (Río Piedras: Editorial Edil, 2004); for a critique of *Insularismo*, see Juan Flores, *Insularismo e ideología burguesa: Una nueva lectura de A. S. Pedreira*, trans. Alberto Nicolás (Río Piedras: Ediciones Huracán, 1980).

57. Pedreira, *Insularismo*, 38.

58. Ibid., 27–28.

59. See Magali Roy-Féquière, *Women, Creole Identity, and Intellectual Life in Early Twentieth-Century Puerto Rico* (Philadelphia: Temple University Press, 2004).

60. See Arcadio Díaz Quiñones, *Sobre los principios: Los intelectuales caribeños y la tradición* (Quilmes: Universidad Nacional de Quilmes Editorial, 2006).

61. See Silvia Álvarez Curbelo and María Elena Rodríguez Castro, *Del nacionalismo al populismo: Cultura y política en Puerto Rico*, ed. Silvia Álvarez Curbelo and María Elena Rodríguez Castro (Río Piedras: Ediciones Huracán, 1993).

8. The Populist Moment

1. Díaz Quiñones, *La memoria rota*, 25.

2. Marianna Norris, *Doña Felisa: A Biography of the Mayor of San Juan* (New York: Dodd, Mead, and Company, 1969).

3. Alana Casanova-Burguess, "Snow in the Tropics," *La Brega*, WNYC Studios, podcast audio, January 6, 2022, https://www.wnycstudios.org/podcasts/la-brega/articles/8-snow-tropics.

4. "Batalla de nieve en el Sixto Escobar degeneró en 'La Batalla de los Chuponazos de China,'" *El Mundo*, January 6, 1953, 1.

5. "Nieve del norte y piraguas del país divierten a niños en batalla en el Escobar," *El Mundo*, January 6, 1954, 1.

6. Carlos de la Torre and Cynthia J. Arnson, eds., *Latin American Populism in the Twenty-First Century* (Baltimore: Johns Hopkins University Press, 2013), 7.

7. Luis A. López Rojas, *Luis Muñoz Marín y las estrategias del poder, 1936–1946* (San Juan: Isla Negra Editores, 2007), 45.

8. Ibid.

9. Ayala and Bernabe, *Puerto Rico in the American Century*, 115–16.

10. Silvestrini and Luque de Sánchez, *Historia de Puerto Rico*, 491.

11. See Luis A. López Rojas, *El debate por la nación: Ascenso y consolidación del muñocismo: Del afán por el poder hasta la discusión por el status entre Luis Muñoz Marín y Gilberto Concepción de Gracia, 1932–1945* (San Juan: Isla Negra Editores, 2011).

12. See Blanca G. Silvestrini, *Los trabajadores puertorriqueños y el Partido Socialista: 1932–1940* (Río Piedras: Editorial de la Universidad de Puerto Rico, 1979), 106; Meléndez-Badillo, *The Lettered Barriada*, 154; Raúl Guadalupe de Jesús, *Sindicalismo y lucha política: Apuntes históricos sobre el Movimiento Obrero Puertorriqueño* (San Juan: Editorial Tiempo Nuevo, 2009), 21–26.

13. Dietz, *Historia económica de Puerto Rico*, 240.

14. See Kenneth Lugo del Toro, *Nacimiento y auge de la Confederación General de Trabajadores, 1940–1945* (San Juan: Universidad Interamericana de Puerto Rico, 2013).

15. Fernando Bayrón Toro, *Historia de los partidos políticos, 1809–2012* (San Juan: Publicaciones Gaviota, 2016), 263.

16. López Rojas, *Luis Muñoz Marín y las estrategias del poder*, 102–4.

17. Victor Rivera Hernández, *Ernesto Ramos Antonini: Una biografía necesaria* (San Juan: Centro de Estudios Avanzados de Puerto Rico y el Caribe, 2004), 56.

18. Carlos R. Zapata Oliveras, "Gilberto Concepción de Gracia, Luis Muñoz Marín y la fundación del Partido Independentista Puertorriqueño, 1936–1946," in *Gilberto Concepción de Gracia: Líder de la libertad, escudero de la patria*, ed. José Luis Colón González (San Juan: Universidad Interamericana de Puerto Rico, 2021), 279–410.

19. For Tugwell, see Norberto Barreto Velázquez, *Rexford G. Tugwell: El ultimo de los tutores* (Río Piedras: Ediciones Hurcán, 2004); Charles True Goodsell, *Administration of a Revolution: Executive Reform in Puerto Rico under Governor Tugwell, 1941–1946* (Cambridge, MA: Harvard University Press, 1965); Francisco A. Catalá Oliveras, *Promesa rota: Una mirada institucionalista a partir de Tugwell* (San Juan: Ediciones Callejón, 2013).

20. Joaquín Villanueva, personal communication with the author, May 24, 2022.

21. See Joaquín Vázquez Brioso, *Eduardo Giorgetti: Precursor del Plan Chardón y el programa Manos a la Obra: Estudio sobre su obra legislativa y el Memorial, 1926* (San Juan: Ediciones Faro de Luz, 2020).

22. Jaime Partsch, *Jesús T. Piñero: El exiliado en su patria* (Río Piedras: Ediciones Huracán, 2006), 68–78.

23. See Partsch, "La lucha por la fortaleza," in *Jesús T. Piñero*, 91–122.

24. See Matthew O. Edel, "Land Reform in Puerto Rico, 1940–1959," *Caribbean Studies Journal* 2, no. 3 (October 1962): 26–61; Rubén Nazario Velasco, *El paisaje y el poder: La tierra en el tiempo de Luis Muñoz Marín* (San Juan: Ediciones Callejón, 2014); Ismael García-Colón, *Land Reform in Puerto Rico: Modernizing the Colonial State, 1941–1969* (Gainesville: University Press of Florida, 2009).

25. Eileen J. Suárez Findlay, *We Are Left without a Father Here: Masculinity, Domesticity, and Migration in Postwar Puerto Rico* (Durham: Duke University Press, 2014), 27.

26. López Rojas, *Luis Muñoz Marín y las estrategias del poder*, 105–6; for the Cold War in Puerto Rico, see Manuel Rodríguez Vázquez and Silvia Álvarez Curbelo, eds., *Tiempos binarios: La Guerra Fría desde Puerto Rico y el Caribe* (San Juan: Ediciones Callejón, 2017); Silvia Álvarez Curbelo, Manuel Rodríguez Vázquez, Yanelba Mota Maldonado, and Rumar Rolón Narváez,

Puerto Rico y el Caribe: Frontera de la Guerra Fría (San Juan: Fundación Luis Muñoz Marín, 2019).

27. See Jorge M. Farinacci Fernós, *La constitución obrera de Puerto Rico: El Partido Socialista y la Convención Constituyente* (Río Piedras: Ediciones Huracán, 2015); Yolanda Martínez Viruet, "María Libertad Gómez Garriga y el proceso de la asamblea constituyente del Estado Libre Asociado de Puerto Rico" (PhD thesis, Universidad del País Vasco, 2016).

28. Francisco Scarano, "La mascarada jíbara y la política de la subalternidad en la forja de la identidad criolla en Puerto Rico, 1745–1823," in *La mascarada jíbara y otros ensayos* (San Juan: Ediciones Laberinto, 2022); Lillian Guerra, "The Jíbaro—Refuge of the Puerto Rican Sou: Elite Discourses of Nostalgia, Incorporation, and Betrayal," in *Popular Expression and National Identity in Puerto Rico: The Struggle for Self, Community, and Nation* (Gainesville: University Press of Florida, 1998).

29. Arlene M. Dávila, "The Institute of Puerto Rican Culture and the Building Blocks of Nationality," in *Sponsored Identities: Cultural Politics in Puerto Rico* (Philadelphia: Temple University Press, 1997), 60–98.

30. Catherine Marsh Kennerly, *Negociaciones culturales: Los intelectuales y el proyecto pedagógico del estado muñocista* (San Juan: Ediciones Callejón, 2008), 19.

31. Soraya Serra Collazo, ed., *Explorando la operación serenidad* (San Juan: Fundación Luis Muñoz Marín, 2011).

32. See Marsh Kennerly, *Negociaciones culturales*; Marcos A. Vélez Rivera, *Las ilustraciones de Los Libros para el Pueblo de la División de Educación de la Comunidad y la modernización de Puerto Rico, 1949–1964* (Carolina: Ediciones UNE, 2016).

33. Marsh Kennerly, *Negociaciones culturales*; Vélez Rivera, *Las ilustraciones de Los Libros para el Pueblo*.

34. Malena Rodríguez Castro, "La década de los cuarenta: De la torre a las calles," in *Frente a la torre: Ensayos del Centenario de la Universidad de Puerto Rico, 1903–2003*, ed. Silvia Álvarez Curbelo and Carmen I. Raffuci (Río Piedras: Editorial de la Universidad de Puerto Rico, 2005), 148–51.

35. Ayala and Bernabe, *Puerto Rico in the American Century*, 134.

36. Rodríguez Castro, "La década de los cuarenta," 168–73.

37. Ibid.

38. Ivonne Acosta Lespier, *La mordaza: Puerto Rico, 1948–1957* (Río Piedras: Editorial Edil, 2008).

39. Kal Wagenheim and Olga Jiménez de Wagenheim, *The Puerto Ricans: A Documentary History* (Maplewood: Waterfront Press, 1988), 204.

40. Edward F. Ryan, *Washington Post*, March 2, 1954, (pp. 1, 12–13) cited in Wagenheim and Jiménez de Wagenehim, *The Puerto Ricans*, 206.

41. División de Educación de la Comunidad, *Emigración* (San Juan: Departamento de Instrucción Pública, 1966); see also Meléndez, *Sponsored Migration*.

42. See Helen Icken Safa, *The Urban Poor of Puerto Rico: A Study in Development and Inequality* (New York: Holt, Rinehart, and Winston, 1974); Zaire Zenit Dinzey-Flores, *Locked In, Locked Out: Gated Communities in a Puerto Rican City* (Philadelphia: University of Pennsylvania Press, 2013), 14–17.

9. The Great Migration

1. For the first-class menu aboard the *Borinquen* steamship, see Matos-Rodríguez and Hernández, *Pioneros*, 20.

2. René Marqués, *La carreta* (San Juan: Francisco Vázquez Editores, 2016); Juan Antonio Corretjer, "Boricua en la luna." For the anonymous worker's name, see Tatiana Pérez Rivera, "Conoce la historia de Lucy y Alicia, las hijas 'del peón de Las Marías y la mujer de Aguadilla' de 'Un boricua en la luna,'" *El nuevo día*, November 14, 2020, https://www.elnuevodia.com /entretenimiento/cultura/notas/conoce-la-historia-de-lucy-y-alicia-las-hijas-del-peon-de-las -marias-y-la-mujer-de-aguadilla-de-un-boricua-en-la-luna/?r=66511; Pedro Pietri, "Puerto Rican Obituary."

3. Teresa Whalen and Vázquez-Hernández, *The Puerto Rican Diaspora*, 37.

4. Meléndez, *Patria*.

5. Hoffnung-Garskof, *Racial Migrations*.

6. Sánchez Korrol, *From Colonia to Community*.

7. Carmelo Rosario Natal, *Éxodo puertorriqueño: Las emigraciones al Caribe y Hawaii, 1900– 1915* (San Juan: Editorial Edil, 2001).

8. Teresa Whalen and Vázquez-Hernández, *The Puerto Rican Diaspora*, 3; for the Jones Act, see McGreevey, *Borderline Citizens*; Erman, *Almost Citizens*; Charles R. Venator-Santiago, *Puerto Rico and the Origins of the U.S. Global Empire: The Disembodied Shade* (New York: Routledge, 2015).

9. Sánchez Korrol, *From Colonia to Community*, 28–30.

10. César Andreu Iglesias, ed., *Memorias de Bernardo Vega: Contribución a la comunidad puer-torriqueña en Nueva York* (Río Piedras: Ediciones Huracán, 2013); Carmen Ana Pont, "'La familia Farallón': Un siglo de vida puertorriqueña en Nueva York," *Revista del Centro de Investigaciones Históricas* 25 (2008): 53–159; Jesús Colón, *A Puerto Rican in New York and Other Sketches* (New York: International Publishers, 1982).

11. Federico Ribes Tovar, *El libro puertorriqueño de Nueva York* (n.p.: Colección Grandes Emigraciones, 1968), 1:129–50.

12. Meléndez, *Sponsored Migration*.

13. Both are cited in Teresa Whalen and Vázquez-Hernández, *The Puerto Rican Dias-pora*, 8.

14. Cited in Duany, *The Puerto Rican Nation on the Move*, 171.

15. Ibid.

16. Ibid., 170.

17. "Socialists Elect 27-Year-Old Leader; Clarence Senior Is Youngest Ever to Hold Position of National Secretary," *New York Times*, July 3, 1929, 28.

18. Duany, *The Puerto Rican Nation on the Move*, 171. Another influential report that also in-formed the government's economic development ideas was Harvey Perloff, *Puerto Rico's Eco-nomic Future: A Study in Planned Development* (Chicago: University of Chicago Press, 1950).

19. Acosta-Belén and Santiago, *Puerto Ricans in the United States*, 66–67. For Chenault, see "Adjustment Challenges: Puerto Ricans in New York City, 1938–1945: The Writings of Patria Aran Gosnell, Lawrence Chenault, and Frances M. Donohue," https://www.thefreelibrary.com

/Adjustment+Challenges%3a+Puerto+Ricans+in+New+York+City%2c+1938-1945.+The. . . -a0589697999.

20. Virgilio Dávila, *Aromas del terruño* (San Juan: Editorial Cordillera, 1979).

21. Meléndez, *Sponsored Migration.*

22. For more contemporary examples of these transnational negotiations of the Puerto Rican identity, see Gina M. Pérez, *The Near Northwest Side Story: Migration, Displacement, and Puerto Rican Families* (Berkeley: University of California Press, 2004); Mérida M. Rúa, *A Grounded Identidad: Making New Lives in Chicago's Puerto Rican Neighborhoods* (Oxford: Oxford University Press, 2002); and Elizabeth M. Aranda, *Emotional Bridges to Puerto Rico: Migration, Return Migration, and the Struggles for Incorporation* (Lanham, MD: Rowman and Littlefield, 2007).

23. Duany, *The Puerto Rican Nation on the Move,* 171.

24. División de Educación de la Comunidad, *Emigración,* 2nd ed. (San Juan: Departamento de Instrucción Pública, 1966).

25. Lilia Fernández, *Brown in the Windy City: Mexicans and Puerto Ricans in Postwar Chicago* (Chicago: University of Chicago Press, 2002), 71–73.

26. Charles R. Venator-Santiago, *Hostages of Empire: A Short History of the Extension of U.S. Citizenship to Puerto Rico, 1989–Present* (Author's edition, 2018). See also Charles R. Venator-Santiago, "The Law That Made Puerto Ricans U.S. Citizens, Yet Not Fully American," *Zócalo,* March 6, 2018, https://www.zocalopublicsquare.org/2018/03/06/law-made-puerto-ricans-u-s -citizens-yet-not-fully-american/ideas/essay/.

27. Cited in Fernández, *Brown in the Windy City,* 5.

28. Ibid.

29. Carmen Teresa Whalen, *From Puerto Rico to Philadelphia: Puerto Rican Workers and Postwar Economies* (Philadelphia: Temple University Press, 2001), 137.

30. Ibid., 173.

31. Lorrin Thomas, *Puerto Rican Citizen: History and Political Identity in Twentieth-Century New York* (Chicago: University of Chicago Press, 2010).

32. José E. Cruz, *Liberalism and Identity Politics: Puerto Rican Community Organization and Collective Action in New York* (New York: Centro Press, 2019), 106. For some examples, see Ribes Tovar, *El libro puertorriqueño de Nueva York,* 276–98.

33. José E. Cruz Figueroa, "Entre West Side Story y los Young Lords," *80 grados,* December 3, 2021, https://www.80grados.net/entre-west-side-story-y-los-young-lords/.

34. Ruth Glasser, *My Music Is My Flag: Puerto Rican Musicians and Their New York Communities, 1917–1940* (Berkeley: University of California Press, 1995).

35. Karen Jaime, *The Queer Nuyorican: Racialized Sexualities and Aesthetics in Loisaida* (New York: New York University Press, 2021), 6.

36. For some important analysis of queerness and Puerto Ricanness, see Lawrence La Fountain-Stokes, *Queer Ricans: Cultures and Sexualities in the Diaspora* (Minneapolis: University of Minnesota Press, 2009); Lawrence La Fountain-Stokes, *Translocas: The Politics of Puerto Rican Drag and Trans Performance* (Ann Arbor: University of Michigan Press, 2021); Lawrence La Fountain-Stokes and Yolanda Martinez-San Miguel, eds., "Revisiting Queer Puerto Rican Sexualities: Queer Futures, Reinventions, and Un-Disciplined Archives," *Centro Journal* 30, no. 2

(Summer 2018): 6–41; and Luis Apontes-Parés, Jossianna Arroyo, Elizabeth Crespo-Kebler, Lawrence La Fountain-Stokes, and Frances Negrón-Muntaner, eds., "Puerto Rican Queer Sexualities," *Centro Journal* 19, no. 1 (Spring 2007).

37. Lawrence La Fountain-Stokes, "The Life and Times of Trans Activist Sylvia Rivera," in *Critical Dialogues in Latinx Studies: A Reader*, ed. Ana Y. Ramos-Zayas and Mérida M. Rúa (New York: New York University Press), 241–53.

38. Ruth Glasser, *Aquí me quedo: Puerto Ricans in Connecticut* (Hartford: Connecticut Humanities Council, 1997).

39. C. Wright Mills, Clarence Senior, and Rose Kohn Goldsen, *The Puerto Rican Journey: New York's Newest Migrants* (New York: Harper & Brothers, 1950), 101.

40. Ismael García-Colón, *Colonial Migrants at the Heart of Empire: Puerto Rican Workers on U.S. Farms* (Berkeley: University of California Press, 2020).

41. See Suárez Findlay, *We Are Left without a Father Here.*

42. Picó, *History of Puerto Rico*, 287.

43. Ayala and Bernabe, *Puerto Rico in the American Century*, 224–25.

44. Pablo José Hernández Rivera, *Compatriotas: Exilio y retorno de Luis Muñoz Marín* (Ponce: Fundación Rafael Hernández Colón, 2020).

45. Ibid., 4.

46. Silvia Álvarez Curbelo, "El centro de todo: Consumo, arquitectura y ciudad," in *San Juan siempre nuevo: Arquitectura y modernización en el siglo XX* (San Juan: Comisión San Juan, 2000), 269.

47. "Puerto Rico: The Bard of Bootstrap," *Time* 71, no. 25 (June 23, 1958), http://content.time.com/time/covers/0,16641,19580623,00.html; "Man of the People," *Time* 53, no. 18 (May 2, 1949), https://content.time.com/time/covers/0,16641,19490502,00.html.

48. Ayala and Bernabe, *Puerto Rico in the American Century*, 273; Picó, *History of Puerto Rico*, 300–301.

49. Jennifer Hinojosa, "Two Sides of the Coin of Puerto Rican Migration: Depopulation in Puerto Rico and the Redefinition of the Diaspora," *Centro Journal* 30, no. 3 (2018): 234.

50. Francisco Rivera-Batiz and Carlos E. Santiago, *Island Paradox: Puerto Rico in the 1990s* (New York: Russell Sage Foundation, 1996), 45; Teresa Whalen and Vázquez-Hernández, *The Puerto Rican Diaspora*, 37.

10. The Cold War and the New Push for Independence

1. For the cultural dimensions of the PPD's discourse, see Eileen J. Suárez Findlay, "Family and Fatherhood in a 'New Era for All': Populist Politics and Reformed Colonialism," in *We Are Left without a Father Here*, 25–59; see also "Discurso preparado para el gobernadora por Arturo Morales Carrión" (October 4, 1953), *Centro de Documentación Histórica Arturo Morales Carrión*, FPH-32–12, Interamerican University of Puerto Rico, http://dspace.cai.sg.inter.edu/xmlui/handle/123456789/11631.

2. Carlos Quiles, *Pupa: Mujer en lucha* (San Juan: Publicaciones Gaviota, 2007), 31.

3. Ibid., 28.

4. Ibid., 31.

5. Ibid., 45.

6. Ibid., 34.

7. Ibid., 53.

8. Paralitici, *Historia de la lucha*, 175–76.

9. Ibid., 173–74.

10. Quiles, *Pupa*, 66–67.

11. Ibid., 56.

12. Ibid., 111–12.

13. For women in the PSP, see Cristina M. Nieves Labiosa, "La mujer en el Partido Socialista Puertorriqueño: Entre la ideología y el género, 1971–77," in *En pie de lucha: Nuevas investigaciones históricas puertorriqueñas*, ed. Evelyn Vélez Rodríguez and Carmelo Campos Cruz (Ponce: Mariana Editores, 2019), 205–40.

14. Juan Ángel Silén, *La nueva lucha de independencia* (Río Piedras: Editorial Edil, 1973).

15. Carmen Gautier Mayoral and Teresa Blanco Stahl, "COINTELPRO en Puerto Rico: Documentos secretos del FBI, 1960–1971," in *Las carpetas: Persecución política y derechos civiles en Puerto Rico*, ed. Ramón Bosque Pérez and José Javier Colón Morera (Río Piedras: Centro para la Investigación y Promoción de los Derechos Civiles, 1997), 255–300; Francisco Pagán Oliveras, "COINTELPRO: Aplicación del programa de contraespionaje doméstico en Puerto Rico, 1960–1971," in *En pie de lucha*, 135–68.

16. Ángel Pérez Soler, *Del Movimiento Pro Independencia al Partido Socialista Puertorriqueño: La transición de la lucha nacionalista a la lucha de los trabajadores: 1959–1971* (San Juan: Publicaciones Gaviota, 2018), 146.

17. Ibid., 123.

18. Cited in ibid., 133.

19. Anne Garland Mahler, *From the Tricontinental to the Global South: Race, Radicalism, and Transnational Solidarity* (Durham: Duke University Press, 2018).

20. Álvaro M. Rivera Ruiz, *Violencia política y subalternidad colonial: El caso de Filiberto Ojeda y el MIRA* (San Juan: n.p., 2020), 182.

21. See Ángel M. Agosto, *Del MPI al PSP: El eslabón perdido* (Río Grande: La Casa Editora de Puerto Rico, 2018).

22. José Atiles Osorio, *Jugando con el derecho: Movimientos anticoloniales puertorriqueños y la fuerza de la ley* (Cabo Rojo: Editora Educación Emergente, 2019), 92.

23. Raúl Álzaga Manresa, "Prólogo al terrorismo de derecha," in *La represión contra el independentismo puertorriqueño: 1960–2010*, ed. Ché Paralitici (San Juan: Publicaciones Gaviota, 2011), 203.

24. Trías Monge, *Puerto Rico*, 136.

25. Ibid., 137.

26. Paralitici, *Historia de la lucha*, 253; Trías Monge, *Puerto Rico*, 138.

27. Cited in Trías Monge, *Puerto Rico*, 139.

28. Ibid., 140.

29. See Norma Tapia, *La crisis del PIP* (Río Piedras: Editorial Edil, 1980).

30. Paralitici, *Historia de la lucha*, 192.

31. Agosto, *Del MPI al PSP*, 79; Ayala and Bernabe, *Puerto Rico in the American Century*, 233.

32. Edwin A. López Tosado, "El Movimiento Obrero Unido: Entre sindicalismo y represión," in *En pie de lucha*, 297.

33. Atiles, *Jugando con el derecho*, 98.

34. Bayrón Toro, *Historia de las elecciones y los partidos políticos de Puerto Rico*, 339, 369.

35. Rachel A. May, Alejandro Schneider, and Roberto González Arana, *Caribbean Revolutions: Cold War Armed Movements* (Cambridge: Cambridge University Press, 2018), 129.

36. Ibid., 131.

37. Cited in ibid., 134.

38. Ángel M. Agosto, *Lustro de gloria: Cinco años que estremecieron el siglo* (Río Grande: La Casa Editora de Puerto Rico, 2013), 182.

39. Agosto, *Del MPI al PSP*, 11.

40. José E. Velázquez, Carmen V. Rivera, and Andrés Torres, eds., *Revolution around the Corner: Voices from the Puerto Rican Socialist Party in the United States* (Philadelphia: Temple University Press, 2021), 38.

41. Ibid., 16.

42. Ibid., 360.

43. Ibid. Emphasis in the original.

44. Cited in ibid.

45. Johanna Fernández, *The Young Lords: A Radical History* (Chapel Hill: University of North Carolina Press, 2020); Darrel Wanzer-Serrano, *The Young Lords and the Struggle for Liberation* (Philadelphia: Temple University Press, 2015); Darrel Enck-Wanzer, ed., *The Young Lords: A Reader* (New York: New York University Press, 2010).

46. Iris Morales, *Through the Eyes of Rebel Women: The Young Lords: 1969–1976* (New York: Red Sugarcane Press, 2016).

47. Emma Francis-Snyder, "The Hospital Occupation That Changed Public Health Care," *New York Times*, October 12, 2021, https://www.nytimes.com/2021/10/12/opinion/young-lords-nyc-activism-takeover.html.

48. Marisol LeBrón, personal communication with the author, May 26, 2022.

49. For other forms of activism, see Mirelsie Velázquez, *Puerto Rican Chicago: Schooling the City, 1940–1977* (Champaign: University of Illinois Press, 2022); María E. Pérez y González and Virginia Sánchez Korrol, *Puerto Rican Studies in the City University of New York: The First Fifty Years* (New York: Centro Press, 2021); Lorrin Thomas, *Puerto Rican Citizen: History and Political Identity in Twentieth-Century New York* (Chicago: University of Chicago Press, 2010); Lorrin Thomas and Aldo Lauria-Santiago, *Rethinking the Struggle for Puerto Rican Rights* (New York: Routledge, 2019).

50. Ayala and Bernabe, *Puerto Rico in the American Century*, 283.

51. Lucila Irizarry Cruz, *CAL: Una historia clandestina* (San Juan: Isla Negra Editores, 2010).

52. Atiles, *Jugando con el derecho*, 98.

53. Ayala and Bernabe, *Puerto Rico in the American Century*, 283.

54. "Operación diez por uno," *Claridad*, April 25, 1971, in *Centro de Documentación de los Medios Armados*, https://cedema.org/digital_items/2046.

55. Luis Nieves Falcón, *Un siglo de represión en Puerto Rico, 1898–1998* (San Juan: Ediciones Puerto, 2009), 165; José Enrique Ayora Santaliz, *Patriotas: Contracanto al olvido* (Cayey: Mariana Editores, 2009), 329; Ché Paralitici, ed., *La represión contra el independentismo puertorriqueño: 1960–2010* (San Juan: Publicaciones Gaviota, 2011), 247.

56. Paralitici, *Historia de la lucha*, 213–14.

57. Nieves Falcón, *Un siglo de represión política*, 156; Atiles, *Jugando con el derecho*, 107; Pedro Reina Pérez, "La primavera nueva y la deuda con Puerto Rico," *80 grados*, May 1, 2015, https://www.80grados.net/la-primavera-nueva-y-la-deuda-con-puerto-rico/; Rosa Mari Pesquera, "Mi hermano Chagui," *80 grados*, March 25, 2011, https://www.80grados.net/mi-hermano-chagui/.

58. José Rafael Reguero, *Alejo y los niños de sangre azul* (N.p.: n.p., 2010); Paralitici, *La represión contra el independentismo puertorriqueño*.

59. Atiles, *Jugando con el derecho*, 108.

60. "Nation: Death at Maravilla," *Time*, May 14, 1979, https://web.archive.org/web/20100728231423/http://www.time.com/time/magazine/article/0,9171,916768,00.html.

61. Ibid.

62. Picó, *History of Puerto Rico*, 290.

63. Ibid., 291.

64. See Ramón Bosque Pérez and José Javier Colón Morera, eds., *Las carpetas: Persecución política y derechos civiles en Puerto Rico* (Río Piedras: Centro para la Investigación y Promoción de los Derechos Civiles, 1997).

65. José Anazagasty, "Las carpetas y la era de la disculpa," *80 grados*, April 6, 2012, https://www.80grados.net/las-carpetas-y-la-era-de-la-disculpa-consideraciones-iniciales/.

11. The Road to Collapse

1. Ayala and Bernabe, *Puerto Rico in the American Century*, 267.

2. Cabrera, *Puerto Rico y su historia íntima*, 2:1019.

3. Ibid., 2:995.

4. Ayala and Bernabe, *Puerto Rico in the American Century*, 268.

5. Picó, *History of Puerto Rico*, 291.

6. Liliana Cotto, *Desalambrar: Orígenes de los rescates de terreno en Puerto Rico y su pertinencia en los movimientos sociales contemporaneos* (San Juan: Editorial Tal Cual, 2006).

7. Bárbara I. Abadía Rexach, "Adolfina Villanueva Osorio, presente," *NACLA*, June 19, 2021, https://nacla.org/adolfina-villanueva-osorio-puerto-rico.

8. Nydia Bauzá, "Viudo de Adolfina Villanueva recuerda su valentía antes de morir a manos de la Policía," *Primera hora*, June 10, 2020, https://www.primerahora.com/noticias/puerto-rico/notas/viudo-de-adolfina-villanueva-recuerda-su-valentia/.

9. "Villa Sin Miedo, destruida," *El país* (Spain), May 19, 1982, https://elpais.com/diario/1982/05/20/internacional/390693623_850215.html.

10. Marisol LeBrón, *Policing Life and Death: Race, Violence, and Resistance in Puerto Rico* (Oakland: University of California Press, 2019).

11. Érika Fontánez Torres, *Casa, suelo y título: Vivienda e informalidad en Puerto Rico* (San Juan: Ediciones Laberinto, 2020), 126–30.

12. Arlene Dávila, *El Mall: The Spatial and Class Politics of Shopping Malls in Latin America* (Oakland: University of California Press, 2016); Rubén Dávila Santiago, *El Mall: Del mundo al paraíso* (San Juan: Ediciones Callejón, 2005).

13. Cabrera, *Puerto Rico y su historia íntima*, 2:1026.

14. Marc D. Joffe and Jesse Martínez, "Origins of the Puerto Rico Fiscal Crisis," Mercatus Research, April 12, 2016, https://doi.org/10.2139/ssrn.3211660.

15. Juan G. Gelpí, *Literatura y paternalismo en Puerto Rico* (Río Piedras: Editorial de la Universidad de Puerto Rico, 1993); Rafael Bernabe, *La maldición de Pedreira: Aspectos de la crítica romántico-cultural de la modernidad en Puerto Rico* (Río Piedras: Ediciones Huracán, 2002); Luis Ángel Ferrao, "Nacionalismo, hispanismo y élite intelectual en el Puerto Rico de la década de 1930," in *Del nacionalismo al populismo: Cultura y política en Puerto Rico*, ed. Silvia Álvarez Curbelo and María Elena Rodríguez Castro (Río Piedras: Ediciones Huracán, 1993), 37–60.

16. María del Carmen Baerga, "Historia crítica, historia autorreflexiva: CEREP y el reto de la teoría," *Claridad*, November 17–23, 2011, 18–19.

17. Carlos J. Carrero Morales, "Reflexionando sobre CEREP y la Nueva Historia Puertorriqueña: A 28 años el final de un proyecto historiográfico" (paper delivered at the Asociación de Estudiantes Graduados de Historia [CEAPRC], March 20, 2016), https://aeghcea.files .wordpress.com/2016/03/20-reflexionando-sobre-cerep3.pdf.

18. Marcia Rivera, Ángel Chuco Quintero Rivera, Arcadio Díaz Quiñones, and Lydia Milagros González, "¿Qué fue CEREP, el centro que tanto aportó a Puerto Rico?" *Voz Alternativa*, Radio Isla 1320, January 23, 2022.

19. Pérez y González and Sánchez Korrol, *Puerto Rican Studies in the City University of New York*, 3.

20. Ibid., 4.

21. Pedro Cabán, "Remaking Puerto Rican Studies at 50 Years," in *Puerto Rican Studies in the City University of New York*, 18.

22. Ibid.

23. Atiles, *Jugando con el derecho*, 114; Rachel A. May, Alejandro Schneider, and Roberto González Arana, *Caribbean Revolutions: Cold War Armed Movements* (Cambridge: Cambridge University Press, 2018), 138.

24. May, Schneider, and González Arana, *Caribbean Revolutions*, 138.

25. Atiles, *Jugando con el derecho*, 114; May, Schenider, and González Arana, *Caribbean Revolutions*, 139.

26. May, Schenider, and González Arana, *Caribbean Revolutions*, 139.

27. Atiles, *Jugando con el derecho*, 115–21.

28. Rubén Berrios Martínez, *La independencia de Puerto Rico: Razón y lucha* (San Juan: Editorial Linea, 1983).

29. Duany, *The Puerto Rican Nation on the Move*; Dávila, *Sponsored Identities*; Marsh Kennerly, *Negociaciones culturales*.

30. Antonio Quiñones Calderón, *Partido Nuevo Progresita: Atecedentes y Fundación* (Río Piedras: Publicaciones Gaviota, 2017), 118.

31. Mario Ramos Méndez, *Posesión del ayer: La nacionalidad cultural en la estadiad* (San Juan: Isla Negra Editores, 2007), 129.

32. Ayala and Bernabe, *Puerto Rico in the American Century*, 280.

33. "Exgobernador Hernández Colón recuerda la visita del Rey a Puerto Rico," *La vanguardia*, June 2, 2014, https://www.lavanguardia.com/politica/20140602/54408617477/exgobernador-hernandez-colon-recuerda-la-visita-del-rey-a-puerto-rico.html.

34. Sociedad Estatal Para la Ejecución de Programas del Quinto Centenario, *Gran regata Colón quinto centenario: programa oficial* (San Juan: n.p., 1992).

35. "Exgobernador Hernández Colón recuerda la visita del Rey a Puerto Rico."

36. Bayrón Toro, *Historia de las elecciones y los partidos políticos de Puerto Rico*, 449.

37. Ibid., 450.

38. Ramos Méndez, *Posesión del ayer*, 149–60.

39. The results were as follows: commonwealth: 823,250; statehood: 785,859; independence: 75,253; blank or nulled votes: 17,025; total: 1,701,395. See Bayrón Toro, *Historia de las elecciones*, 469.

40. Petra R. Rivera-Rideau, *Remixing Reggaeton: The Cultural Politics of Race in Puerto Rico* (Durham: Duke University Press, 2015), 36; Zaire Zenit Dinzey-Flores, *Locked In, Locked Out: Gated Communities in a Puerto Rican City* (Philadelphia: University of Pennsylvania Press, 2013), 29; LeBrón, *Policing Life and Death*.

41. LeBrón, *Policing Life and Death*, 64.

42. José Fusté, "Colonial Laboratories, Irreparable Subjects: The Experiment of (B)ordering San Juan's Public Housing Residents," *Social Identities* 16, no. 1 (2010): 41–59.

43. Dinzey-Flores, *Locked In, Locked Out*, 16–17.

44. Rivera-Rideau, *Remixing Reggaeton*, 36.

45. Dinzey-Flores, *Locked In, Locked Out*, 30

46. Scarano, *Puerto Rico*, 994.

47. Ibid., 995.

48. Bayrón Toro, *Historia de las elecciones*, 475.

49. Ibid., 491.

50. Juan Cruz Ricart, *Memoria corta: Una breve historia de Puerto Rico, 1800 a 2000* (San Juan: Ediciones Situm, 2006), 135–39.

51. Cited in Bayrón Toro, *Historia de las elecciones*, 492.

52. Ayala and Bernabe, *Puerto Rico in the American Century*, 299.

53. Lirio Márquez and Jorge Fernández Porto, "El impacto ambiental de las actividades de la Marina de Guerra de los Estados Unidos en la isla-municipio de Vieques," *Exégesis* (2001), http://www.uprh.edu/exegesis/fernandezporto.pdf.

54. Marie Cruz Soto, "The Making of *Viequenses*: Militarized Colonialism and Reproductive Rights," *Meridians* 19, no. 2 (2020): 362.

55. Márquez and Fernández Porto, "El impacto ambiental de las actividades de la Marina de Guerra."

56. Ayala and Bernabe, *Puerto Rico in the American Century*, 301–3.

57. See LeBrón, *Policing Life and Death*.

58. Office of the Inspector General, "Chapter Three: Chronology of Events in the Surveillance and Arrest Operation," in *A Review of the September 2005 Shooting Incident Involving the Federal Bureau of Investigation and Filiberto Ojeda Ríos*, August 2006, https://oig.justice.gov/sites/default/files/archive/special/s0608/chapter3.htm.

59. Paralitici, *Historia de la lucha*, 284.

12. Broken Promises and Ongoing Resistance

1. Juan R. Torruella, "Ruling America's Colonies: The Insular Cases," *Yale Law and Policy Review* 32, no. 1 (2013): 84, https://digitalcommons.law.yale.edu/ylpr/vol32/iss1/3; Jennifer Wolff, "Debtors' Island: How Puerto Rico Became a Hedge Fund Playground," *New Labor Forum* 25, no. 2 (2016): 48–55.

2. Joel Cintrón Arbasetti, Carla Minett, Alex V. Hernández, and Jessica Stites, "100 Years of Colonialism: How Puerto Rico Became Easy Prey for Profiteers," *In These Times*, November 13, 2017.

3. Jorell Meléndez-Badillo, "Commemorating May Day in Puerto Rico," *NACLA* 51, no. 3 (2019): 301–5.

4. "Papel Machete—Jorge Díaz Ortiz," *Visible*, n.d., https://www.visibleproject.org/blog/project/papel-machete/.

5. "Ninguno para gobernador," *Actipedia*, n.d., https://actipedia.org/project/ninguno-pa%E2%80%99-gobernador.

6. "Acevedo Vilá agradecido con el pueblo," *El Nuevo Día*, December 2, 2008, https://www.elnuevodia.com/noticias/politica/notas/acevedo-vila-agradecido-con-el-pueblo/.

7. Bayrón Toro, *Historia de las elecciones y los partidos políticos en Puerto Rico*, 542.

8. Wanda I. Ocasio-Rivera, "Metáforas extremas del neoliberalismo en la literatura latinoamericana" (PhD diss., University of Illinois at Urbana-Champaign, 2015); Fionnuala Murphy, "Un sueño para vender: The Economics of Memory and the Malvinas War in Argentinian Political Discourse, 1989–2015" (Honors thesis, Dartmouth College, 2021).

9. For CAREF, see Jorell Meléndez-Badillo, "The Puerto Rican Experiment: Crisis, Colonialism, and Popular Response," in *The End of the World as We Know It? Crisis, Resistance, and the Age of Austerity*, ed. Deric Shannon (Oakland: AK Press, 2014), 165–81. For criollo bloc, see Joaquín Villanueva and Martín Cobián, "Beyond Disaster Capitalism: Dismantling the Infrastructure of Extraction in Puerto Rico's Neo-Plantation Economy," *Antipode Online*, June 25, 2019, https://antipodeonline.org/2019/06/25/beyond-disaster-capitalism/.

10. Meléndez-Badillo, "The Puerto Rican Experiment."

11. Marc D. Joffe and Jesse Martínez, "Origins of the Puerto Rico Fiscal Crisis," Mercatus Research, April 12, 2016, https://doi.org/10.2139/ssrn.3211660.

12. Meléndez-Badillo, "The Puerto Rican Experiment," 172.

13. "Ley 7 fue adversa para la economía," *Primera hora*, April 19, 2011, https://www.primerahora.com/noticias/gobierno-politica/notas/ley-7-fue-adversa-para-la-economia/.

14. Ibid.

15. Yarimar Bonilla and Rafael A. Boglio Martínez, "Puerto Rico in Crisis: Government Workers Battle Neoliberal Reform," *NACLA*, January 5, 2010, https://nacla.org/article/puerto-rico-crisis-government-workers-battle-neoliberal-reform.

16. Ibid.

17. Cited in ibid.

18. "Concluye el paro sin mayores incidentes," *El nuevo día*, October 15, 2009, https://www.elnuevodia.com/noticias/locales/notas/concluye-el-paro-sin-mayores-incidentes/.

19. "Tensa situación entre estudiantes y Policía en el expreso Las Américas," *Primera hora*, October 15, 2009, https://www.primerahora.com/noticias/gobierno-politica/notas/tensa-situacion-entre-estudiantes-y-policia-en-el-expreso-las-americas/.

20. Rima Brusi, "A New, Violent Order at the University of Puerto Rico," *Graduate Journal of Social Science* 8, no. 1 (June 2011): 45.

21. "Descontento en Puerto Rico por la privatización del aeropuerto," *Univisión*, February 28, 2013, https://www.univision.com/noticias/noticias-de-latinoamerica/descontento-en-puerto-rico-por-privatizacion-del-aeropuerto.

22. Wolff, "Debtors' Island," 48–55.

23. United States General Accounting Office, "Tax Policy: Puerto Rico and the Section 936 Tax Credit," Report to the Chairman, Committee on Finance, U.S. Senate, June 1993, https://www.gao.gov/assets/ggd-93-109.pdf; Yarimar Bonilla, "The Coloniality of Disaster: Race, Empire, and the Temporal Logics of Emergency in Puerto Rico, USA," *Political Geography* 78 (April 2020), https://doi.org/10.1016/j.polgeo.2020.102181; Stephen Kim Park and Tim R. Samples, "Puerto Rico's Debt Dilemma and Pathways toward Sovereign Solvency," *American Business Law Journal* 54, no. 1 (Spring 2017): 9–60; Rafael Bernabe, "Puerto Rico: Economic Reconstruction, Debt Cancellation, and Self-Determination," Committee for the Abolishment of Illegitimate Debt, December 13, 2018, http://www.cadtm.org/Puerto-Rico-Economic-reconstruction-debt-cancellation-and-self-determination#nb9.

24. Joan Benach, Marinilda Rivera Díaz, Nylca J. Muñoz, Eliana Martínez-Herrera, and Juan Manel Pericás, "What the Puerto Rican Hurricanes Make Visible: Chronicle of a Public Health Disaster Foretold," *Social Science & Medicine* 238 (October 2019), https://doi.org/10.1016/j.socscimed.2019.112367; see also José Fusté, "Repeating Islands of Debt: Historicizing the Transcolonial Relationality of Puerto Rico's Economic Crisis," *Radical History Review* 128 (May 2017): 91–120.

25. CNN Money, "Gorbenador de Puerto Rico: 'La deuda es impagable,'" CNN, June 29, 2015, https://cnnespanol.cnn.com/2015/06/29/gobernador-de-puerto-rico-la-deuda-es-impagable/; Ed Morales, *Fantasy Island: Colonialism, Exploitation, and the Betrayal of Puerto Rico* (New York: Bold Type Books, 2019), 119.

26. "Puerto Rico," *Last Week Tonight with John Oliver*, HBO, April 25, 2016, https://www.youtube.com/watch?v=Tt-mpuR_QHQ&ab_channel=LastWeekTonight.

27. Francisco J. Fortuño Bernier, "Cerrar para abrir: Puerto Rican Student Struggles and the Crisis of Colonial-Capitalism," *Viewpoint Magazine*, April 27, 2017, https://viewpointmag.com/2017/04/27/cerrar-para-abrir-puerto-rican-student-struggles-and-the-crisis-of-colonial-capitalism/.

28. Lyle Denniston, "Opinion Analysis: Setback for Puerto Rico's Independent Powers," *SCOTUSblog*, June 9, 2016, https://www.scotusblog.com/2016/06/opinion-analysis-setback-for-puerto-ricos-independent-powers/. Another case decided that same week, *Puerto Rico v. Franklin*, noted that municipalities in Puerto Rico could not declare bankruptcy; see Lyle Denniston, "Opinion Analysis: Puerto Rico's Debt Woes Left to Congress," *SCOTUSblog*, June 13, 2016, https://www.scotusblog.com/2016/06/opinion-analysis-puerto-ricos-debt-woes-left-to-congress/.

29. Cited in Morales, *Fantasy Island*, 141.

30. Ronald Mann, "Justices Side with Puerto Rico's Financial Oversight Board in Public Records Dispute," *SCOTUSblog*, May 15, 2023, https://www.scotusblog.com/2023/05/justices-puerto-rico-public-records-dispute/; also, Carlos Edil Berríos Polanco, "Supreme Court: Puerto Rico's Fiscal Control Board Has 'Sovereign Immunity,'" *Latino Rebels*, May 12, 2023, https://www.latinorebels.com/2023/05/12/supremecourtjuntasovereignimmunity/.

31. Marisol LeBrón, "People before Debt," *NACLA Report on the Americas* 48, no. 2 (2016): 116.

32. Luna Olavarría Gallegos, "Puerto Rican Activists Shut Down the First Scheduled PROMESA Conference in San Juan," August 31, 2016, https://remezcla.com/culture/promesa -conference-protest-san-juan/; "Puerto Rican Activists Protest First #PROMESA Conference," September 4, 2016, https://www.latinorebels.com/2016/09/04/puerto-rican-activists-protest -first-promesa-conference-democracy-now-video/; "Puerto Rico: 6 Arrested Protesting Pro-PROMESA Media Coverage," August 30, 2016, https://www.democracynow.org/2016/8/30 /headlines/puerto_rico_6_arrested_protesting_pro_promesa_media_coverage.

33. Arys Rodríguez Andino, "Escritora denuncia que Ricky Rosselló la plagió," July 31, 2014, https://www.primerahora.com/noticias/gobierno-politica/notas/escritora-denuncia-que -ricky-rossello-la-plagio/.

34. "El escándalo de Ricky Rosselló," August 31, 2012, https://www.noticel.com/80-grados /blogs/opiniones/20120831/el-escandalo-de-ricky-rossello/.

35. Cited in A. W. Maldonado, *Boom and Bust in Puerto Rico: How Politics Destroyed an Economic Miracle* (Notre Dame: University of Notre Dame Press, 2021), 118.

36. Ibid., 128–29.

37. Aurora Santiago Ortiz, "Apuntes sobre la charterización y cierre de escuelas en Puerto Rico," in *Políticas educativas y justiciar social: Entre lo global y lo local*, ed. Carmen Rodríguez-Martínez, Fernanda Saforcada, and Javier Campos-Martínez (Madrid: Ediciones Morata, 2020), 70–71.

38. "Puerto Rico's Debt Crisis Claims Another Casualty: Its Schools," *New York Times*, May 10, 2017.

39. Centro para la Reconstrucción del Habitat, *Cierre de escuelas públicas en Puerto Rico: Impactos comunitarios y recomendaciones*, August 2020, https://ntc-prod-public-pdfs.s3.us-east -2.amazonaws.com/XZjUc0k1f3xq4__zcjGQR3G8_ls.pdf.

40. Cited in Fortuño Bernier, "Cerrar para abrir."

41. José Caraballo Cueto, "UPR: Mitos y realidades," *80 grados*, April 7, 2017. See also Universidad de Puerto Rico, *Presupuesto Puerto Rico*, https://presupuesto.pr.gov/PRESUPUESTO PROPUESTO2020-2021/PresupuestosAgencias/Universidad%20de%20Puerto%20Rico .htm.

42. Juan C. Dávila, "Students of Puerto Rico Lead Resistance against Promesa," *Huff Post*, April 9, 2017, https://www.huffpost.com/entry/students-of-puerto-rico-lead-resistance-against -promesa_b_58e851c1e4b00dd8e016ec0e.

43. Ibid.

44. Fortuño Bernier, "Cerrar para abrir."

45. Gabriela Carrasquillo Piñeiro, "Cronología: Caso contra estudiantes tras la huelga de la UPR en 2017," February 5, 2020, https://pulsoestudiantil.com/cronologia-caso-contra -estudiantes-tras-la-huelga-de-la-upr-en-2017/.

46. José Karlo Pagán Negrón, "Huelga 2017: 72 días en defensa de la UPR," *Diálogo*, June 8, 2017, https://dialogo.upr.edu/huelga-2017-72-dias-en-defensa-de-la-upr/; "Cronología de la huelga en la UPR," *Metro Puerto Rico*, June 5, 2017, https://www.metro.pr/pr/noticias/2017/06 /05/cronologia-la-huelga-la-upr.html.

47. Meléndez-Badillo, "Commemorating May Day," 303.

48. For more on her case, see Marisol LeBrón, "Policing *Coraje* in the Colony: Toward a Decolonial Feminist Politics of Rage in Puerto Rico," *Signs* 46, no. 4 (2021): 801–26.

13. The Night Everything Went Silent

1. Dánica Coto, "Report: FEMA Fumbled in Puerto Rico after Storms Irma, María," AP News, October 1, 2020, https://apnews.com/article/puerto-rico-hurricane-irma-storms-latin -america-hurricanes-8bfd2865519e79a2109bab7edb625436.

2. Saidiya Hartman, *Scenes of Subjection: Terror, Slavery, and Self-Making in Nineteenth-Century America* (New York: Oxford University Press, 1997); Saidiya Hartman, "Venus in Two Acts," *Small Axe* 12, no. 2 (June 2008): 1–14; Some writers have experimented with the meaning of Hurricane María through literature. See Xavier Navarro Aquino, *Velorio: A Novel* (New York: HarperVia, 2022); Xochitl González, *Olga Dies Dreaming: A Novel* (New York: Flatiron Books, 2022).

3. For a discussion about the etymology of the word "hurricane," see Schwartz, *Sea of Storms*, 6–7.

4. Amarilys Arocho Barreto, "La invasión de San Ciriaco," *Proyecto 1867*, https://www .proyecto1867.com/la-invasioacuten-de-san-ciriaco.html.

5. Coralys Molina Rodríguez, "Los siete huracanes más devastadores de la historia de Puerto Rico," *Pulso estudiantil*, September 29, 2020, https://pulsoestudiantil.com/los-siete-huracanes -mas-devastadores-en-la-historia-de-puerto-rico/. There were twenty hurricanes that menaced Puerto Rico throughout the twentieth century; see Luis Caldera Ortiz, *Historia de los ciclones y huracanes tropicales en Puerto Rico* (Lajas: Editorial Akelarre, 2014).

6. Álvarez Guedes, "Álvarez Guedes y huracanes," YouTube, May 2, 2019, https://www .youtube.com/watch?v=leUX4Yr0zB8&ab_channel=AndyPonce.

7. Aurora Santiago Ortiz, "Testimonio as Stitch Work: Undoing Coloniality through Auto-ethnography in Puerto Rico," *Chicana/Latina Studies: The Journal of Mujeres Activas en Letras y Cambio Social* 20, no. 2 (2021): 131.

8. Levi Gahman, "In the Caribbean, Colonialism and Inequality Mean Hurricanes Hit Harder," *The Conversation*, September 20, 2017, https://theconversation.com/in-the-caribbean -colonialism-and-inequality-mean-hurricanes-hit-harder-84106.

9. Michael Deibert, *When the Sky Fell: Hurricane Maria and the United States in Puerto Rico* (New York: Apollo Publishers, 2019), 114.

10. Homeland Security Operational Analysis Center, "Hurricanes Irma and Maria: Impact and Aftermath," RAND Corporation, https://www.rand.org/hsrd/hsoac/projects/puerto-rico -recovery/hurricanes-irma-and-maria.html.

11. National Resources Defense Council, "Threats on Tap: Drinking Water Violations in Puerto Rico," https://www.nrdc.org/sites/default/files/threats-on-tap-drinking-water-puerto -rico-ip.pdf.

12. Christine Santillana, "AES Puerto Rico: 20 años de contaminación por cenizas de carbón," *Earth Justice*, January 13, 2022, https://earthjustice.org/from-the-experts/2022-january/aes -puerto-rico-tras-20-anos-de-contaminacion-por-cenizas-de-carbon#:~:text=AES%2DPR%20

produce%20un%20promedio,de%2012%20pisos%20de%20altura; Omar Alfonso, "Viven y jue-
gan entre el arsénico de las cenizas de AES," *Centro de Periodismo Investigativo* and *La Perla del Sur*, August 20, 2019, https://periodismoinvestigativo.com/2019/08/viven-y-juegan-entre-el-arsenico-de-las-cenizas-de-aes/.

13. "Así fue la visita de Trump a Puerto Rico," *TelemundoPR*, October 4, 2017, https://www.telemundo51.com/noticias/noticias-destacados/el-presidente-donald-trump-visitara-puerto-rico-el-martes/138929/.

14. Aaron Blake, "Trump's Half-Baked Puerto Rico Photo Op, Annotated," *Washington Post*, October 3, 2017, https://www.washingtonpost.com/news/the-fix/wp/2017/10/03/trumps-half-baked-puerto-rico-press-conference-annotated/.

15. Omaya Sosa Pascual and Jeniffer Wiscovitch, "Aparecen decenas de muertos no contados por el huracán María," *Centro de Periodismo Investigativo*, November 16, 2017, https://periodismoinvestigativo.com/2017/11/aparecen-decenas-de-muertos-no-contados-por-el-huracan-maria/.

16. "Morgue de Puerto Rico aun con cadavers sin reclamar desde el paso de María," *El Heraldo*, June 11, 2018, https://www.elheraldo.co/mundo/morgue-de-puerto-rico-aun-con-cadaveres-sin-reclamar-desde-el-paso-de-maria-505560.

17. "Piden más timepo para estudiar las muertes por el huracán María," *El nuevo día*, May 21, 2018, https://www.elnuevodia.com/noticias/locales/notas/piden-mas-tiempo-para-estudiar-las-muertes-por-el-huracan-maria/.

18. Nishant Kishore, Domingo Marqués, Ayesha Mahmud, et al., "Mortality in Puerto Rico after Hurricane Maria," *New England Journal of Medicine*, no. 379 (July 12, 2018): 162–70.

19. Hilda Llorens, "US Media Depictions of Climate Migrants: The Recent Case of the Puerto Rican 'Exodus,'" in *Aftershocks of Disaster*, 127.

20. Frances Negrón Muntaner, "Our Fellow Americans: Why Calling Puerto Ricans 'Americans' Will Not Save Them," in *Aftershocks of Disaster*, 117.

21. Ibid., 118–19.

22. Deibert, *When the Sky Fell*, 145.

23. Jamelle Bouie, "Why Trump Doesn't Care about Puerto Ricans," *Slate*, October 1, 2017, https://slate.com/news-and-politics/2017/10/trumps-poor-response-to-puerto-rico-is-no-surprise.html.

24. "Estudio confirma FEMA trajo chatarra a PR," *Noticel*, June 14, 2018, https://www.noticel.com/huracanes/el-tiempo/la-calle/top-stories/20180614/estudio-confirma-fema-trajo-comida-chatarra-a-pr/.

25. Jacqueline Villarrubia-Mendoza and Roberto Vélez-Vélez, "Centros de Apoyo Mutuo: Reconfigurando la asistencia en tiempos de desastre," *Centro Journal* 32, no. 3 (Fall 2020): 89–117.

26. Ibid.

27. Sarah Molinari, "Authenticating Loss and Contesting Recovery: FEMA and the Politics of Colonial Disaster Management," in *Aftershocks of Disaster*, 287.

28. Ibid., 294.

29. Ibid.

30. Joel Cintrón Arbasetti, *El local* (San Juan: Instituto de Cultura Puertorriqueña, 2017).

31. Saritha R, "Punk, Self-Determination, and Solidarity Post-Maria: An Interview with Félix Rodríguez of El Local," *Boston Hassle*, September 12, 2018, https://bostonhassle.com/punk-self-determination-and-solidarity-post-maria-an-interview-with-felix-rodriguez-of-el-local/; "Sobre El Local," *El Local en Santurce*, https://ellocalensanturce.com/sobre-el-local/.

32. Jhoni Jackson, "The Rock Club That Helped Feed San Juan after Hurricane Maria," January 11, 2018, https://pitchfork.com/thepitch/the-rock-club-that-helped-feed-san-juan-after-hurricane-maria/.

33. Blanca Ortiz Torres, "Decoloniality and Community-Psychology Practice in Autonomous Organizing (*autogestion*) and Self-determination," *International Review of Psychiatry* 32, no. 4 (2020): 359–64.

14. The Storm after María

1. Cited in Diebert, *When the Sky Fell*, 118.

2. "Leptospirosis," Centers for Disease Control and Prevention, https://www.cdc.gov/leptospirosis/infection/index.html.

3. Alexa S. Dietrich, Adriana María Garriga-López, and Claudia Sofía Garriga-López, "Hurricane Maria Exposes Puerto Rico's Stark Environmental and Health Inequalities," *Items*, October 3, 2017, https://items.ssrc.org/just-environments/hurricane-maria-exposes-puerto-ricos-stark-environmental-and-health-inequalities/.

4. Frances Solá Santiago, "This Puerto Rican Town Went Viral for Its SOS Call after Maria. This Is Its Message Today," *Remezcla*, August 8, 2018, https://remezcla.com/culture/this-puerto-rican-town-went-viral-for-its-sos-call-after-maria-this-is-its-message-today/.

5. Manuel Ernesto Riva, "Hallan millones de botellas de agua abandonadas en una pista de Puerto Rico a un año del paso de María," *Univisión*, September 12, 2018, https://www.univision.com/local/puerto-rico-wlii/hallan-millones-de-botellas-de-agua-abandonadas-en-una-pista-de-puerto-rico-a-un-ano-del-paso-de-maria.

6. "FEMA jutifica decomiso de miles de botellas de agua," *NotiUno*, July 29, 2019, https://www.notiuno.com/noticias/gobierno-y-politica/fema-justifica-decomiso-de-miles-de-botellas-de-agua/article_11f1dc0e-b26f-11e9-92b8-6f668853e591.html.

7. Victor Martínez, "The Diaspora Helps Rebuild Puerto Rico," *Centro: Center for Puerto Rican Studies*, n.d., https://centropr.hunter.cuny.edu/events-news/rebuild-puerto-rico/policy/diaspora-helps-rebuild-puerto-rico.

8. "Our Story," María Fund, https://www.mariafund.org/about.

9. "Encuentran vagones con suministros dañados en Puerto Rico," *Telemundo 51*, August 12, 2018, https://www.telemundo51.com/noticias/local/encuentran-vagones-con-suministros-danados-en-puerto-rico/168326/; "Encuentran vagones con suministros dañados en la CEE," *El Vocero*, August 10, 2018, https://www.elvocero.com/gobierno/encuentran-vagones-con-suministros-da-ados-en-la-cee/article_7c012a32-9cdb-11e8-b507-73f5ba82ebda.html.

10. Melissa Correa Velázquez, "Apunta el FBI a Unidos por Puerto Rico," *El Vocero*, July 16, 2019, https://www.elvocero.com/ley-y-orden/apunta-el-fbi-a-unidos-por-puerto-rico/article_4ed8e534-a77c-11e9-a7e0-ff53b7a5f82b.html.

11. Wilma Maldonado Arrigoitía, "Cargos contra Raúl Maldonado son un patrón de persecución, dice su abogada Mayra López Mulero," *Endi*, January 19, 2022, https://www.elnuevodia .com/noticias/locales/notas/cargos-contra-raul-maldonado-son-un-patron-de-persecucion -dice-su-abogada-mayra-lopez-mulero/.

12. Javier Moya, "¿Qué tiene que ver Beatriz Rosselló con todo esto?" WKAQ, June 25, 2019, https://www.univision.com/radio/puerto-rico-wkaq-am/wkaq-580-am/que-tiene-que-ver -beatriz-rossello-con-todo-esto-raul-maldonado-acusa-al-gobernador-de-cambiar-reporte-de -vagones-para-ayudar-a-su-esposa-vid.

13. "Beatriz Rosselló reacciona a expresiones de hijo de Raúl Maldonado," *Metro Puerto Rico*, June 25, 2019, https://www.metro.pr/pr/noticias/2019/06/25/beatriz-rossello-dice-expresiones -raulie-maldonado-falsas.html.

14. Moya, "¿Qué tiene que ver Beatriz Rosselló con todo esto?"

15. See Karrieann Soto Vega, "The Imperious Rule of Julia Keleher: Gender, Race, and Colonialism in the Corruption of Public Education in Puerto Rico," *Centro Journal* 34, no. 2 (Summer 2022): 123–44.

16. Carmen Lydia Arcelay Santiago, *La agenda inconclusa de Ricardo Rosselló Nevarez* (Hato Rey: Publicaciones Puertorriqueñas, 2020), 80–82; "Arrestan a la Secretaria de Educación Julia Keleher," *Primera hora*, July 10, 2019, https://www.primerahora.com/noticias/gobierno-politica /notas/arrestan-a-la-exsecretaria-de-educacion-julia-keleher/.

17. Carlos Rubén Rosario, *¡Ricky Renuncia!: Crónicas del Verano del '19* (N.p: n.p., 2020), 70.

18. Arcelay Santiago, *La agenda inconclusa de Ricardo Rosselló Nevares*, 83–84.

19. Rubén Rosario, *¡Ricky Renuncia! 69*.

20. Ibid., 80.

21. Ibid., 81–83.

22. Ibid., 100.

23. Luis J. Valentín Ortiz and Carla Minet, "The 889 Pages of the Telegram Chat between Rosselló Nevares and His Closest Aides," Centro de Periodismo Investigativo, July 13, 2019, https://periodismoinvestigativo.com/2019/07/the-889-pages-of-the-telegram-chat-between -rossello-nevares-and-his-closest-aides/.

24. "Calculan que 500,000 personas se manifestaron ayer contra Rosselló," *El Nuevo Día*, July 18, 2019, https://www.elnuevodia.com/noticias/locales/notas/calculan-que-500000 -personas-se-manifestaron-ayer-contra-rossello/.

25. "Escalera pide reunión con organizadores de protestas contra Rosselló," *El Nuevo Día*, July 19, 2019, https://www.elnuevodia.com/noticias/seguridad/notas/escalera-pide-una -reunion-con-organizadores-de-protestas-contra-rossello/?utm_term=Autofeed&utm _medium=Social&utm_source=Facebook&fbclid=IwAR1OT4EDlQVAr0YzJeLfkSkxGfNX wkKp8-9-BblkZ_UzzSQwM1WhiutCS5c#Echobox=1563579354; Aurora Santiago Ortiz and Jorell Meléndez-Badillo, "Puerto Rico's Multiple Solidarities: Emergent Landscapes and the Geographies of Protest," *The Abusable Past*, July 22, 2019, https://www.radicalhistoryreview.org /abusablepast/puerto-ricos-multiple-solidarities-emergent-landscapes-and-the-geographies -of-protest/.

26. For rage, see Marisol LeBrón, "Policing *Coraje* in the Colony: Toward a Decolonial Feminist Politics of Rage in Puerto Rico," *Signs* 46, no. 4 (2021): 801–26.

27. Hugo J. Delgado Martí, "La noche es pa'l combate," *Bandera Roja*, July 23, 2019, https://www.bandera.org/la-noche-es-pal-combate/?fbclid=IwAR3mU_mcjEKCdjYWVNH2d2JQF9i6cQxaAoTxNLtjmQNrFD51HppKQRVQd7g.

28. Frances Rosario, "Denuncian que el gobierno violenta los derechos constitucionales de los manifestantes," *Primera hora*, July 19, 2019, https://www.primerahora.com/noticias/gobierno-politica/notas/denuncian-que-el-gobierno-violenta-los-derechos-constitucionales-de-los-manifestantes/.

29. Rubén Rosario, *¡Ricky Renuncia!* 168.

30. Santiago Ortiz and Meléndez-Badillo, "Puerto Rico's Multiple Solidarities."

31. Aurora Santiago Ortiz and Jorell Meléndez-Badillo, "*La Calle Fortaleza* in Puerto Rico's *Primavera de Verano*," *Society and Space Journal*, February 25, 2020, https://www.societyandspace.org/articles/la-calle-fortaleza-in-puerto-ricos-primavera-de-verano.

32. Aurora Santiago Ortiz, "La Colectiva Feminista en Construcción Are Leading the Puerto Rican Resistance," *Open Democracy*, January 14, 2020, https://www.opendemocracy.net/en/oureconomy/la-colectiva-feminista-en-construccion-are-leading-the-puerto-rican-resistance/; see also Rocío Zambrana, "Black Feminist Tactics: On La Colectiva Feminista en Construcción's Politics without Guarantees," *Decolonial Geographies of Puerto Rico's 2019 Summer Protests*, online forum edited by Marisol LeBrón and Joaquín Villanueva, *Society and Space Journal* (February 25, 2020), https://www.societyandspace.org/articles/black-feminist-tactics-on-la-colectiva-feminista-en-construccions-politics-without-guarantees.

33. Rubén Rosario, *¡Ricky Renuncia!* 201–2.

34. Ibid., 200. "Shep Smith Presses Puerto Rico's Governor: Attacks on Your Own People Are Not Mistakes," Fox News, July 22, 2019, https://www.youtube.com/watch?v=trQatZPmULk&ab_channel=FoxNews; Frances Rosario, "Alcalde de San Sebastían desmiente a Ricardo Rosselló," *Primera hora*, July 22, 2019, https://www.primerahora.com/noticias/gobierno-politica/notas/alcalde-de-san-sebastian-desmiente-a-ricardo-rossello/.

35. Santiago-Ortiz and Meléndez-Badillo, "*La Calle Fortaleza* in Puerto Rico's *Primavera de Verano*."

36. Patricia Mazzei and Frances Robles, "Ricardo Rosselló anunció su renuncia a la gobernación de Puerto Rico," *New York Times*, July 24, 2019, https://www.nytimes.com/es/2019/07/24/espanol/america-latina/rossello-renuncia-puerto-rico.html.

37. Patricia Mazzei, "Who Is Pedro Pierluisi, Who Has Been Sworn in as Puerto Rico's Next Governor?" *New York Times*, August 1, 2019, https://www.nytimes.com/2019/08/01/us/puerto-rico-governor-pedro-pierluisi.html; Associated Press, "El tribunal superior de Puerto Rico dictamina que Pedro Pierluisi no puede ser gobernador," *Los Angeles Times*, August 8, 2019, https://www.latimes.com/espanol/eeuu/articulo/2019-08-08/el-tribunal-superior-de-puerto-rico-dictamina-que-pedro-pierluisi-no-puede-ser-gobernador; Alejandra Rosa, Patricia Mazzei, and Frances Robles, "Puerto Rico Supreme Court Ousts New Governor, and Another Is Sworn In," *New York Times*, August 7, 2019, https://www.nytimes.com/2019/08/07/us/puerto-rico-governor-wanda-vazquez.html.

38. Jacqueline Villarrubia-Mendoza and Roberto Vélez-Vélez, "Puerto Rican People's Assembly Shift from Protest to Proposal," *NACLA*, August 20, 2019, https://nacla.org/news/2019/08/22/puerto-rican-people%E2%80%99s-assemblies-shift-protest-proposal.

39. Aurora Santiago Ortiz is working on addressing this in a book manuscript in progress titled "Circuits of Self-Determination: Mapping Solidarities and Radical Political Pedagogies in Puerto Rico."

40. Pedro Lebrón Ortiz, "Against the Mythological Machine, Towards Decolonial Revolt," *Theory & Event* 24, no. 3 (July 2021): 809.

41. "Puerto Rico Earthquakes," *Center for Disaster Philanthropy*, December 3, 2020, https://disasterphilanthropy.org/disaster/puerto-rico-earthquakes/.

42. Nicholas Van Der Elst, Jeanne L. Hardebeck, and Andre J. Michael, "Potential Duration of Aftershocks of the 2020 Southwestern Puerto Rico Earthquake," *USGS Numbered Series* (2020), https://doi.org/10.3133/ofr20201009.

43. Daniel Edgardo Adorno Cruz, "Terremoto en Puerto Rico demuestra que el gobierno no puede manejar una crisis," *Open Democracy*, January 15, 2020, https://www.opendemocracy.net/es/democraciaabierta-es/terremoto-en-puerto-rico-demuestra-que-el-gobierno-no-puede-manejar-una-crisis/.

44. Hilda Llorens, *Making Livable Worlds: Afro-Puerto Rican Women Building Environmental Justice* (Seattle: University of Washington Press, 2021).

45. Ibid., 122.

46. "Educación registra 16,105 estudiantes menos que el año pasado," *Noticel*, October 2, 2020, https://www.noticel.com/educacion/ahora/top-stories/20201002/educacion-registra-16105-estudiantes-menos-que-el-ano-pasado/; "Colegio de Ingenieros advierte que solo 500 escuelas están reforzadas contra terremotos," *El Nuevo Día*, January 8, 2020, https://www.elnuevodia.com/noticias/locales/notas/colegio-de-ingenieros-advierte-que-solo-500-escuelas-estan-reforzadas-contra-terremotos/?r=24893.

47. "Cinco mil puertorriqueños siguen sin hogar tras el terremoto de 6,4 grados de magnitud," *Democracy Now*, January 15, 2020, https://www.democracynow.org/es/2020/1/15/titulares/5_000_puerto_ricans_still_homeless_after_64_magnitude_earthquake.

48. Adorno Cruz, "Terremoto en Puerto Rico demuestra que el gobierno no puede manejar una crisis."

49. "Habla el León Fiscalizador sobre el video que sacudió al país," *Primera hora*, January 20, 2020, https://www.primerahora.com/noticias/puerto-rico/notas/habla-el-leon-fiscalizador-sobre-el-video-que-sacudio-al-pais/.

50. Marisol LeBrón, *Against Muerto Rico: Lessons from the Verano Boricua* (Cabo Rojo: Editora Educación Emergente, 2021), 14–15.

51. Joaquín Villanueva, Martín Cobián, and Félix Rodríguez, "San Juan, the Fragile City: Finance Capital, Class, and the Making of Puerto Rico's Economic Crisis," *Antipode* 50 (2018): 1419.

52. LeBrón, *Against Muerto Rico*, 17.

15. Broken Memories and Future-Oriented Histories

1. Damaris Suárez, "Publicist Edwin Miranda Tried to Conceal His Propaganda Work, but Reports Say Otherwise," *Centro de Periodismo Investigativo*, January 21, 2020, https://periodismoinvestigativo.com/2020/01/publicist-edwin-miranda-tried-to-conceal-his-propaganda-work-but-reports-say-otherwise/.

2. Page 868 from the chat, which can be accessed here: Luis J. Valentín Ortiz and Carla Minet, "The 889 Pages of the Telegram Chat between Rosselló Nevares and His Closest Aides," *Centro de Periodismo Investigativo*, July 13, 2019, https://periodismoinvestigativo.com/2019/07/the-889-pages-of-the-telegram-chat-between-rossello-nevares-and-his-closest-aides/.

3. Teresa Whalen, *From Puerto Rico to Philadelphia*, 137.

4. Donald Yacovone, *Teaching White Supremacy: America's Democratic Ordeal and the Forging of Our National Identity* (New York: Pantheon Books, 2022); Carol Anderson, *White Rage: The Unspoken Truth of Our Racial Divide* (New York: Bloomsbury, 2016); Angela J. Davis, ed., *Policing the Black Man: Arrest, Prosecution, and Imprisonment* (New York: Pantheon Books, 2017); Keeanga-Yamatha Taylor, *From #BlackLivesMatter to Black Liberation* (Chicago: Haymarket Books, 2016).

5. Jennifer Hinojosa, Edwin Meléndez, and Kathya Severino Pietri, *Population Decline and School Closure in Puerto Rico*, May 2019, p. 5, https://centropr-archive.hunter.cuny.edu/research/data-center/research-briefs/population-decline-and-school-closure-puerto-rico.

6. World Population Review, https://worldpopulationreview.com/states/puerto-rico-population.

7. Nellie Bowles, "Making a Crypto Utopia in Puerto Rico," *New York Times*, February 2, 2018, https://www.nytimes.com/2018/02/02/technology/cryptocurrency-puerto-rico.html.

8. Naomi Klein, *The Battle for Paradise: Puerto Rico Takes on the Disaster Capitalists* (Chicago: Haymarket Books, 2018), 20.

9. Bowles, "Making a Crypto Utopia in Puerto Rico."

10. Jillian Crandall, "Blockchains and the 'Chains of Empire': Contextualizing Blockchain, Cryptocurrency, and Neoliberalism in Puerto Rico," *Design and Culture: The Journal of the Design Studies Forum* 11, no. 3 (2019): 287.

11. Ibid., 286.

12. Ibid., 283.

13. José Atiles, "The Paradise Performs: Blockchain, Cryptocurrencies, and the Puerto Rican Tax Haven," *South Atlantic Quarterly* 121, no. 2 (2022): 616.

14. Coral Murphy Marcos and Patricia Mazzei, "The Rush for a Slice of Paradise in Puerto Rico," *New York Times*, January 31, 2022, https://www.nytimes.com/2022/01/31/us/puerto-rico-gentrification.html.

15. José Orlando Delgado Rivera, "Identifican sobre 22,000 habitaciones de alquileres a corto plazo en Puerto Rico," *El Nuevo Día*, April 23, 2022, https://www.elnuevodia.com/negocios/turismo/notas/estudio-revela-la-existencia-de-sobre-22000-habitaciones-de-alquileres-a-corto-plazo-en-puerto-rico/.

16. Discover Puerto Rico, "Annual Report, 2020–2021," https://www.discoverpuertorico.com/media/589356, 33.

17. "Puerto Rico superará a la economía a la economía en general en los próximos 10 años," Puerto Rico Tourism Company, June 14, 2022, https://prtourism.com/2022/06/14/pronostican-que-el-sector-de-viajes-y-turismo-en-puerto-rico-superara-a-la-economia-en-general-en-los-proximos-10-anos-2/.

18. Atiles, "The Paradise Performs."

19. Jennifer A. Marcial Ocasio, "Gobernadora de Puerto Rico pide restringir espacio aereo y uso de aeropuertos," *Orlando Sentinel*, March 18, 2020, https://www.orlandosentinel.com

/elsentinel/os-es-gobierno-puerto-rico-pide-cerrar-aeropuertos-20200318-swuzchrs6vgg
pngqrujesffi6m-story.html.

20. "Puerto Rico registra año record en turismo," *EFE: Agencia EFE*, September 27, 2021,
https://www.efe.com/efe/america/economia/puerto-rico-registra-ano-record-en-turismo
/20000011-4639343.

21. Yarimar Bonilla, "Las turistas 'aterradoras,'" *El Nuevo Día*, March 19, 2021, https://www
.elnuevodia.com/opinion/punto-de-vista/las-turistas-aterradoras/.

22. Comisión Estatal de Elecciones del Estado Libre Asociado de Puerto Rico, *Informe Es-
tadístico: Elecciones generales, 5 de noviembre de 2000*, https://ww2.ceepur.org/sites/ComisionEE
/es-pr/Informe%20Estadstico/ESTADISTICAS%20DE%20LAS%20ELECCIONES%20
2000.pdf, 1; Centro Estatal de Elecciones de Puerto Rico, "Resultados Isla: Gobernador,"
https://elecciones2020.ceepur.org/Escrutinio_General_93/index.html#es/default
/GOBERNADOR_Resumen.xml.

23. Comisión Estatal de Elecciones del Estado Libre Asociado de Puerto Rico, "Resultados
Isla: Gobernador," http://168.62.166.179/EG2012/REYDI_Escrutinio/index.html#es/default
/GOBERNADOR_ISLA.xml.

24. Matthew Goldstein, "Judge in Puerto Rico's Debt Lawsuit Handled Major Financial
Crises," *New York Times*, May 5, 2017, https://www.nytimes.com/2017/05/05/business
/dealbook/judge-puerto-rico-case.html.

25. Michelle Kaske, "Puerto Rico's Bankruptcy Is Ending, What Comes Next?" *Washington
Post*, January 29, 2022, https://www.washingtonpost.com/business/puerto-ricos-bankruptcy
-is-ending-what-comes-next/2022/01/26/44215fa6-7ea0-11ec-8cc8-b696564ba796_story
.html.

26. Natalie Jaresko and David Skeel, "Getting Puerto Rico's Financial House in Order: The
Territory's Crushing Debt Load Has Been Lifted," *Wall Street Journal*, January 24, 2022, https://
global-factiva-com.ezproxy.library.wisc.edu/redir/default.aspx?P=sa&an=WSJO0000
20220124ei1o00691&cat=a&ep=ASE.

27. "Gobernadores, legisladores, secretarios y alcaldes: Wanda Vázquez se une a la larga lista
de funcionarios acusados por fraude y corrupción desde 2020," *Univisión*, August 4, 2022,
https://www.univision.com/local/puerto-rico-wlii/corrupcion-puerto-rico-legisladores
-secretarios-alcaldes-ppd-pnp-fotos.

28. José Atiles, Gustavo A. García López, and Joaquín Villanueva, "Beyond Corruption and
Anti-corruption Narratives: Introducing a Critical Research Agenda for Puerto Rican Studies,"
Centro Journal 34, no. 2 (Summer 2022): 13–14.

29. See Villanueva, "The Criollo Bloc," 13–14.

30. Gustavo J. Bobonis, Luis Raúl Cámara Fuertes, Harold J. Toro, and Julie Wilson, "Development and Decay: Political Organization and Municipal Corruption in Puerto Rico, 1952–
2015," *Centro Journal* 34, no. 2 (Summer 2022): 281.

31. Atiles, García López, and Villanueva, "Beyond Corruption," 18.

32. José Atiles, "From Anti-corruption to Decolonial Justice: A Sociolegal Analysis of the
Puerto Rican Summer of 2019," *Centro Journal* 34, no. 2 (Summer 2022): 353–80.

33. Alex Figueroa Cancel, "Autoridades confirman que manifestante fue herido con una bala
viva en Aguadilla," *El Nuevo Día*, January 31, 2023, https://www.elnuevodia.com/noticias

/seguridad/notas/autoridades-confirman-que-manifestante-fue-herido-con-una-bala-viva-en
-aguadilla/.

34. Manuel Guillama Capella, "Exgobernador Alejandro García Padilla será abogado de los
desarrolladores del condohotel en Aguadilla," *El Nuevo Día*, March 11, 2023, https://www
.elnuevodia.com/noticias/locales/notas/exgobernador-alejandro-garcia-padilla-sera-abogado
-de-los-desarrolladores-de-condohotel-en-aguadilla/.

35. "Hijo del Gobernador Pierluisi controla negocio AirBnB y alquileres," *En Blanco y Negro*,
February 8, 2023, https://sandrarodriguezcotto.substack.com/p/hijo-del-gobernador-pierluisi
-controla?sd=pf.

36. "Erradiquemos la violencia de la cotidianidad," *El Nuevo Día*, January 27, 2023, https://
www.elnuevodia.com/opinion/editorial/erradiquemos-la-violencia-de-la-cotidianidad/.

37. "El Apagón," track 16 on *Un verano sin ti*, Universal Music Publishing Group, Warner
Chappel Music, Inc. Bad Bunny. Songwriters: Benito Antonio Martínez Ocasio, Hector L.
Pagán, Joselly Rosario, and Marco Daniel Borrero, 2022.

SELECTED THEMATIC BIBLIOGRAPHY

General Histories of Puerto Rico

Ayala, César, and Rafael Bernabe. *Puerto Rico in the American Century: A History since 1898.* Chapel Hill: University of North Carolina Press, 2007.

Bayrón Toro, Fernando. *Historia de las elecciones y los partidos políticos de Puerto Rico, 1809–2012.* San Juan: Publicaciones Gaviota, 2016.

Brau, Salvador. *Historia de Puerto Rico.* Río Piedras: Editorial Edil, 2000.

Cabrera, Gilberto R. *Puerto Rico y su historia íntima: 1500–1995.* 2 vols. San Juan: Academia Puertorriqueña de la Historia, 1997.

Díaz Quiñones, Arcadio. *La memoria rota: Ensayos sobre cultura y política.* Río Piedras: Ediciones Huracán, 1993.

Díaz Soler, Luis M. *Puerto Rico: Desde sus orígenes hasta el cese de la dominación española.* Río Piedras: Editorial de la Universidad de Puerto Rico, 1994.

Dietz, James L. *Historia económica de Puerto Rico.* Río Piedras: Ediciones Huracán, 1989.

Duany, Jorge. *The Puerto Rican Nation on the Move: Identities on the Island and in the United States.* Chapel Hill: University of North Carolina Press, 2002.

———. *Puerto Rico: What Everyone Needs to Know.* Oxford: Oxford University Press, 2017.

Figueroa, Loida. *Breve historia de Puerto Rico.* 2 vols. Río Piedras: Editorial Edil, 1979.

Jiménez de Wagenheim, Olga. *Puerto Rico: An Interpretive History from Pre-Columbian Times to 1900.* Princeton: Markus Wiener, 2006.

Morales Carrión, Arturo. *Historia del pueblo de Puerto Rico: Desde sus orígenes hasta el siglo XVIII.* San Juan: Editorial Cordillera, 1983.

Picó, Fernando. *History of Puerto Rico: A Panorama of Its People.* Princeton: Markus Wiener, 2014.

Scarano, Francisco. *Puerto Rico: Cinco siglos de historia.* Mexico City: McGraw-Hill Interamericana Editores, 2008.

Schwartz, Stuart B. *Sea of Storms: A History of Hurricanes in the Greater Caribbean from Columbus to Katrina.* Princeton: Princeton University Press, 2015.

Silén, Juan Ángel. *Historia de la nación puertorriqueña.* Río Piedras: Editorial Edil, 1980.

Silvestrini, Blanca G., and María Dolores Luque de Sánchez. *Historia de Puerto Rico: Trayectoria de un pueblo.* San Juan: Ediciones Cultural Panamericana, 1992.

Teresa Whalen, Carmen, and Víctor Vázquez-Hernández, eds. *The Puerto Rican Diaspora: Historical Perspectives.* Philadelphia: Temple University Press, 2005.

Trías Monge, José. *Puerto Rico: The Trials of the Oldest Colony in the World.* New Haven: Yale University Press, 2007.

Pre-Columbian Societies

Altman, Ida. *Life and Society in the Early Spanish Caribbean: The Greater Antilles, 1493–1550.* Baton Rouge: Louisiana State University Press, 2021.

Chanlatte Bail, Luis A. *Proceso y desarrollo de los primeros pobladores de Puerto Rico y Las Antillas*. San Juan: n.p., 1986.

Gómez, Labor, and Manuel Ballesteros Gabrois. *Culturas indígenas de Puerto Rico*. Río Piedras: Editorial Cultural, 1978.

Moscoso, Francisco. *Sociedad y economía de los Taínos*. Río Piedras: Editorial Edil, 2003.

Oliver, José R. *Caciques and Cemí Idols: The Web Spun by Taíno Rulers between Hispaniola and Puerto Rico*. Tuscaloosa: University of Alabama Press, 2009.

Robiou Lamarche, Sebastián. *Tainos and Caribs: The Aboriginal Cultures of the Antilles*. Trans. Grace M. Robiou Ramírez de Arellano. San Juan: Editorial Punto y Coma, 2019.

Rouse, Irving. *The Tainos: Rise and Decline of the People Who Greeted Columbus*. New Haven: Yale University Press, 1992.

Sued Badillo, Jalil. *Agüeybaná el Bravo*. San Juan: Ediciones Puerto, 2008.

———. *Caribe taíno: Ensayos históricos sobre el siglo XVI*. San Juan: Editorial Luscinia C.E., 2020.

———. *La mujer indígena y su sociedad*. Rev. ed. Río Piedras: Editorial Cultural, 2010.

Early Colonial Period (1508–1800)

Delgado Negrón, Juan Alberto. *La visión y misión evangelizadora del obispo Alonso Manso en Las Américas*. Lajas: Centro de Estudios e Investigaciones del Sur Oeste, 2020.

Díaz Soler, Luis M. *Historia de la esclavitud negra en Puerto Rico*. Río Piedras: Editorial de la Universidad de Puerto Rico, 1981.

Gelpí Báez, Elsa. *Siglo en blanco: Estudio de la economía azucarera en Puerto Rico, siglo XVI*. Río Piedras: Editorial de la Universidad de Puerto Rico, 2000.

López Cantos, Ángel. *Los puertorriqueños: Mentalidad y actitudes, siglo XVIII*. San Juan: Ediciones Puerto, 2001.

———. *Mi tío, Miguel Enríquez*. San Juan: Ediciones Puerto, 2006.

———. *Miguel Enríquez*. San Juan: Ediciones Puerto, 1998.

Morales Carrión, Arturo. *Puerto Rico y la lucha por la hegemonía en el Caribe*. Río Piedras: Editorial de la Universidad de Puerto Rico, 2003.

Moscoso, Francisco. *Agricultura y sociedad en Puerto Rico, siglos 16 al 18*. San Juan: Instituto de Cultura Puertorriqueña, 2001.

———. *El hato: Latifundio ganadero y mercantilismo en Puerto Rico, siglos 16 al 18*. San Juan: Publicaciones Gaviota, 2020.

———. *Fundación de San Juan en 1522*. San Juan: Ediciones Laberinto, 2020.

Rodríguez López, Miguel. *El indio borincano y el rey emperador: Un encuentro para la historia, 1528*. San Juan: Editorial EDP, 2021.

Sued Badillo, Jalil, and Ángel López Cantos. *Puerto Rico negro*. Río Piedras: Editorial Cultural, 2007.

Tapia y Rivera, Alejandro. *Biblioteca histórica de Puerto Rico, que contiene varios documentos de los siglos XV, XVI, XVII y XVIII*. San Juan: Editorial Mundo Nuevo, 2010.

Taveras de León, Jose Aridio. *San Germán: Comunidad, parroquia y misión, 1511–1556*. Author's edition, 2021.

Torres, Bibiano. *La isla de Puerto Rico*. San Juan: Instituto de Cultura Puertorriqueña, 1968.

Nineteenth Century and Turn of the Twentieth Century

Altagracia Espada, Carlos. *La utopía del territorio perfectamente gobernado: Miedo y poder en la época de Miguel de la Torre. Puerto Rico, 1822–1837*. N.p.: n.p., 2013.

Álvarez Curbelo, Silvia. *Un país del porvenir: El afán de modernidad en Puerto Rico, siglo XIX*. San Juan: Ediciones Callejón, 2005.

Baerga, María del Carmen. *Negociaciones de sangre: Dinámicas racializantes en el Puerto Rico decimonónico*. Madrid: Iberoamericana Vevuert, 2015.

Baralt, Guillermo. *Esclavos rebeldes: Conspiraciones y sublevaciones de esclavos en Puerto Rico, 1795–1873*. Río Piedras: Ediciones Huracán, 1981.

Cancel, Mario R. *El laberinto de los indóciles: Estudios sobre historiografía puertorriqueña del siglo 19*. Cabo Rojo: Editora Educación Emergente, 2021.

———. *Segundo Ruiz Belvis: El prócer y el ser humano*. Bayamón: Editorial Universidad de América, 1994.

Cruz Monclova, Lidio. *Historia de Puerto Rico, siglo XIX*. 3 vols. Río Piedras: Universidad de Puerto Rico, 1970.

Findlay, Eileen. *Imposing Decency: The Politics of Sexuality and Race in Puerto Rico, 1870–1920*. Durham: Duke University Press, 1999.

Quintero Rivera, Ángel G. *Patricios y plebeyos: Burgueses, hacendados, artesanos y obreros: Las relaciones de clase en el Puerto Rico de cambio de siglo*. Río Piedras: Ediciones Huracán, 1988.

Meléndez, Edgardo. *Patria: Puerto Rican Revolutionary Exiles in Late Nineteenth Century New York*. New York: Centro Press, 2020.

Moscoso, Francisco. *La revolución puertorriqueña de 1868: El Grito de Lares*. San Juan: Instituto de Cultura Puertorriqueña, 2003.

Ojeda Reyes, Félix. *El desterrado de París: Biografía del doctor Ramón Emeterio Betances*. San Juan: Ediciones Puerto, 2001.

Rodríguez Silva, Ileana. *Silencing Race: Disentangling Blackness, Colonialism, and National Identities in Puerto Rico*. New York: Palgrave Macmillan, 2012.

The Long Twentieth Century (1898–2005)

Álvarez Curbelo, Silvia, and Carmen I. Raffuci, eds. *Frente a la torre: Ensayos del Centenario de la Universidad de Puerto Rico, 1903–2003*. Río Piedras: Editorial de la Universidad de Puerto Rico, 2005.

Ayala, César J. *American Sugar Kingdom: The Plantation Economy of the Spanish Caribbean, 1898–1934*. Chapel Hill: University of North Carolina Press, 1999.

Dávila, Arlene M. *Sponsored Identities: Cultural Politics in Puerto Rico*. Philadelphia: Temple University Press, 1997

Del Moral, Solsiree. *Negotiating Empire: The Cultural Politics of Schools in Puerto Rico, 1898–1952*. Madison: University of Wisconsin Press, 2013.

Erman, Sam. *Almost Citizens: Puerto Rico, the U.S. Constitution, and Empire*. Cambridge: Cambridge University Press, 2019.

García, Gervasio L., and Ángel G. Quintero Rivera. *Desafío y solidaridad: Breve historia del movimiento obrero puertorriqueño*. Río Piedras: Ediciones Huracán, 1997.

García Muñiz, Humberto. *Sugar and Power in the Caribbean: The South Porto Rico Sugar Company in Puerto Rico and the Dominican Republic, 1900–1921*. Río Piedras: Editorial de la Universidad de Puerto Rico, 2010.

Hernández, Jesús Manuel. *Nilita Vientós Gastón y la legitimación de las disidencias políticas bajo su presidencia en el Ateneo Puertorriqueño, 1946–1961*. San Juan: Disonante, 2018.

Lugo del Toro, Kenneth. *Nacimiento y auge de la Confederación General de Trabajadores, 1940–1945*. San Juan: Universidad Interamericana de Puerto Rico, 2013.

Marsh Kennerly, Catherine. *Negociaciones culturales: Los intelectuales y el proyecto pedagógico del estado muñocista*. San Juan: Ediciones Callejón, 2008.

McGreevey, Robert. *Borderline Citizens: The United States, Puerto Rico, and the Politics of Colonial Migration*. Ithaca: Cornell University Press, 2018.

Medina Báez, Bianca M. *Teresa Angleró Sepúlveda: Primera organizadora de las trabajadoras de la industria de la aguja en Puerto Rico*. San Juan: Publicaciones Gaviota, 2019.

Meléndez-Badillo, Jorell. *The Lettered Barriada: Workers, Archival Power, and the Politics of Knowledge in Puerto Rico*. Durham: Duke University Press, 2021.

Nazario Velasco, Rubén. *La historia de los derrotados: Americanización y romanticismo en Puerto Rico, 1898–1917*. San Juan: Ediciones Laberinto, 2019.

Paralitici, Ché. *Historia de la lucha por la independencia de Puerto Rico: Una lucha por la soberanía y la igualdad social bajo el dominio estadounidense*. Río Piedras: Publicaciones Gaviota, 2018.

Pérez Soler, Ángel. *Del Movimiento Pro Independencia al Partido Socialista Puertorriqueño: La transición de la lucha nacionalista a la lucha de los trabajadores: 1959–1971*. San Juan: Publicaciones Gaviota, 2018.

Suárez Findlay, Eileen J. *We Are Left without a Father Here: Masculinity, Domesticity, and Migration in Postwar Puerto Rico*. Durham: Duke University Press, 2014.

Thompson, Lanny. *Imperial Archipelago: Representations and Rule in the Insular Territories under U.S. Dominion after 1898*. Honolulu: University of Hawai'i Press, 2010.

The Puerto Rican Diaspora

Acosta-Belén, Edna, and Carlos E. Santiago. *Puerto Ricans in the United States: A Contemporary Portrait*. 2nd ed. Boulder, CO: Lynne Rienner Publishers, 2018.

Cruz, José E. *Liberalism and Identity Politics: Puerto Rican Community Organization and Collective Action in New York*. New York: Centro Press, 2019.

Duany, Jorge. *The Puerto Rican Nation on the Move: Identities on the Island and in the United States*. Chapel Hill: University of North Carolina Press, 2002.

Fernández, Johanna. *The Young Lords: A Radical History*. Chapel Hill: University of North Carolina Press, 2020.

Fernández, Lilia. *Brown in the Windy City: Mexicans and Puerto Ricans in Postwar Chicago*. Chicago: University of Chicago Press, 2002.

Fernández-Jones, Delia. *Making the MexiRican City: Migration, Placemaking, and Activism in Grand Rapids, Michigan.* Champaign: University of Illinois Press, 2023.

García-Colón, Ismael. *Colonial Migrants at the Heart of Empire: Puerto Rican Workers on U.S. Farms.* Berkeley: University of California Press, 2020.

Glasser, Ruth. *My Music Is My Flag: Puerto Rican Musicians and Their New York Communities, 1917–1940.* Berkeley: University of California Press, 1995.

Hoffnung-Garskof, Jesse. *Racial Migrations: New York City and the Revolutionary Politics of the Spanish Caribbean.* Princeton: Princeton University Press, 2019.

La Fountain-Stokes, Lawrence. *Queer Ricans: Cultures and Sexualities in the Diaspora.* Minneapolis: University of Minnesota Press, 2009.

Matos Rodríguez, Felix V., and Pedro Juan Hernández. *Pioneros: Puerto Ricans in New York City, 1896–1948.* Charleston: Arcadia Publishing, 2001.

Meléndez, Edgardo. *Sponsored Migration: The State and Puerto Rican Postwar Migration to the United States.* Columbus: Ohio State University Press, 2017.

Pérez, Gina M. *The Near Northwest Side Story: Migration, Displacement, and Puerto Rican Families.* Berkeley: University of California Press, 2004.

Rosario Natal, Carmelo. *Éxodo puertorriqueño: Las emigraciones al Caribe y Hawaii, 1900–1915.* San Juan: Editorial Edil, 2001.

Rúa, Mérida M. *A Grounded Identidad: Making New Lives in Chicago's Puerto Rican Neighborhoods.* Oxford: Oxford University Press, 2002.

Sánchez Korrol, Virginia. *From Colonia to Community: The History of Puerto Ricans in New York City.* Berkeley: University of California Press, 1994.

Teresa Whalen, Carmen. *From Puerto Rico to Philadelphia: Puerto Rican Workers and Postwar Economies.* Philadelphia: Temple University Press, 2001.

Thomas, Lorrin. *Puerto Rican Citizen: History and Political Identity in Twentieth-Century New York.* Chicago: University of Chicago Press, 2010.

Valdés, Vanessa. *Diasporic Blackness: The Life and Times of Arturo Alfonso Schomburg.* Albany: State University of New York Press, 2017.

Velázquez, José E., Carmen V. Rivera, and Andrés Torres, eds. *Revolution around the Corner: Voices from the Puerto Rican Socialist Party in the United States.* Philadelphia: Temple University Press, 2021.

Velázquez, Mirelsie. *Puerto Rican Chicago: Schooling the City, 1940–1977.* Champaign: University of Illinois Press, 2022.

The Collapse (2005–23)

Atiles, José. *Profanaciones del verano del 2019: Corrupción, frentes comunes y justicia decolonial.* Cabo Rojo: Editora Educación Emergente, 2020.

Bonilla, Yarimar, and Marisol LeBrón, eds. *Aftershocks of Disaster: Puerto Rico Before and After the Storm.* Chicago: Haymarket Books, 2019.

Deibert, Michael. *When the Sky Fell: Hurricane Maria and the United States in Puerto Rico.* New York: Apollo Publishers, 2019.

Klein, Naomi. *The Battle for Paradise: Puerto Rico Takes on Disaster Capitalists*. Chicago: Haymarket Books, 2018.

LeBrón, Marisol. *Against Muerto Rico: Lessons from the Verano Boricua*. Cabo Rojo: Editora Educación Emergente, 2021.

———. *Policing Life and Death: Race, Violence, and Resistance in Puerto Rico*. Oakland: University of California Press, 2019.

Llorens, Hilda. *Making Livable Worlds: Afro-Puerto Rican Women Building Environmental Justice*. Seattle: University of Washington Press, 2021.

Powers Guimond, Christopher. *4645*. Cabo Rojo: Editora Educación Emergente, 2020.

Rodríguez Castro, Malena. *Poéticas de la devastación y la insurgencia: María y el Verano del 19*. Cabo Rojo: Editora Educación Emergente, 2022.

Serán dueñas de la tierra. Dir. Juanma Pagán Teitelbaum. San Juan: Producciones Libélula, 2022.

Simulacros de liberación. Dir. Juan C. Dávila Santiago. San Juan: República 21 Media, 2021.

Zambrana, Rocío. *Colonial Debts: The Case of Puerto Rico*. Durham: Duke University Press, 2021. Translated to Spanish: *Deudas coloniales: El caso de Puerto Rico*. Cabo Rojo: Editora Educación Emergente, 2022.

INDEX

Note: "PR" refers to Puerto Rico. Page numbers in italic type indicate illustrations.

Brazil, 22, 31, 105
bregar (struggle), 24
Brigades of Honor, 61
Brookings Institution, 91
Bulletin, 126
Bureau of Insular Affairs (United States), 84, 92
Burke, John, 68
Bush, George H. W., 138

cabildos, 17–19, 31–32, 35
cabotage laws, 84
Cabral, Amílcar, 137
caciques (chiefs): relations among, 1, 9, 14; relations with colonizers, 1–2, 6, 10, 14; resistance from, 12, 14; role of, 4–5, 224n8
Caguas, PR, 187
CAL. *See* Comandos Armados de Liberación
Calderón, Sila María, 164
Camacho, Julio, 99
Campeche, José, 41
CAMs. *See* Centros de Apoyo Mutuo
Camuy, PR, 46
Canales, Blanca, 115
Cancel Miranda, Rafael, 116, 169
Cancel-Sepúlveda, Mario R., 26
cannibalism, 5, 7
Cánovas del Castillo, Antonio, 55–57
Caonabo, 8
Caparra, PR, 10–12, 14, 17
Capetillo, Luisa, 79–80, 88
capitalism, 51, 88, 143, 213, 217
Caraza, Diego de, 20
Caribbean archipelago: as European theater of war, 19, 22; map of, *viii*
Carib Indians: attacks on Spaniards by, 14, 18, 20; relations with indigenous population of Borikén, 5, 7, 12
carpetas (files), 148–49
Carrasquillo, Agustín, 151
Carrión, José, III, 177
Carrión, Richard, 177
Carroll, Henry K., 75

caserío, El, 117
caseríos (public housing units), 117, 160
Castro, Fidel, 135–37, 139
Castro, Ramón de, 33
Catholic Church, 23, 75, 151
cattle ranching, 18, 20
Cédula de Gracias, 35
Celso Barbosa, José, 54
cemís (sculptures), 4, 7
Central Intelligence Agency (CIA), 137
Centro: Center for Puerto Rican Studies, 154–55, 205
Centro de Estudios de la Realidad Puertorriqueña (Center for the Study of Puerto Rican Reality [CEREP]), 153–55
Centro de Periodismo Investigativo (CPI), 184–85, 194, 203
Centros de Apoyo Mutuo (CAMs), 187–88
CEREP. *See* Centro de Estudios de la Realidad Puertorriqueña
Cerro Maravilla, 147–48, 155
Céspedes, Juan de, 20
CGT. *See* Confederación General de Trabajadores
Chardón, Carlos, 92
Charles I, King of Spain, 9, 16–17
Charles II, King of Spain, 24
Charles IV, King of Spain, 31
Charlie, Rey, 196
Chenault, Lawrence, 123
Chicago, Illinois, 120, 124, 126, 144
Chicano civil rights movement, 143
Chile, 45, 71
cholera, 44
Christianity, 6, 9, 75. *See also* Catholic Church; religion
CIA. *See* Central Intelligence Agency
cimarrones (runaways), 17
citizenship, xii, 71, 82–85, 121, 126, 129, 186, 204
Civil Code (Puerto Rico), 75
Civil Guard, 54
civil rights movement, 143, 158
Claridad, 135, 138, 141–42
Clinton, Bill, 164

Villa Sin Miedo (squatter settlement), 151–52
vocational schools, 91
voter turnout, 209, 211–12
voting rights, 50, 58, 77–80

wages, 90, 94, 171, 175
Wall Street Journal, 197, 212
War of 1898, 63–66, 81, 83
War of Succession, 24, 28
Washington, D.C., voting rights of, 131
Washington Post, 197
water, xii, 17, 180, 182–83, 187, 190
Wells Fargo, 155
Weyler, Valeriano, 56–57, 58
Whalen, Carmen Teresa, 126
Wheat, David, 226n6
whiteness, 26
white supremacy, 204
Wilbur Cartwright Bill, 98
Wilson, Woodrow, 83, 85
Winship, Blanton, 97
Wolf, Eric R., 2
women: and divorce, 75; intellectual
    engagement of, 53; middle-class, 77–78;
    political engagement of, 47, 48, 77–80,
    104, 112; and sexism, 193–94; social
    status and exclusion of, 53, 76–77; in
    sugar industry, 76; in Taíno society,
    5; and unions, 78–79; voting rights of,

77–80; in workforce, 76, 78–79. *See also*
    feminism
Worcester, Massachusetts, 132
workers: agency of, 76–77; attitudes toward,
    82; education of, 61, 76, 79–80; forced
    labor, 8–9, 13; immigrant experiences
    of, 126, 129, 132, 204; laws aimed at, 40;
    migration of, 81, 121; political and intel-
    lectual engagement of, 51, 61, 66–68,
    76–81, 88, 93; PPD and, 107–8; protections
    for, 167, 175; social hierarchy among, 62;
    union leaders' relations with, 76, 88,
    93–95; U.S. affinity of, 68, 76; in U.S.-
    governed Puerto Rico, 84–85; women
    among, 76, 78–79. *See also* exploitation of
    indigenous population: labor; strikes;
    unemployment; unions; wages
World Bank, 172, 213

xenophobia, xiv, 70–71, 82, 85, 95, 102–3, 124,
    205. *See also* race

Yager, Arthur, 85, 122
Yauco uprising, 60–61, 62
yellow fever, 48
"Yo no me dejo" generation, 215
Young Lords Organization, 126, 143
Young Lords Party, 128, 143–44
Yulín Cruz, Carmen, 186

A NOTE ON THE TYPE

This book has been composed in Arno, an Old-style serif typeface in the classic Venetian tradition, designed by Robert Slimbach at Adobe.